Purefoy Letters

VOLUME II

Plate 15. THE KING'S HEAD, ISLINGTON

Frontispiece II

Purefoy Letters

1735–1753

Edited by G. Eland
F.S.A.

VOLUME II

London
Sidgwick & Jackson, Ltd
1931

PRINTED IN GREAT BRITAIN

58254

CONTENTS

VOLUME II

Chap. IX London Agents . . . . . *page* 213

 X Family Affairs 239

 XI Books, Newspapers, Etc. 273

 XII Clothing 295

 XIII Medical, Dental, Optical: Visits to Bath and London 325

 XIV The Shrievalty 363

 XV Neighbours and Social Matters . . . 372

 XVI Purlieu Hunting 405

Appendix A Rules for Management of Open Fields . . 434

 B Suggested Sale of the Estate . . . 439

 C List of Subscribers to Sheriff's Fund . . 441

 D Undertaking by Servant who contracts Small Pox 444

 E Lotteries 444

Index 447

Pedigree . . . . *at end*

LIST OF ILLUSTRATIONS

VOLUME II

PLATE

15. The King's Head, Islington   *frontispiece*

16. Henry Purefoy the elder as Cupid   *to face p.* 244

17. Mrs Christopher Hales   „   „   260

18. Knightley Purefoy   „   „   268

19. Mrs Knightley Purefoy   „   „   270

20. Henry's Study   „   „   282

21. Facsimile of Letter No. 499   „   „   332

22. Finmere House   „   „   362

23. Henry when High Sheriff   „   „   368

24. Astrop Well   „   „   388

25. Facsimiles of Letter No. 582, (*a*) from the Letter-
Book, (*b*) from the letter actually sent   „   „   396

26. The Second Duke of Grafton   „   „   404

27. Dunney Baxter's Quart Pot   „   „   416

28. Fiennes Trotman   „   „   430

*** Notes on these Plates will be found in Volume I, pp. xi–xiv.

CHAPTER IX

LONDON AGENTS

WHEN the letters begin the principal agent in London was Mr Robotham who had married an old servant of Mrs Purefoy's family;[1] he was the licencee of the "King's Head" in Islington, which is mentioned several times by Mr Pepys: under 27 Mar. 1664 he says that his father used to take him "to Islington, to the old man's, at the King's Head, to eat cakes and ale, (his name was Pitts) ".[2] It was evidently still an important house in 1747,[3] and Mr Robotham appears to have been a trustworthy, if easy-going, man. There was a considerable exchange of presents between Shalstone and Islington, but there is no evidence that Mr Robotham was paid for his services, though he had the use of money left in his hands. After his death there was apparently a small balance against him, for which his niece by marriage was rather unmercifully dunned.

Mr Peter Moulson, the other agent, was an eminently respectable wine-merchant with successive addresses in Cursitor's Street, Billingsgate, and Wood Street; at the last address the Purefoys spent some time with him during a visit to London. According to the records of the Vintners' Company, he was apprenticed to Robert Witham and became a freeman of the Vintners' Company on 5 Feb. 1717.[4] He was evidently a man of tact and character, and able to keep on good terms with great men's great men, so that his indirect influence was invoked on more than one occasion. He had a daughter married to a Mr Vaughan, and when she had a son Henry Purefoy conceived the great joke of calling him "George the Second", a piece of wit which he never failed to revive when referring to him.

One forms the idea that Mr Robotham was the more jovial and probably good company, because he used to stay at Shalstone for a week or two at a time and be taken about a good deal. Mr Moulson was a graver person with more solid qualities: but both of them were wholly devoted to the Purefoys and cheerfully undertook the most varied types of commissions for them. As a rule the mother wrote to Mr Robotham, and the son to Mr Moulson.

The letters in this chapter are of a very miscellaneous character, and cannot be conveniently grouped elsewhere.

1 See Letter No. 371 where she is called "Mrs Millesent Clarke who liv'd with my father & afterwards with me".
2 Wheatley's edition, 1904, vol. IV, p. 84.
3 See Letter No. 362.
4 For these particulars the editor is indebted to Lt.-Col. E. T. Lea.

No. 338. E. P. *to* THOMAS ROBOTHAM

Shalstone [&c.]
Sunday January ye 11th 1735

I rece^d Mr Robotham's letter of the 30th of last month with a quarter of lamb & the oranges & lemons & a Barrell of Sturgeon wch wee have not yet tapt; But if it be as good as that Mrs Robotham sent last year there never was finer sturgeon eaten, for this kind present wee return you thanks. Mrs Robotham shall not faill of some hog puddings when wee kill our other hog. Wee are very sorry to hear of your surprize at the Rogues attempt to break into your house But are glad you have now gott shutters wch was always my advice & I hope you have got them backwards as well as forwards & wee heartily wish you may never come under the Lash of such villains. I desire you will pay Mr Belchier of St Paul's Church yard eleven pounds & five shillings & take a receipt in full of all accounts of him—when you go to Town call on him & pay him. Wee shall be glad of the Chain to my son's watch as soon as may be. Wee rece^d the coffeeberries & the receipt But the receipt had no date of ye year but shall want more things soon then will have a receipt in full of Mr Cossins. My son & self join in our service to yourself & Mrs Robotham wishing you both an happy new Year & many of them & I am

Your humble serv^t
E. P.

Direct your L^{res} to Buckingham so as you used to do. Just as I concluded I received the two Lobsters, & the chain of my son's watch, for wch return thanks.

To Mr Robotham...
London

No. 339. E. P. *to* THOMAS ROBOTHAM

Shalstone [&c.]
Wensday July ye 14th 1736

I rece^d Mr Robotham's letter of the 8th instant & my son has his repeating watch safe agen, it goes true at present. Pray pay Mr Belchier four pounds & take a receipt in full of all Demands from him. I have better health than I had but my leg will not be well. Wee shall be glad to see Mrs Robotham at Shalstone when it suits with her conveniency & I thank you for doing my errand to Mr Porter. My son has returned you five pound this next week by Mr Webster who comes into Town on Tuesday next about noon & my son desires you will subscribe four pounds for four Lottery Tickets for him & hee will return you the money for the other subscriptions in due time.

This long Vacation I desire you will enquire out the lowest price of a second hand chair for 2 men to carry mee to church in. Pray get mee 4 dozen yards of lace the same to ye pattern, if you can't have it ready made there is a man keeps a little lace shop over against St Clements Church on ye side of the street next ye Thames, hee will make it at two & twenty pence or two shillings the dozen yards.

I desire you will buy mee the last Book that came out about the Scarborough Spaw Waters, I think it was wrote by one Dr Shaw.[1] Wee both join in our service & respect to yourself & Mrs Robotham & I am

Your humble serv^t

ffor /
Mr Robotham...
London

E. P.

No. 340. E. P. *to* THOMAS ROBOTHAM

Shalstone [&c.]
Sunday 27th Novr 1737

I rece^d Mr Robotham's letter together with my son's 2 Lottery tickets & the other things I sent for, together with your kind present of codling & Lobster ffish & oysters, which were all very good but ye lobsters wch when boyled the flesh was tender like a Jelly. They came to us dead & I beleive it may be attributed to the boyling them when dead; I mention this because I beleive your ffish-monger did not do right by you. Wee both return you thanks for this & all other favours. Wee have killed a pig & have sent you the neck chine & a couple of pulletts, with an hare & a woodcock (carriage paid) by this return of Webster, which wee desire you to accept on; Webster comes into Town on Tuesday morning.

1 This is presumably *An Enquiry into the...Virtues and Uses of Scarborough Spaw Waters,* by Peter Shaw, physician, 1734.

14-2

Wee intend you a small present[1] against X^t'mas & desire to know whether you would have it sent on X^t'mas day or on the Sunday before X^t'mas day. Pray let mee know what sort of mourning[2] will be proper for my son who will have but one suit for the whole six months & wear it every day, & pray send him some patterns of Cloath which will oblidge

Your humble serv^t
E. P.

P.S. /

Wee both join in service & respect to you & Mrs Robotham.

ffor /
 Mr Robotham...
   London

No. 341. E. P. *to* THOMAS ROBOTHAM

Shalstone [*&c.*]
ffebruary ye 26th 1737

I received both Mr Robotham's Łres & his kind presents of oranges lemons & sturgeon & a Barrell of Oysters, wch were all good & pray accept of our thanks for them. I should have wrote to you before now but wee have been in daily expectation of an Hare which you shan't faill of if wee can get one, there are now seven packs of hare hounds kept hereabouts, which has made ye scarcity.

My son would sell his 2 blank Lottery tickets when you think they will sell best, which pray acquaint us with, & send 6 pounds of grounds to powder Periwigs, & 2 gallons of spiritts of wine. My son has sent his diamond ring & silver watch to be mended, & pray tell Mr Mulford when you carry 'em to him that the watch never went right well for any time & the Diamond slipt out quickly after wee had it, desire it may be set stronger next time. I desire when you go to Town to pay Mr William Coryndon, in Naked Boy court near ye new Church in ye Strand, Three pounds four shillings

---

1 Eventually a chine, a cock turkey, a couple of pullets, and a goose were sent. In return Mr Robotham offered "a present of lamb", but was told that "wee have lamb in the countrey", and a barrel of oysters would be more welcome.
2 The Queen (Caroline of Brandenburg-Anspach), died on 20 Nov. 1737, a week before this letter was written.

on my account[1] & take a receipt in full of him. If the Lottery tickets don't sell let us have your account in your next & will order you some money, & with our best service & respects to yourself & Mrs Robotham I am

Your humble serv^t
E. P.

ffor /
  Mr Robotham...
        London

No. 342. E. P. to THOMAS ROBOTHAM

Shalstone [&c.]
June ye 8th 1738

I received Mr Robotham's letter of the 6th of Aprill last & therewith my son's watch & ring & the grounds & spiritts of wine, for procuring wch wee return you thanks as likewise for your kind present of a Tobacco box wch is very pretty. Shall be glad to hear in your next what ye Lottery tickets fetched. Pray pay Mr Mulford ye nine shillings, but let him know ye silver watch will not go right. I hope you have paid Mr Willson in St Paulls Church yard & Mr Budd ye stationer & took a rec^t in full of them. Pray pay Mr Crutchfeild at a colour shop on Holborn bridge Two pounds thirteen shillings & fourpence, but you must abate twenty pence of it wch hee has set down for two brushes & two toolls, & tell him I never paid for them but hee always gave mee them into ye Bargain, & take a receipt in full of him.

They say Sallet Oyll is very cheap in London, if so pray buy mee 2 gallons; pray send some patterns of Cloath of a fashionable colour for second mourning for my son & let mee know if they wear coat, wastcoat, & Breetches all alike or wear black wastcoat & breetches. Pray send mee as much white sattin as will make up that sattin I bought for a wrapper a gown & Petticoat, of which I have sent you a pattern; be sure it be of the colour with ye pattern. Mrs Robotham was with mee when I bought it; she knows ye shop, they are most likely to match it there, it cost mee eight shillings a yard. My nephew Leonard Porter is dead so wee mourn somewhat ye longer on that account, they say hee was a

1 This was a dentist's bill, see Letter No. 521.

very fine youth. This is ye first letter I have had from my sister since I saw you. Wee both join in our service & respect to you & Mrs Robotham & I am

Your humble serv^t

E. P.

ffor /
    Mr Robotham...
        London

The satten I have is 11 yards.

No. 343. E. P. *to* THOMAS ROBOTHAM

Shalstone [&c.]
Tuesday 5th Septemb^r 1738

Wee are heartily glad to hear Mr Robotham got safe to London & that Mrs Robotham is well & that wee shall have the pleasure of seeing her here; let mee know when she comes that wee may meet her. I am glad you found the Hare sweet & that it was acceptable, my son has had ye good fortune to catch a brace of hares as yesterday wch hee has sent you this day (the carriage paid,) by William Eagles the son, ye Buckingham carrier....I sent by Webster 6 pound of Butter this week as you ordered. I would have wrote last post but could not have your letter. I desire you will set the workmen to work on ye wall between Mr Wishaw & mee, I question not but you will make as wise a Bargain as you can. Pray my son's & my service to M^r & Mrs Wishaw. In your next I hope to hear of Mr Bernard's Resolution about ye house. More about ye watch in my next or when wee hear about ye allarum. When Mrs Robotham comes I desire she will bring mee 2 pounds of new roasted Coffee berries & half a pound of Hyson tea & a fashionable hoop from Long's warehouse. She must tell them 't is for one who is not half an Ell[1] in ye wast & I beleive she can guesse at the length. Wee both join in service & respect to you & Mrs Robotham, wishing her a good journey down wch concludes mee

Your humble serv^t

E. P.

1 An ell was 45 inches.

P.S. /

I will send half a dozen pounds of butter a week as you order / Let them know at ye warehouse ye Hoop is for mee.

ffor /
   Mr Robotham...
        London

No. 344. H. P. *to* PETER MOULSON

Shalstone...
Septemb^r ye 17th 1738

Sir! /

I hope you & Mr Price got well to Town[1] tho' your horses went from our House without any Corn wch is a concern to my mother & self; for ye future I hope you will take ye Liberty as I do wherever I go (that is) To command what meat you judge proper for your horses & to order your servant to call for it. It is such a thing as never happened with us before & I am really ashamed of it. I have had the good fortune to catch a Brace of young hares & desire your acceptance of them with a shoulder of venison, being of the last Buck wch was killed in ye fforest this season, or otherwise it might have been a better peice. They are sent this day (carriage paid) by ye Buckingham carrier....

Wee both join in our service & respect to you & Miss Moulson, not forgetting Mr Price & I am, Sir!

Your very humble serv^t
H. P.

ffor /
   Mr Moulson
   on Saint Mary Hill
   near Bishopsgate
        London

No. 345. E. P. *to* THOMAS ROBOTHAM

Shalstone [&c.]
ffebruary the 3^d 1739

I received Mr Robotham's letter of the 25th of last December & therewith your kind present of sturgeon, oysters, oranges, & lemons for which wee return you & Mrs Robotham many thanks.

1 According to the Diary, Mr Moulson and Mr Price ("a vintner on Ludgate hill who came along with him") were at Shalstone on the afternoon of 14 September, so they were presumably on a journey, and made no stay.

Wee are heartily sorry to hear your Cough is encreased & hope when this hard Weather is gone you will be better. I have sent you a spare ribb, a couple of pulletts, a goose, a cream cheese, & another cheese, all which wee desire your acceptance of. Wee intended hog puddings for Mrs Robotham but the hard Weather prevented us so that wee could get no Herbs. Wee have had a Letter from Mr Barnard wherein hee sais hee has paid for the Paving the street by the Door, but does not tell the summe it came to; pray when you go to Town see it is done & ask him what it comes to, as also what my share for the drawing his Lease came to; it is only for engrossing the lease & for Parchm^t & stamps; Wee sent him the draft out of the Countrey so I suppose it cannot come to much, when you have enquired let mee know, as likewise whether Mr Willson, the grocer at the 3 sugar loaves in St Paulls Church yard be dead or no,[1] for there is such a Report here. I have put up some cannisters which I desire you to keep for mee. The above things are sent this day with your butter by Mr Eagles the carrier (carriage paid). Wee heartily wish you a speedy Recovery of your Health and with my sons & my best service & respects to yourself & Mrs Robotham I am

Your humble servant
E. P.

ffor /
  Mr Robotham...
        London

No. 346. E. P. *to* THOMAS ROBOTHAM

Shalstone [&c.]
November ye 2^d 1740

I rece^d Mr Robotham's Łre of the 16th of last Septr together with the Silver Lace & Bohea tea & shall be glad of a yard of Grogram if to be had. The herrings proved exceeding good, for which wee return thanks & have sent you this day with your butter by Eagles a cheese & an hare wch is the first my son has catcht since you went; hee was up yesterday morning at 6 a clock to try for another, but had no successe. I desire when you send

1 See Letter No. 103.

again to send 6 pounds of Grounds to powder wiggs with, & a fine fashionable Leghorn hat for myself. They wear them here small crowns and narrow Brimms. I am about thirty shillings in debt to Mͬ Crutchfeild at a colour shop on Holborn Bridge, wᶜʰ I desire you will call on him and pay. I don't exactly know what it is by reason hee sent no bill. With our best services to yourself & Mͬˢ Robotham I am in hast

Your humble servᵗ

ffor /

Mͬ Robotham...
    London

E. P.

No. 347. H. P. *to* PETER MOULSON

Shalstone [&c.]
January the 10ᵗʰ 1740

Sir! /

My mother received the half hogshead of mountain wine & with it the Chocolate & the money that you sent. She is a little snuff¹ that you sent money when she owed you money, she thanks you for letting her have the Chocolate; on the ballance of the account my mother owes you £7. 10ˢ 6ᵈ and desires you will receive the quarter's rent due from Mͬ Barnard according to the underwritten order, & if there be any Taxes due to pay them on his delivering you the vouchers for them. Wee desire your acceptance of an hare & a Goose, & a couple of Pulletts, sent this day (carriage paid) by the Buckingham carrier.... Your present had been better but that my mother had a dreadfull fall down stairs² which had like to have cost her her Life, wee live in hopes she is in a way of recovery. However 'ere long wee hope wee shall get something better for you. I shall be glad when you write to know the ffate of my Lottery ticketts, & with our compliments of the Season to self & Miss Moulson I am, with much esteem, Sir!

Your very hie servant

ffor /

Mͬ Moulson...
    London

H. P.

1 So far as is known, the adjectival use of this word, with the meaning of the modern colloquialism "sniffy", is peculiar.

2 See Letter No. 493.

[On the same sheet]

Shalstone
January the 10ᵗʰ 1740

Mͬ Barnard

Sir! /

I pray pay to Mͬ Moulson of Sͭ Mary hill the summe of ten pounds & ten shillings for your quarter's rent due at Christmas last & his receipt shall be a sufficient discharge to you for the same from

Your humble servant

ffor /
Mͬ Barnard...
    London

E. P.

No. 348. H. P. *to* PETER MOULSON

Shalstone [&c.]
August the 30ᵗʰ 1741

Sir! /

I have just catched a brace of hares wᶜʰ I desire you to accept of & hope they will come sweet to you. The claw of the hither fore foot of each of them is cut of[f], that they may not be changed. They are sent this day by the Buckingham carrier, . . . the carriage paid. Pray reconcile yourself to your servant's mistake, for if you should light of a servant that makes no mistake you would have better luck than anybody in this age. I have only time to tell you as soon as I have an opportunity I will return you the money due to you,[1] & with our compliments to yourself & Miss Moulson am, Sir!

Your very humble servᵗ

ffor /
Mͬ Moulson...
    London

H. P.

1 A sum of £11. 7s. 6d. was sent a fortnight later, and it was mentioned in the letter that it balanced an account which included "3 Lottery Tickets in this State Lottery".

No. 349. E. P. *to* THOMAS ROBOTHAM

Shalstone [&c.]
November the 22th 1741

I received a present this day of Codling & shrimps wch by the direction I suppose came from Mr Robotham & before they came this morning had the good fortune to catch a brace of Hares, being the first wee have catched since you left Shalstone, wch wee desire you & Mrs Robotham to accept of together with a Cock Turkey, wch are sent with your Butter by Mrs Eagles, carriage paid. The turkey cock is of my own ffeeding & therefore I cut of[f] his head because I would not put him to pain. Wee return you thanks for the above & all your other kind presents. I hope to hear you have been at Bellbar & seen the house in Grublane & that you have spoke with M^r ffish in order to the sale thereof. The little black coach horse is perfectly sound & no ill Quality attends him, if you know of a chap I will sell him for twelve pounds. At X$^{t'}$mas I intend you a present of a chine & desire to know if you would have it sent on y^e Saturday or Wensday before X$^{t'}$mas day or on the Saturday after X$^{t'}$mas day.

The length of the brasse fender is 4 foot 1 inch & an half, you will hardly light of anything of that length second hand, but if it is 3 foot it will do, but nothing under that.

My son & self join in our hearty Service & respects to yourself & Mrs Robotham & I am

Your humble serv^t
E. P.

ffor /
   Mr Robotham...
          London

The three next letters give very different reasons for sending single hares to London. The first of them is also of interest for its mention of the death of the Rector, who was no favourite at the Manor House. Letters regarding the appointment of his successor were given in Chapter 1 (Nos. 19 to 23).

No. 350. E. P. *to* THOMAS ROBOTHAM

Shalstone [&c.]
Octob^r 23^d 1742

I desire Mr Robotham's acceptance of an Hare wch I send you this day with the butter by Mr Meads ye Carrier. My son was

within an ace of catching another had not poor Gip on flinging
herself at the hare tumbled arse over head & hurt herself. With
both our services am in hast

Your life serv^t

E. P.

P.S. Pray tell Mr Potts the newsman my name is Purefoy and
not Burefoy as hee has directed.

On Tuesday last at 8 at night our Rector, the Revd Mr Townsend [1]
departed this life.

ffor /
    Mr Robotham...
                London

No. 351. H. P. *to* PETER MOULSON

Shalstone [&c.]

Novemb^r the 2^d 1742

Sir! /

I am favoured with yours of the 21st of last month & wee have
rece^d the half hogshead of mountain wine, you shall have an
answer to your letter when I have tapt it.

In the mean time I desire your acceptance of an Hare sealed
at the knot of Direction with my coat of arms, carriage paid, &
sent by the Buckingham carrier....I would have made it a brace
but now the green wheat is come up the hares grow stout & are
exceeding hard to catch. Wee both join in our best respects to
yourself & Miss Moulson & I am with reall esteem Sir! /

Your very humble servant

ffor /   H. P.
    Mr Moulson...
                London

No. 352. E. P. *to* THOMAS ROBOTHAM

Shalstone [&c.]

Novemb^r the 7th 1742

I rece^d Mr Robotham's letter of the 2^d instant & wee thank
you for your kind present of ffish & oysters, they were all exceeding
good. Wee desire your acceptance of the old Turkey Cock & a

1 The Rev. Richard Townsend was inducted, 8 September 1705, on the
presentation of Mrs Purefoy.

Banging hare wch ran above a mile course, sent with your butter by Mr Meads.

When my son's things come they will be acceptable because hee wants the Tops for his Boots. Wee both join in our service & respects to yourself & Mrs Robotham & I am

Your humble servant
E. P.

ffor /
Mr Robotham...
   London

Two days later a "brace of banging hares" was sent to Mr Robotham, so presumably they were to be found in spite of the green wheat—or because of it, according to the poacher's song in *Alton Locke*.

Wright (*Dialect Dictionary*) defines "banging" as "an expletive expressive of size; large, huge". Cf. "thumping" and schoolboys' "whacking big", "whopping".

No. 353. E. P. *to* THOMAS ROBOTHAM

Shalstone [*&c.*]
March ye 20th 1742

I rece^d Mr Robotham's Łre of the 15th of ffebruary last with my son's repeating watch & the rest of the things with it, as also the Barrell of Oysters & the tale[1] of fresh salmon for all which wee return you thanks. I should have wrote before this had not Mr Willis said at Mr Rodds at Torcester that I had promised Mrs Robotham the next presentation of my son's Living at Shalstone 3 years before the late Mr Townsend died & that you & Mrs Robotham promised it him, & that hee never had bought[2] the Vicarage of little Billing had it not been within distance of & a prospect to Shalstone living. I can't but resent this & thought I never would write to you more, that amongst you you should be an Instrument to make mee such a base Body & a Countrey Talk when I am an innocent person; instead of going to buy boots at Northampton I understand since you went to little Billing to dispose of my son's living. If I should sell your Beer & wine & take ye money for it you would not like it. Mr Willis has the character of a civilized person, so I must beleive it to be all your

1 This may refer to a fish of such size as to be sold by "tale", i.e. over 26 inches in length. *O.E.D.*

2 The Rev. Wm. Willis was instituted to Little Billing in April 1741; he became rector of Overston in 1746 and held both livings until his death.

own. My pleasure is I have never yet forfeited my word on any account, nor hope I never shall. My son has been confined to his Chamber these 14 weeks past but wee got him out in the Coach this last week & I thank God his Gout dos not return. On Wednesday night last I sent you a large hare sealed at the knot of the Direction & carriage paid by M.ʳ Meads yᵉ carrier, & this day I send you another large hare carriage paid & sealed at the knot of the Direction with your Butter, which wee desire you to accept on & hope to retain my Integrity whilst I am

ffor M.ʳ Robotham...   E. P.
   London.

No. 354. E. P. *to* THOMAS ROBOTHAM

Shalstone [&c.]
Aprill the 30ᵗʰ 1743

I received M.ʳ Robotham's kind Present of a Barrell of oysters w.ᶜʰ were as good as could be expected for the Time of the year. Wee have an Hare came to hand which was shot in the fore legs & wish it may be acceptable to you, 't is sent carriage paid with your Butter.

'T is pity your freind M.ʳ Willis should reflect so much upon you, but I had it from very good Hands & beleive what I wrote to you ab.ᵗ him to be true, with our service & respects to you both am

           Your humble servant
ffor /   E. P.
 M.ʳ Robotham...
   London

One presumes that Mr Robotham somehow managed to exonerate himself from the charge, for we hear no more about it; just as a generous person is always indignant at an accusation of meanness Mrs Purefoy was particularly sensitive at the suggestion that she had broken her word.

No. 355. E. P. *to* MRS MOULSON

from M.ʳ Langley's in
little Lincoln's inne ffeilds
August the 25ᵗʰ 1743

Madam /

Upon telling the money over again I found a 2 guinea piece w.ᶜʰ was told by mistake for a 36.ˢ piece, w.ᶜʰ six shillings makes

the money right. I could not be easy till I let you know of this
& with my son's & my compliments, begging Mr Moulson & you
will excuse all this trouble wee have given you I am, Madam,

Your oblidged ħħe servant

ffor /   E. P.
 Mrs Moulson...
   London

The 36*s.* piece was a Portuguese coin, issued in the reign of John V,
its nominal value was 6,400 reis, but this had to be reckoned at 20 per
cent. more. There was a scarcity of our own coinage at this date, and
the currency of genuine foreign coins was determined by Proclamation,
so that they obtained semi-official recognition. (Information kindly
supplied by Mr J. O. Manton.)

No. 356. H. P. *to* PETER MOULSON

Shalstone [&c.]
Sir! /   *January the 18th 1743*

I have received the Runlet of wine & the account & my mother
will order you payment soon. Wee heartily congratulate you &
your daughter on her marriage & wish the young couple all the
ffelicity this world can afford & our best service waits on them.
Wee shall be sure to make use of Mr Vaughan when wee want
anything in his way. My mother little thought hee was to be
ye happy man tho' she used the shop many years.

The reason I write to you before I send an order for ye money
is that I have a ffriend who has two Livings fell to him & hee
wants to be a Nobleman's Chaplain to qualifie him to hold them
both. As you are intimate with my Lord Shaftesburie's Steward
& other Noblemen who may deall with you for wine I do imagine
now the Parliament sits you might have interest enough to procure
a Scarf for him on paying what is usuall in that case; if the English
Peers should chance to be full a Scotch peer will do. This will be
a ffavour both to mee and the gentleman, if in your power. The
Benefice being vacant I entreat you would let mee know in a
week's time whether you are like to succeed in this affair.[1]

1 An allusion in a later letter shows that it would prove a decidedly "difficult
affair". Mr F. H. L. Errington, C.B., kindly informs the editor that in 1743 the
law in the matter was that laid down by 21 Hen. VIII Ch. 21 Sec. 14 et seq. By
this Act the number of chaplains a nobleman could have was regulated, and each
such chaplain might purchase a licence or dispensation to hold two benefices.

Wee both join in our best services & respects to you & I am
Sir!

Your very humble serv.^{t}
H. P.

ffor /
Mr Moulson...
            London

Mrs Purefoy's letters of condolence are inimitable: amidst its becoming
sables the word "indulgent" is a neatly-barbed shaft.

No. 357. E. P. *to* THOMAS ROBOTHAM

Shalstone [&c.]
November the 9.th 1745

I received Mr Robotham's lre of the 1.st instant with the sorrowfull account of Mrs Robotham's death, you have lost the most
indulgent & best of wives & I am afraid Nelly has lost her best
ffreind and I am sure my son & I have lost a very good one &
I beleive all her acquaintance may say the same. If sorrow would
bring her again I beleive wee should soon have her amongst us;
but as that can't be wee must go to her and in the mean time
reconcile ourselves as well as wee can to our Losse of her. Wee
received your kind present of sack & ffish for which wee return
you thanks, they were all exceeding good. Since I wrote to you
last I have sent you three hares with this, wch I desire you to accept.

If your health is no better than usuall I fear you will not be
able to go on with your Businesse, except Nelly can be capable
of assisting you. Wee thank you for your kind proffers of service,
& all other ffavours, & send you the measure you desire. Our
service & best wishes attend yourself & Nelly & I am

Your humble servant
E. P.

ffor /
Mr Robotham...
            London

No. 358. E. P. *to* THOMAS ROBOTHAM

Shalstone [&c.]
Octob.^{r} the 29.th 1746

I received Mr Robotham's letter of the 23.^{d} instant and am very
sorry to hear of your Indisposition & glad you are better. Wee

received your kind present of Oysters & Herrings for which wee return you thanks, & desire your acceptance of a side of Doe Venison, an hare & a goose sent by ye Buckingham carrier (carriage paid)....The time for the Butter is out at Allhallowtide & I am sorry I cannot serve you any longer for my two cows will not do it & I durst not buy any cows, the Distemper being within 5 or 6 miles of us.[1]

You said you forgot Mrs Robotham's fine ffan.

'T is Wartime & Deal Poles are hard to come by so I will have patience till they grow cheaper.

I desire you will enquire out the price of a Tin Tunnell with a weather cock thing to it & how to put it upon the Chimney, & pray when you send agen send a pound of the best flower of mustard seed. With our service & Respects to yourself & Nelly I am

Your humble servant
E. P.

ffor /
Mr Robotham...
    London

No. 359. E. P. *to* THOMAS ROBOTHAM

Shalstone [&c.]
Decemb^r the 24th 1746

I received Mr Robotham's Łre of the 18th instant & wee hope in your next to hear ye pain in your arm will be gone. The asses milk has done mee a great deall of good both for my sicknesse & faintnesse wch made mee think it might do you good, & that you might have an opportunity of keeping it in the Close behind your yard; &, shutting the little ass in your yard a nights, you will have milk enough next morning to serve 3 or 4 folks. Then, by putting up the young ass at 10 a clock, you will have milk enough at 4 or 5 in the afternoon. I desire your acceptance of a Chine of our own hog, a Turkey, a Goose, & a couple of Pulletts, together with the Complements of the Season & our Respects to Nelly. I hope, if my other cow calves speedily, I may be able to let you have six pounds of butter a week; however you may have what I can spare. I have had 2 Barrells of oysters from ye fishmongers wch wee like very well, hee charges 3^s a Barrell. If you

1 See Letter No. 585.

think hee can't afford them at half a crown a barrell pray pay him & tell him to send them on once in a fortnight, which will oblidge

Your humble servant

ffor /
   Mᴿ Robotham

E. P.

No. 360. E. P. *to* THOMAS ROBOTHAM

Shalstone [*&c.*]
January yᵉ 11ᵗʰ 1746

I have received Mᴿ Robotham's letter of the 6ᵗʰ instant. The same day I received it came a man from Mᴿ Jones for the ass & Jack ffoall, wᶜʰ hee had away with him, & I gave him what instructions I could how to manage them on the Road & to give her good Corn & Hay. Had I had timely notice I would have chused to have had her shod before, but I told the man that if it was required hee should have it done. I heartily wish she may come well to you for she is a fine ass & gives a great deall of milk. You must not expect her to give so much till she has rested; wee don't give her anything but what she gets among the cows (vizᵗ) Hay & Grasse, & wee hope the milk will do you good. I have had no oysters but 2 barrells wᶜʰ pray pay for & order the ffish-monger to send a Barrell of oysters once a fortnight when the weather will permit. I am contented to give 3 shillings a barrell for them; & let him send a dozen or 2 of herrings with them when there be any. I have sent you this week 6 pounds of butter. Pray call on Cousin Harry ffish for two pounds & five shillings of the money remaining from the Lottery tickets, as also from the half year's rent due from the house in Grub Lane. Wee give you & Nelly the Compliments of the Season & I am

Your humble servant
E. P.

P.S. The dogs made a shift to catch an hare which I have sent wᵗʰ the Butter carriage paid; you should have more but they are very scarce. I hope you receᵈ the hare I sent before with your butter.

ffor /
   Mᴿ Robotham...
            London
   With an hare carriage paid

No. 361. E. P. *to* THOMAS ROBOTHAM

Shalstone [&c.]
Aprill the 12ᵗʰ 1747

I received Mʳ Robotham's Letter of the 24ᵗʰ of last month & am glad to hear the asses milk dos you good & I hope you receive Benefit by yᵉ Tarwater.

Wee received your kind Present of Salmon, Herrings, & Sevill oranges wᶜʰ were all very good. I doubt hares will be scarce this next Season; our dogs killed a little Leverett in yᵉ late snow which, as is reported, has destroyed a great many of them. Wee han't catched one since the last wee sent you but hope our Countrey will shortly afford something to make a return of your kind present. Pray tell the ffishmonger to send no more Oysters this season; his oysters in generall have been too small & watry. I desire you will pay him for them & take a receipt in full of him. My son joins with mee in our Respects to yourself & Nelly & I am

Your humble servant
E. P.

ffor /
Mʳ Robotham...
          London

This letter was the last thing which this "Countrey" or this world afforded Mr Robotham; a letter to Mr Wallbank from Henry, which appears next but was cancelled, contains the following passage:

"Wee had an account that Mʳ Robotham departed this life on Monday night last about 6 a clock, & retained his senses to the last moment, having read a letter that came from my mother but a quarter of an Hour before hee died".

Our next letter, to "Nelly", is one of Mrs Purefoy's letters of condolence which certainly never gave way to sentiment.

No. 362. E. P. *to* MRS RUSSELL

Shalstone [&c.]
Aprill the 21ᵗʰ 1747

I received Mʳˢ Russell's letter & wee are sorry to hear of Mʳ Robotham's Death, but it is what I expected long ago, for I thought him very bad when hee was here last.

I have been told when hee married your Aunt she settled an

hundred pounds upon you in Trustees' hands, if so I think unlesse
you marry it will be an hard venture for you to keep such a Publick
house as yours. I hope hee has left you what hee had tho' I
beleive they did not save much, & should be glad to know how
it is. I have sent the butter & am

Your humble servant

ffor /   E. P.
  Mrs Russell...
      London

No. 363. E. P. *to* MRS RUSSELL

Shalstone [&c.]
Aprill the 26th 1747

I received Mrs Russell's łre of the 23^d instant & am sorry to
hear Mr Robotham died in such bad circumstances. It will be
right in you to remove your cloaths & anything else that is yours
out of the house immediately, for if the Landlord, for rent or any
Execution, should come on ye Premisses they will take what they
find thereon to satisfie their Debt. There is nobody shall wrong
you if I can help it. Mr Robotham told mee hee gave you all
your Aunt's linnen and cloaths wch will be necessary for you to
secure, & I shall be glad to know if there is any writing drawn
to settle the hundred pounds on you, for Ralph Porter told mee
Mr Robotham sealed such a writing & if you can find any such
thing I will endeavour to see you have justice done you, if there
is anything left after payment of debts. For the butter account
it stands thus:—

	£	s	d
From the 13th Septr 1746 to the 1st of Novr following, being 8 weeks butter at 2^s 6^d a week	1	0	0
From 8th Novr 1746 to 21st March following, being 20 weeks butter at 3^s a week, all but one week when there was but 4 pounds sent.	2	19	0
From 28th March 1747 to 25th Aprill following 5 weeks butter at 2^s 6^d a week	0	12	6
	£4	11	6

On the 11ᵗʰ of September 1746 Mʳ Robotham reckoned here at Shalstone with mee & my son & gave us a receipt in full & wee gave him one,[1] so wee desire to know what hee has laid out for us since that time. I don't know anything hee could pay for us unlesse it be Mʳ Potts yᵉ newsman and for the Oysters. My son joins with mee in our service to you & should be glad to hear how you go on, & wish you may find it better than you expect. I suppose some of the Creditors will administer but you must not meddle with anything but what is your own. I shan't send any more butter; wᶜʰ concludes mee   Your freind to serve you

E. P.

P.S. Pray let mee know if your uncle was buried where your aunt is.

ffor /
  Mʳˢ Russell...
        London

No. 364. E. P. *to* MRS RUSSELL

Shalstone [&c.]
May the 10ᵗʰ 1747

I received Mʳˢ Russell's Łre of the 2ᵈ instant & wee have had but 6 Barrells of Oysters from Mʳ Curtis, as appears by Mʳ Jones yᵉ Carrier's bill, who brought them down; so I suppose the 18 shillings paid for them all, but if Mʳ Curtis has made a mistake & insists upon it wee must comply with it, tho' wee never had oysters but once in a fortnight of him, so there must be an over reckoning in this last nine shillings. The £3. 9ˢ is my son's money wᶜʰ Mʳ ffish paid Mʳ Robotham by his order, I think the Ballance of your account as follows:—

	£	s	d
Due for butter	4	11	6
By cash received of Mʳ ffish	3	9	0
	8	0	6
Cʳ By paymᵗˢ to Mʳ Curtis & Potts & for mustard seed	2	9	6
So there remains due to mee on yᵉ ballance	5	11	6
Proof	8	0	6

1 "For nine pounds thirteen shillings & a penny In ffull for Butter & all other Accounts & Demands" (extract from 'Instruments Executed' book).

This five pounds eleven shillings & six pence I desire you will pay to Mʳ Peter Moulson in Woodstreet, Cheapside, & take a recᵗ of him for it. My son has ordered him to buy some Lottery Tickets for him.

I am sorry you can't find the writing that was made to give you £100, I fancy your Aunt let your Uncle destroy it, ffor such a thing there was & if you could find it you would come in for that before any of the Creditors. As for Porter's debt it is as I suppose worth nothing, for hee died insolvent & worse than nothing by some thousands of pounds.

I wish the businesse of the house turns out as you expect since your Uncle & Aunt got nothing but lost there considerably. I doubt you will find it difficult to borrow money and pay interest & get a livelihood too out of the businesse of that house; however as you have been used to it you must be the best Judge. I never heard Mʳ Robotham had a mother before, but I have heard him talk of his sister. My son joins with mee in our services to you & I am

Your humble servant

ffor /
  Mʳˢ Russell...
    London

E. P.

No. 365. E. P. *to* MRS RUSSELL

Shalstone [&c.]
May the 28ᵗʰ 1747

I wrote to Mʳˢ Russell on the 10ᵗʰ of this instant May wherein I desired her to pay yᵉ money due to my son & self to Mʳ Moulson in Woodstreet in Cheapside. If you have not paid it already pay ffive pounds¹ to Mʳ Moulson & let yᵉ rest lie in your hands. I mistook sixpence in the account. Wee can't find Mʳ Potts's receipt for the last money Mʳ Robotham paid him, if you have it let us know. If you han't leisure to pay Mʳ Moulson wee must get somebody to call upon you for it. My son joins with mee in our Service & good wishes for you & I am

Your humble servant

ffor /
  Mʳˢ Russell...
    London

E. P.

1 See Letter No. 332.

Mrs Russell did not pay the £5, so Mr Fish was ordered to collect the account in July, by which time Mrs Russell had become Mrs Mason. Mr Fish was not successful, so when Mr Land, the attorney, went to London he was told to try, and even to threaten them "with the Law". On 6 Feb. 1747 O.S. Mr Land collected the money and paid it to the Purefoys, but nearly eighteen months later Mr Mason started a counter-claim, which produced our next letter.

No. 366. E. P. *to* MR MASON

Shalstone [&c.]
October the 9ᵗʰ 1748

I received Mʳ Mason's ſre of the 29ᵗʰ of last month. Had I thought I had owed you anything I should have wrote to you before now. The rect. that you sent of Mʳ Potts's I have accounted with your spouse for, and the article in your spouse's letter & account is Dec. 31ᵗʰ 1746 paid Mʳ Potts for news £1. 1ˢ. This amongst other articles of the account is under her own hand; if you have any scruple about it I will send her letter up to a ffreind in Town to show it you. I doubt if I had not chanced to have kept her letter by mee I must have paid it again. Wee had a leaf to ourselves in Mʳ Robotham's account book & our little affair was always posted, so it will be easily found there.

My son joins with mee in our service to yourself & Mʳˢ Mason & I am

Your humble servant
E. P.

ffor /
Mʳ Mason at the King's
head against the Church
in Islington near
London

No. 367. H. P. *to* PETER MOULSON

Shalstone [&c.]
Octobʳ the 15ᵗʰ 1748

Sir! /

Herewith I send you Mʳˢ Vaughan's Lace wᶜʰ she has paid my mother for, I hope it will prove to her satisfaction. You was so kind when you was here to offer to buy mee anything I wanted in Town, wᶜʰ occasions mee to venture to entreat the favour of you to get mee at your leisure a Chrystall Button made & set in

Gold exactly the same to the Button I send you herewith in a little box; I had the misfortune to loose the other button when I was on Purlieu hunting. As also to buy mee a quart of large Rouncivall Peas & four pounds of la Lucern Grasse¹ seed at 1ˢ 6ᵈ the pound, if the grasse seed won't come at that price you may send a lesse Quantity, for I will have but 6 shillings worth of it; tell yᵉ seedsman if the Grasse seed hitts I shall want more.

And I must beg you to get mee a gallon or two of ffrench Brandy, it must be good because it is to infuse my Rheubarb & Hiera Picra² therein for my Gout, and please to place these things to my account. My mother joins with mee in our service & respects to yourself & Mʳ & Mʳˢ Vaughan, & I beg you'll excuse this Trouble from, Sir!

Your very humble servᵗ

H. P.

P.S. Desire your acceptance of an hare sealed at the knot of yᵉ Direction & carriage paid, & the Lace & Chrystall button is tied to the hare.

ffor /
Mʳ Moulson...
London
with an hare & a small parcell tied to it. Carriage paid.

The old bachelor's advice in the following letter to a grandfather on the rearing of his grandson is extremely edifying.

No. 368. H. P. *to* PETER MOULSON

Shalstone [&c.]
ffebʳʸ 27ᵗʰ 1749

Sir! /

I am favoured with yours of the 24ᵗʰ instant with the two £res of Attorney, but your name was inserted Poulson instead of Moulson; I have altered it & hope it will passe. I send you again

1 This was a fairly early date for the use of lucerne in England; for example a footnote to Lisle, *Observations in Husbandry*, 1757, p. 241, says that it was very little known in Lisle's day, he died in 1722; the text quotes Varro and does not prove that Lisle knew it at first hand. "Rouncival" peas were a large variety; the name may be derived from Roncesvalles, it was used by Tusser.

2 An Account-book has the following entry under 13 August 1748: "Paid Mʳ Wallbank (the Surgeon) of Buckingham for Rheubarb & Hiera Picra and in ffull——00..07..04½". *Hiera picra* is still in the British Pharmacopœia, and is made up of 4 parts of powdered aloes and 1 part of canella bark.

inclosed the Ł̄res of Attorney post paid & desire when you have
sold the Annuities to buy East India Bonds, & let 'em be under
your care till wee order 'em otherwise; when you have setled this
affair pray favour us with a line or two. I desire you will order
your sadler M.ʳ Turner to send mee a black leather head stall and
reins for my heavy bit w.ᶜʰ has silver bosses to it, & a note what
it comes to, & let him know y.ᵉ Day Jones sets out of Town. My
mother is very glad to hear George the Second & his mama have
so good health, & wishes she may be able to suckle him till hee
has bred his Teeth, & when hee is on breeding his Teeth she
desires his back Door may be kept a little open with some Syrrup
of Violets & if that dos not do give him at a Time from a quarter
of an ounce to half an ounce of manna according as it operates,
& heartily wishes George y.ᵉ 2.ᵈ blessings of health & long life. Wee
both join in our compliments to yourself & M.ʳ & M.ʳˢ Vaughan
& with thanks for all favours I am Sir! /

Your oblidged hfe serv.ᵗ
H. P.

ffor /
  M.ʳ Moulson in
     London

No. 369. H. P. *to* PETER MOULSON

Shalstone [*&c.*]
Aprill the 29.ᵗʰ 1750

Sir! /

   I am favoured with both your Letters & had answered your first
sooner but knew you would do for mee as you would for yourself.
My mother has been ill of this Epidemick cold for 20 weeks last
past, sixteen weeks of which she has been confined to the House,
and I am now indisposed with a feverish Disorder & scarcely
qualified to write. You may be assured yourself, M.ʳ and M.ʳˢ
Vaughan & George the Second & his maid will be as wellcome
here as you will be at your own houses without our thinking it
any Trouble.

   Wee were really under great concern for you on account of the
Earthquake[1]—I have sent you enclosed the two permitts signed

1 "Between 12 and 1 o'clock an earthquake was felt throughout London and
Westminster; in the new buildings about Grosvenor Square people ran out of
their houses, chairs shaking, and pewter rattling on the shelves." (*Gentleman's
Magazine*, vol. xx, p. 89.) Shocks were felt in January, February, and April 1750.

by my mother and self. Wee both join in our Compliments to you
with thanks for this and all other favours & I am Sir!

Your oblidged h̄īe serv^t

ffor /
   Mr Moulson in
      London

H. P.

No. 370. H. P. *to* GEORGE VAUGHAN

Shalstone [&c.]
August the 26th 1753

Sir!

On the 16th of this instant August I wrote to Mr Moulson for
half an hogshead of white mountain wine & I have a Letter subscribed W. L. that I should have the wine sent to Jones ye carrier
on Tuesday morning. In pursuance whereof I sent my Team to
Buckingham for it on Thursday morning last, but when they came
to the carrier's there was no wine sent. I had another letter by
ye Post, subscribed also W. L., purporting that the wine was not
sent that day but should be sent the Saturday following. Whether
't is a man or woman who subscribes this W. L. I can't tell, but
Mr Moulson did not use to leave his affairs in such person's hands
as would not subscribe their name at length to a letter, but I hope
by this time Mr Moulson is returned safe home that wee may have
some good wine for wee stand in need of it.[1] What I require of
you is if hee is not come home to see that the wine is sent & to
favour mee with a line or two by ye post the name of the person
who acts for Mr Moulson in his absence.

Wee both desire to join in our Compliments to yourself &
Mrs Vaughan & to excuse this trouble from

Your very humble serv^t

ffor /
   Mr George Vaughan
   at the Golden ball near Arundell
   Street in the Strand
      London

H. P.

---

1 This is the true cause of this querulous letter; an earlier one to "Mr W. L."
was begun but abandoned, perhaps because of the difficulty of directing it.

CHAPTER X

FAMILY AFFAIRS

ON the Purefoy side there was no near relative living in England at the time of our letters: those who subsequently became Henry's heirs were descended from his grandfather's sister who had married Thomas Jervoise, of Herriard, Hants. A few letters to the Jervoises are printed, at first to Thomas, son of the Thomas just mentioned, and afterwards to his son. These letters have a stately formal politeness which never attains cordiality.

Mrs Purefoy was less fortunate in her relatives; a sister had married injudiciously, which brought forth a remarkable letter of condolence (No. 393) when she died. But the great scandal was caused by a nephew who was not merely a ne'er-do-well but an actual *mauvais sujet*, causing the greatest alarm and consternation in the peaceful Manor House of Shalstone, where he was at one time in high favour. His escapades were not of the venial sort and we are lucky in having a very full account of them, and some very characteristic letters from the out-spoken aunt leave us with no illusions as to the young attorney's character.

There is included in this chapter a letter of great importance to Browne Willis; this is formally acknowledged by the great antiquary in his *History of the Hundred of Buckingham*. This is not intended to be a family history, and excessive genealogical data would be out of place, but all the pedigrees which have been published[1] contain many errors, and it has been thought worth while to include one which at all events shows the Purefoy descents of Shalstone, and sets out the relationship of our letter-writers to their heirs and successors. First by *Inquisitiones post mortem* and subsequently by entries in parish registers every entry has official sanction.

The Rev. Geo. H. Jervoise added the name of Purefoy upon suc-ceeding to Shalstone, afterwards reassuming the name of Jervoise; he married the daughter of the Rev. Wright Hawes, rector of Shalstone, whose name often appears in the diaries. In his diary of 16 Apr. 1752 Henry notes that he was "At the Rev.ᵈ Mr. Haws's house on Christening his daughter Miss Mary"; he is little likely to have thought that his ultimate heir would marry this young lady and that later successors in the estate would be descended from her.

1 E.g. the Visitation pedigrees and those given in Nichols: *Leicestershire*, and in Lipscomb: *Buckinghamshire*. There are two amongst the Browne Willis MSS, and a printed proof of one intended for his *History of Buckingham*, but never actually included; all are considerably at fault, the one given by Nichols is the best.

No. 371. E. P. *to* CHRISTOPHER FARMER

Shalstone [&c.]
May the 9ᵗʰ 1736

I receᵈ Mᶦ ffarmer's Letter of the 1ˢᵗ instant & am sorry to hear you left York since the Southwark air disagrees with you so much. My son & self wish you better health & shall be very glad to see you at Shalstone when it suitts with your conveniency—if you don't know it Mʳˢ Millesent Clarke who liv'd with my ffather & afterwards with mee lives at the Kings Head Tavern over against the Church in Islington which house she keeps & is married again to one Mᶦ Robotham & my nephew Porter (who lives in Chancery Lane) hath married an heiress out of Lincolnshire of £6000 fortune as he sais. Her maiden name was Cunington & she lived at Lincoln when he married her. Pray if you know anybody of that countrey enquire if their be any such place as the mannor of Cainby which he sais is devolved to him & his wife's sister by the death of their Uncle. This will oblidge

Your humble servᵗ
E. P.

PS /
My son joins with mee in our service to you.

ffor /
Mᶦ Christopher ffarmer
at yᵉ back of Guy's Hospitall
Southwark

No. 372. E. P. *to* THOMAS ROBOTHAM

Shalstone [&c.]
May the 9ᵗʰ 1736

I receᵈ Mᶦ Robotham's Letter of the 13ᵗʰ of Aprill last & am sorry to hear Mʳˢ Robotham continues so ill as to keep her chamber & shall be glad to hear of her perfect recovery. Pray let mee have your account the first opportunity as I may send your note when I have the receipts &c. Pray send mee 6 pounds of grounds to powder periwiggs with. I had a letter from Mᶦ Porter wherein hee tells mee the mannor of Cainby in Lincolnshire is devolved to his wife & her sister by the death of her uncle to the vallue of £9.000, enquire out if it be so & if it be let mee know. He has a great desire I should give his wife & him an Invitation to Shalstone & if it did not suit with my conveniency to communicate my mind to you that you might tell him again. Pray acquaint him when my son & self come to Town wee will let him & his spouse know wee are there. tell him this privately & not before M[rs] Porter, with our love & service to them both. I am not very well no more than my son & can't tell how to entertain strangers at present. However don't let that frighten M[rs] Robotham from coming for I shall be glad to see her & you said she should come to Shalstone some time this summer. Our hearty wishes are for M[rs] Robotham's speedy & perfect recovery & wee both join in our services to you & her. Pray let us know where M[r] Porter has taken an house & if you & M[rs] Robotham have been at it w[ch] will oblidge

Your humble serv[t]
E. P.

ffor M[r] Robotham at the
    King's Head &c.

"M[r] Porter" is the scapegrace nephew, of whom we shall hear a great deal: villain though he was, this story of his wife's fortune is entirely correct, as will be seen from the following extract from an article[1] by Canon Maddison on *The Tournays of Caenby*; the manor of Caenby was owned by the Tournays from the fourteenth century until the death of George Tournay in 1736: "the coheirship would have vested in his two sisters, Jane, wife of Rev. Thos. Cunnington, and Mary...but they pre-deceased him, the representation therefore was in Mrs Cunington's two daughters, her sister having died childless. These were Jane... and Mary, who married Ralph Porter, who was lost at sea, returning from Jamaica, without issue, August 1743; his widow apparently survived till 1752, when 'Mary Porter' was buried at Glentham. The Court Rolls of Caenby-cum-Glentham give in 1737 Jane Cunnington, spinster, and Ralph Porter and Mary his wife as 'Lord and Ladies of the Manor',—till Ralph Porter's death."

From our Letter No. 374 it appears that Ralph Porter had a girl who evidently did not live, if the above account is correct.

Letter No. 380 is addressed to "M[rs] Jane Conington", who, on 30 Dec. 1743, married Laurence Monck, and their only child Jane married Sir Charles Middleton, Bart., of Belsay Castle, Northumberland.

1 In *Lincolnshire Notes and Queries*, 1907, vol. IX, p. 248.

No. 373. E. P. *to* THOMAS ROBOTHAM

Shalstone [&c.]
Tuesday, June ye 15^(th) 1736

I rece^d Mr Robotham's of the 29^(th) of last month together with
the Turbott & couple of lobsters w^(ch) were very good & wee thank
you for them, & since have received your account w^(ch) is right &
on the Ballance thereof you owe mee £5. 11^s 1½^d.

I shall send you next Saturday my son's repeating watch by
Webster together with your note for that you gave mee. Hee
desires you to carry ye watch to Mr Mulford in Cursitors Alley,
who got it for him, & desire him to get it mended, for young
Mr Gregg has done it never the better; its fault is it gets above
an hour in 24 tho' you turn the spring as backward as may be.

Wee are glad M^(rs) Robotham is so well as to go to visit M^(rs)
Porter—'t is well hee has got such a good wife & an house well
furnished which I hope hee will be contented with. Hee has wrote a
letter here & sais wee mistrust ye truth of what he said. Wee never
said anything about him but to you, therefore I pray advise him to
be at rest for wee never did nor shall ever say or do anything to his
prejudice. The more he has the better it is for him, for I desire to
know no more about it which pray let him know. I have at present
a very bad state of health, I beleive it is a fever on my spiritts.

I must desire you to call on Mr Belchier in St Pauls Churchyard
to know what I am in debt for the last Chimney glasse in three
peices that hee sent, packing and all. I know what hee said hee
would have for the glasse but I don't know what ye packing will
come to. Wee both join in service to yourself & M^(rs) Robotham,
wishing her perfect health, & am   Your humble serv^t
                                                      E. P.
ffor /
   Mr Robotham...
            London

No. 374. E. P. *to* RALPH PORTER

Shalstone [&c.]
January ye 26^(th) 1736

Dear Nephew /

I rece^d yours of the 23^d instant with a Poney mare w^(ch) is come[1]
in a seasonable time for I wanted one, & if it proves fit for mee

1 The Account-book under 28 Jan. 1736 reads: "Gave Mr Porter's Clerke
when he brought the mare....10s.". See Letter No. 523.

to ride I will pay you for it, if it dos not I will send it to a fair and sell it & give you the money for it, if you have no desire of having of it again, which if you have let mee know by Letter. I am very glad your little Girl pleases you so. My son & self shall be glad to see you & Mrs Porter here a night or two as you go to Lincoln. I have been lame & ill some time & under a Physician & a surgeon & am now somewhat better & have found great Benefit by drinking asses' milk & my son has had a sharp fit of ye gout. Wee both join in love & service to you & Mrs Porter, which concludes mee

Your affect. Aunt
E. P.

P.S.

At present wee have the small pox in ye parish wch put us in some fear.

ffor /
  Mr Porter Attorney[1]
  at law in Chancery lane
    London

No. 375. E. P. *to* RALPH PORTER

Shalstone [&c.]
Aprill the 3^d 1737

Dear Nephew,

I received your letter and the small pox has been very much here and all who have had it (but one) died. But at present 't is out of our town. When your fears are over shall be glad to see you & Mrs Porter at Shalstone. Jenny mare at present is in great favour but I have not rode her yet, my leg has been so bad. My son joins with mee in love & service to you both & I am

Your affecte Aunt
E. P.

ffor /
  Mr Porter...
    London /

1 It is worth noting perhaps that according to the official list of solicitors kept by the Law Society Mr Porter was not admitted until 12 Feb. 1736.

No. 376. E. P. *to* RALPH PORTER

Shalstone [*&c.*]
June 5ᵗʰ 1737

Dear Nephew /

I received your Łre on yᵉ 2ᵈ instant & am sorry to hear Mʳˢ Porter is afraid of the Small pox, it has broke out in our Town again at John Hobcrafts & wee have never been at Church since, 't is now three weeks since they first had 'em so I hope there is no danger. As to your travelling, the Ailesbury stage coach goes out from the Bell inne in Holborn every Tuesday at 6 in yᵉ morning & comes to Ailesbury that night, next day it comes to the Lord Cobham's Arms at Buckingham & there our Coach may meet you. But how to get you from Shalstone to Northampton I know not for wee have a ffarm fell in our hands so our horses are workt down, neither do I know whether that is the road to Lincoln or no. My son & self join in love and service to you & Mʳˢ Porter & I am

Your affect. Aunt
E. P.

P.S. /

I well hoped you would have come in your own Chaise & pair.

ffor /
Mʳ Porter...
    London

No. 377. H. P. *to* THOMAS ROBOTHAM

Shalstone [*&c.*]
June yᵉ 14ᵗʰ 1737

This requests Mʳ Robotham as soon as you can after you receive this to go to my cousin Porter & acquaint him that my mother is again much indisposed, and that wee can't have any Thoughts of his coming to Shalstone till my mother has better health. I would have wrote to him myself but was afraid the letter might by chance miscarry. Wee are in great hurry having a ffarme of an hundred pound a year fell into our hands, which, joined to this other misfortune, makes it impossible for us to entertain anybody; pray give our Love & Service to Mʳ & Mʳˢ Porter. If you have

To face p. 244

Plate 16. HENRY PUREFOY THE ELDER AS CUPID

not paid M.ʳ Mulford already pray pay him, as also M.ʳ Gamull
& let mee know yᵉ price of 2 Tickets in yᵉ Bridge Lottery as also
let us have your account that I may know what money to return.
My mother & self join in Service & Respect to you & M.ʳˢ Robotham
& I am

Your very humble serv.ᵗ

ffor /
M.ʳ Robotham...
   London

H. P.

No. 378. E. P. *to* THOMAS ROBOTHAM

Shalstone [&c.]
March yᵉ 14ᵗʰ 1738

I received both M.ʳ Robotham's letters together with the Locks,
Buttons, & workmen's receipts, & I hope you have not forgot to
take the 11 shillings 5 pence three farthings of the plummer, wᶜʰ
was due to mee from him for the lead of the Summerhouse. With
your last wee receᵈ your kind present of fish wᶜʰ were exceeding
good, wee return you & M.ʳˢ Robotham many thanks for them.
When you go that way pray pay M.ʳ Mulford for mending my
son's repeating watch & take a receipt in ffull of him & at your
leisure let mee have your account. Wee are very sorry for the losse
of my Cozen Monger,¹ wee design to mourn 3 months for him.
I wonder his Death was not put in the news considering hee was
a Lievetent Coll.ˡˡ & had been so long in the service. Wee both
join in our service & respect to yourself & M.ʳˢ Robotham & I am

Your humble serv.ᵗ

ffor /
M.ʳ Robotham...
   London

E. P.

1 The earliest Account-book has some pages (in a writing which is not Mrs
Purefoy's) filled with executor's expenses upon the death of Capt. Ben. Monger,
who died 4 March 1699 apparently in London, and an inquest had to be held
on him. The details are full and curious, but too voluminous to be given here.
The name of Charles Monger often occurs, and he may have been the Lt.-
Colonel of forty years later.

No. 379. E. P. *to* MRS PORTER

Shalstone [*&c.*]
Octobr the 21st 1739

Dear Sister /

I received yours a considerable time ago and am glad to hear your son Porter & his spouse were to visit you. Wee should have been glad if it had been in our power to have done your younger son any acceptable service, but as it is now War Time I hope you will find it no difficulty to have your Expectations answered as to him, as he has been bred to sea affairs. All our ffreinds who could have served him are either dead or who [*sic*] have no interest at Court. I have my health pretty well now, all but a sore Leg which has been very bad as I have been in health. It is a Scorbutick humour & I cannot learn when it is to be well. My son presents his Duty to you & wee both desire our love & service to your ffamily & shall be glad to hear of all your healths, which concludes mee

Your affect. sister
E. P.

ffor /
Mrs Porter
at
Scarborough
in Yorkshire
By London /

No. 380. E. P. *to* MRS JANE CUNNINGTON

Shalstone [*&c.*]
December the 31th 1740

Madam /

I recd yours of the 20th instant & in answer thereto I do assure you I have never given my nephew Ralph Porter one farthing of money since hee has been married nor some time before, nor never shall give him anything for I have a son of my own & if I had ten times what I have I would leave it him. My nephew lost my favour on account of some little Indiscretions here, & soon after I heard hee had bought chambers at Barnards Inne, or rather built them at a great expence & put himself in a garb of velvet silk, gold & silver, & a fine Diamond ring at a greater Expence, & after that I discarded him knowing that his circumstances could

not bear anything of that kind, ffor I suppose my sister Porter
has £40 a year in land at old Newton in Yorkshire for her life,
& hee has it after her in ffee, & I suppose my sister may have
to the vallue of £1.000 besides at her disposall, as hee told mee
for I have not seen my sister Porter since the year 1716.

As to what Dr Trimnell[1] said about my giving my nephew a
great summe of money I heard it from severall of my neighbours
that Dr Trimnell should say so, & when the D^r was at Astrop
Wells last season I took care to send him word there was nothing
in it. I look on the Doctor to be a very worthy gentleman & am
sorry to hear my nephew has used him as hee has. I doubt my
nephew takes his basenesse from the Porters, for I never knew any
of my ffather or mother's kindred behave as hee has done. I think
his father made a poor Improvement of the fortune hee had with
my sister, for hee had £3.000 with her at my ffather's death
besides what hee had with her before.

I once thought my nephew Porter as likely to get an Estate by
his Businesse as any young fellow whatsoever, & if I could have
prevailed on him to have been advised by mee & my son wee
thought no otherwise than to have encouraged him & to have
been kind to him.

I hope Mrs Porter as an Heiresse has kept her land to herself
at least. Hee reported when hee came to Town & bought the
Chariot & fine equipage that hee had £400 a year in land left
him by the Conington family, exclusive of you & there was a
report that hee had got your money in his hands, wch came from
a merchant in the City & that hee had put £800 thereof in the
late Alderman Childs hands to take up to pay Tradesmen, and
hee once gave out hee had my will in his keeping wch is entirely
false. I aver this for Truth and wish it may be serviceable to you.

I am, Madam,

Your humble servant

E. P.

ffor /
Mrs Jane Conington
To be left at Mrs Ruxtons
in the ffishmarket below the
Hill in Lincoln in Lincolnshire
By London

1 For particulars of the Rev. Doctor see Letter No. 572. Astrop Wells is
described on pp. 388–392.

The Diary of 5 March 1740 records that there came "a stranger gentleman who said hee came from my cousin Ralph Porter, & that his name was Kent, & that hee was an attorney of Grantham in Lincolnshire". The gentleman himself was innocuous but proved to be the harbinger of events which gravely disturbed the placid life of Shalstone. Our first letter gives us a very exact picture of the caller; it gives small hint of the anxiety roused by the call.

No. 381. E. P. *to* THOMAS ROBOTHAM

Shalstone [&c.]
March ye 8th 1740

I received Mr Robotham's letter of the 14th of ffebruary last with half a dozen of oranges, a dozen of Delft plates, & 2 shoe Brushes wch do very well, 2 of the plates were broke. I thank you for the oranges. I thank God I am pretty well recovered of my fall, the losse of my blood was by my ffall, my right arm ever since has been very weak.

I know you used to have acquaintance of Lincolnshire gentlemen & I desire you would enquire if there be such a Person as Mr Kent an Attorney of Grantham in Lincolnshire & what character hee bears in that Countrey, & what sort of a person of a man hee is.

A stranger man came to us as from Mr Porter on the 5th of this instant March at 7 in ye morñ), & said his name was Kent, and that hee was an attorney of Grantham in Lincolnshire. Hee came as hee pretended upon a very impudent Errant from Mr Porter, which you shall know more of when I have the character of the man. As to his Person hee was very near six foot high, of a fair & fresh complexion, with a white perriwigg, a short loose great-coat, & a blue-grey coat with gold Buttons, & a black Wastcoat & a coloured handkercheif about his neck, & had a young fellow with him about 20 years old in a black cap. Both of them were very well mounted & they lay the night before they came here at the Lord Cobham's Inne, as hee said. When you have enquired if there is such a person & his character let mee know by the post as soon as may be, wch will oblidge

Your humble servant
E. P.

P.S. Our service & respects are with yourself & Mrs Robotham.

ffor /
  Mr Robotham...
      London

No. 382. E. P. *to* THOMAS ROBOTHAM

Shalstone [&c.]
March the 18ᵗʰ 1740

I receḋ Mʳ Robotham's letter of the 12ᵗʰ instant, I am glad to hear Mʳ Cant is a man of good character for hee came in such a manner I was afraid hee was an Incendiary, his coming so early in the morning & refusing to send in his businesse, and desiring to speak with mee alone without any bodies letter or name to introduce him, very much surprized mee, till my son looking out of yᵉ window & asking him his businesse hee said hee came from Mʳ Porter, upon which my son asked him to walk in, & wee went down to him. Upon my enquiring his Businesse hee told mee hee came from Mʳ Porter who said that I would be bound with him for £3000, and that one Mʳ Preston was to advance the money & asked if such a person did not live hereabouts. I told him there was no such person as Mʳ Preston in this Countrey, & that I would not be bound with Mʳ Porter for 3 farthings, & that I had not seen him these 7 years. Mʳ Cant seemed shocked when I told him I had not seen Mʳ Porter for 7 years, & that I would not be bound with him, & so took his leave, & I could not help telling him hee came with the tale of a Tubb without a bottom.¹ Too be sure Mʳ Porter must tell him some strange story to give him an assurance to come in such a manner. I desire you will write to Mʳ Porter & let him know that Mʳ Cant called here on the 5ᵗʰ of March last in this manner & that unless Mʳ Porter writes mee word by the Post that hee never had any Will of mine in his keeping & that I never was bound with him nor for him for any summe of money whatsoever, nor ever promised to be bound with him, & that hee never asked mee to be bound with him, & that I never gave him any summe of money more than 2 or 3 guineas² at a time, and that I have not seen him these 7 years last past,—if Mʳ Porter dos not comply with this & that soon too I shall be oblidged to advertize something of this nature in the newspapers.

1 This particular phrase does not seem to be in the *O.E.D.* but "The Tale of a Tub" was used long before Swift's marine application of it. Presumably "without a bottom" means that it will "not hold water", as we say nowadays of an untenable proposition.
2 Henry's Account-book, under "22ᵗʰ Janʳʸ 1732", has the entry: "paid my mother my share of what wee gave Cousen P—r— 00 : 10 : 6".

I seldom go into any Company in this countrey but I am told M.ʳ Porter reports I gave him £4000 this last year, besides other summs before, w.ᶜʰ you know is false. I pray you would not spare M.ʳ Porter but inform him of all these particulars, for I am really apprehensive hee has some mischeivous design against me, to prevent w.ᶜʰ I am advised by my ffreinds to advertize what I have mentioned unlesse hee makes mee the above acknowledgement, for I think if M.ʳ Porter has no ill design in this matter it is well if hee is in his right senses, for I never heard of such a thing in my Life before. Wee both join in our service & respects to yourself & M.ʳˢ Robotham & I am

Your humble servant
E. P.

P.S. I entreat M.ʳˢ Robotham if she lights of such a penny-worth of cambrick as she did before to buy me 3 or 4 yards.

ffor /
 M.ʳ Robotham...
   London

No. 383. E. P. to THOMAS ROBOTHAM

Shalstone [&c.]
March the 22.ᵗʰ 1740

I hope by this time M.ʳ Robotham has my letter of the 18.ᵗʰ instant. I desire you will accept of a neck chine which I have sent with the Butter & am sorry I can get neither Pidgeons nor ffowlls to send with it. I used to have early pidgeons, but the catt got into the Dovehouse & almost destroyed them.

Wee happening to say in our ffamily that that was a young gentleman who came with M.ʳ Cant, a servant who lett them in at the Gates said that could not be, for the young man asked where hee might set his master's horses, upon which the footman was called to show him where, & hee came into the kitchen at the back door with the ffootman & set down by the fire. But when hee heard M.ʳ Cant & my son & self talk in our little parlour hee jumpt up & came as far as the brick passage window, & the servants thought hee was coming into the parlour. This has so ill a look that I apprehend M.ʳ Porter has some mischeivous Design against mee. Pray don't you send M.ʳ Porter the letter that I sent

you last, but write to him yourself & desire a speedy answer, for
if I am not satisfied by him speedily in this affair I will certainly
advertize him. Our respects & services are with yourself & M:rs
Robotham & am

Your humble serv:t
E. P.

ffor /
    M:r Robotham...
         London

On 21 May Mr Robotham had been asked to "enquire of M:r James
Whitfeild at the Golden Cock in lower Holloway about a mechanical
churn that is to be seen there which was invented by M:r Newsham,
the engine maker, & is said to churn quicker & easier than other
churns". Richard Newsham (d. 1743), was a noted maker of fire-
engines: one made by him was presented to Brackley by Sir Paul
Methuen, M.P. for the borough; the letter promising it to the Mayor,
Sam:l Harding, is dated 28 Dec. 1725. The engine is still preserved by
the Town, and Mrs Purefoy must have been familiar with it. (Information kindly supplied by Dr Parkhurst.)

No. 384. E. P. *to* THOMAS ROBOTHAM

Shalstone [&c.]
June the 13th 1741

I received M:r Robotham's letter of the 26:th of May last with the
Turbott which was very good & for which wee return you thanks.

You sent mee word you would let mee know the price of the
churn next week but I have heard nothing of it. I should be glad
to hear about it for our old churn is quite rotten & makes y:e
butter tast of y:e wood, w:ch I suppose you are sensible of. I was
forced to churn twice this week in a little churn so hope your
butter will be very good this week. Wee have set all our Land wee
design to set, so that a churn that will churn two dozen pounds
& an half of butter at a time will be bigg enough, pray let mee
know about it & the price or else I must have one made in y:e
Countrey.

I have never heard from M:r Porter but I think hee might have
mentioned something to you if hee had not writt to mee, but it
is like the rest of his proceedings; I can't join with you in sorrow
for M:r Porter, but am glad Justice has overtook him that there
may be some hopes that something may be saved for his wife.
I am sorry I have so vile a person so near a kin to mee, and shall

not trouble my head to advertize him now his circumstances are such. I am in hopes of seeing a gentleman soon who will give mee an account of everything.

Next week my son will send his repeating watch with the butter as also his pocket book, pray carry the watch to M.͏ͬ Mulford to be mended & the ffigures in the Diall plate to be done with black wax. It gets[1], notwithstanding you turn the spring ever so much backwards, so I suppose the spring is quite loose; & carry the pockett book at your leisure to M.͏ͬ Samuell Saunders at the 7 Stars & half Moon on the south side of S.͏ͭ Paulls Church near Watling Street, to have y.͏ᵉ spring of the bolt mended that shoots thro' the clasp, and to be mended elsewhere if it wants. Wee both join in our service & respects to yourself & M.͏ʳˢ Robotham & I am

Your hte serv.͏ͭ
E. P.

P.S. If the alteration of the churn is only the brasse boxes for the iron to go in wee make such here.

ffor /
   M.͏ͬ Robotham...
       London
with a parcell of butter

No. 385. E. P. *to* THOMAS ROBOTHAM

Shalstone [&c.]
December the 23.͏ᵗʰ 1741

I received M.͏ͬ Robotham's letter of the 1.͏ˢᵗ instant and at y.͏ᵉ time you mentioned have sent you a Chine & a couple of Turkeys & [a blank] this day by M.͏ʳˢ Eagles, the Buckingham carrier (who comes into London on ffriday in the afternoon,) carriage paid, w.͏ᶜʰ I desire you to accept on.

I shall be glad to hear if M.͏ͬ ffish has got a purchaser for y.͏ᵉ house in Grub Lane. My son has 3 tickets in the present State Lottery, the numbers whereof are N.͏ᵒ 11 m 501, N.͏ᵒ 11 m 502, N.͏ᵒ 11 m 503, when the Lottery is all drawn I desire you will examine at some office & see what they come up & let mee know.

Since I wrote to you last here has been a man who has assumed the name of ffysh & pretended to buy the Mannor House of

1 That is: "gains time"; this is the 18th meaning in the *E.D.D.*

Souldern[1] near Bircester, in Oxfordshire, & other estates of 5 or 6 hundred a year, & to pay for 'em on a day certain. But before the day of payment came hee absconded. Hee has run in Debt (as the Countrey sais) at Oxford, Banbury, Bircester, & Souldern to the sum of 5 or 6 hundred pounds & on Tuesday the 8th of this December, about 4 a clock in the morning hee went towards London with a good deall of Plate & money. The Countrey is in pursuit of him & would be glad to know where hee is. The Saturday before hee went of[f] a gentleman came to us who had a writt out against him by the name of Ralph Porter alias ffysh, which surprized us very much & hee told us hee should be at Brackley on Wensday following, where hee should serve ye writt upon him. To convince myself I sent the ffootman who lived here when Mr Porter was here & my own present footman to see if hee could know him, but hee smelt a rat & went of[f] a day before.

Whoever hee is hee is a consummate Rascall, for hee has given a note subscribed R. Fysh to one Mr James Gibbs (a Grazier & one that wee deall with,) for £60, who has a wife & seuall[2] children, & hee has not satisfied the said note.

Hee went attended with 3 servants on horseback & one [of] them (to witt) Paull[3] sais his master never went out without 3 brace of pistolls about him, & his 3 servants armed with the like. Hee has seuall[2] times with his men rode thro' Shalstone by our Gates & rounded the Town feilds & the Townspeople took notice of them & brought us word that they thought they were Highway-

---

1 There is a curious confirmation of this in a letter from Ralph Verney (afterwards Earl Verney), to his father Lord Fermanagh (in *Verney Letters of the Eighteenth Century*, 1930, vol. II, p. 190).
The letter is dated 31 Dec. 1741: "Mr Souldern is bit in the Sale of his House at Souldern as are several tradesmen round about. The Pretended Purchaser was discovered by Mrs Purefoy of Shawson to whom twas said he was Related. He proves to be an Attorney's Cleark worth nothing and is gone off.... He had had goods from several Tradesmen, who will be losers by him, particularly a Silversmith, who had deliver'd a large Quantity of Plate".
There is apparently a slip here, the owners of Souldern were not themselves named Souldern at this date; the Manor House belonged to a Cox, who had married a Kilby, herself connected with the Weedons who had been there since the sixteenth century. The other Souldern family was named Gough. See J. C. Blomfield, *History of Souldern*, 1893, pp. 16–26.
2 The "u" with an upward flourish does duty for "ver" in this word on both occasions.
3 See Letter No. 193.

men. And this Paull the servant sais his master gives out that in case my son dies without children hee is heir of Shalstone in spite of any body, & Paull tells openly such secrets of his master's ffamily that I must think it is Ralph Porter.

Pray let mee know M⁫ Porter's agent's name & find out if you can whether hee carries any correspondence with him now. This has put us into y᪱ utmost Consternation & Paull & another of the servants lie about y᪱ Countrey still, as is supposed for no good. All the while you was here last hee was no further of[f] than at the Crown inne at Brackley at Bed & Board. Wee are told that the whole City of London will ring of him for that his creditors design to advertize him. I could wish poor M⁫ Gibbs had his money again. When I see you you shall have more of this at large; with our compliments for the season of the year to you both am in hast

Your humble serv⁫
E. P.

ffor /
M⁫ Robotham....
London /

No. 386. H. P. *to* JAMES GIBBS

Shalstone
Sunday, Dec⁫ the 27ᵗʰ 1741

M⁫ Gibbs /

Wee have had a strange man who took up his Quarters at a lone house in this Parish & will be known by no name but that of Thomas wᶜʰ hee sais is his Christian Name. As to his person hee is ab⁫ the tallnesse of Kirton Gostello,[1] but lathy & thin in the body. Hee is of a tawny complexion, black longish hair that just curls up at the end & his face is pitted with the small pox, especially on y᪱ forehead, & hee has a roundish face & a Roman nose, & about 45 years of age. Hee wears a blueish grey broad cloath coat & wastcoat & a white ffrock over, buttoned at the hands like a shirt. His stockings were the colour of his cloaths & hee had on a Buckskin pair of Breetches & silver shoe buckles & silver clasps to his neck, & silver buttons to his shirt, & 2 holland shirts & 2 very good necks. Hee sais hee came from within 2 miles of Grantham in Lincolnshire.

1 See Letter No. 229.

Some of our neighbours suppose him to be one of M.ᵣ ffysh his men, whom hee had at Souldern with him. I made a shift to dislodge him yesterday & hee said hee would go to the Posthouse at Buckingham & stay there till hee had a letter out of his own Countrey. Hee said hee came away for debt but when wee examined him hee contradicted himself in everything hee said. I will tell you more of him when I see you. I shall be glad to know whether you think it one of M.ᵣ ffysh's men, for if hee is not I imagine him to be guilty of some crime.

I thought fit to let you know this that if anybody had any desire to see him they might know where to find him, I shall be glad to hear you have succeeded at Astrop & to see you here when you come this way & am in hast, wishing a merry X.ᵗmas

Your humble servant
H. P.

ffor /
    M.ᵣ James Gibbs at
        Souldern
            This

No. 387. e. p. *to* THOMAS ROBOTHAM

Shalstone [&c.]
March 25ᵗʰ 1742

I rece.ᵈ M.ᵣ Robotham's letter of the 13ᵗʰ instant and all the things you mention but the charger for the Blunderbuss & the swan shott, which wee could find nothing on. Pray send them as soon as possible for wee can't use y.ᵉ Blunderbusse till wee have them.

Wee thank you & M.ʳˢ Robotham for your kind present of the salmon & anchovy & oranges, & likewise for your trouble in procuring the other things. I am much surprized at M.ᵣ Porter's proceedings; they say hee carries correspondence still at Brackley with one Matt. Onion, who pulls out a great many Łres out of his pocketts & sais they all come from his master Porter. 'Tis said this Matt. Onion is as like to betray him as any man; I should be glad to hear M.ᵣ Porter was got beyond sea. I shall send you next Wensday by M.ʳˢ Eagles some hog puddings & a chine (carriage paid) & if you send to the George inne in Smithfeild on the

ffriday following in the evening you may have them. My son has
had so dangerous a fit of the Cholick that I thought I should have
lost him, but I thank God hee is now somewhat better. Pray send
a yard & a half of stuff the same to the pattern wch will be in y^e
Baskett. Wee both join in our hearty respects & service to yourself
and Mrs Robotham and I am

Your humble servant
E. P.

ffor /
  Mr Robotham...
      London

P.S. I thank you for selling my son's Lottery tickett. When you
send again pray send a gallon of the best ffrench Brandy for mine
& my son's own drinking.

No. 388. H. P. *to* HARRY FISH

Shalstone [*&c.*]
March the 30th 1742

Sir! /

I wrote to you in August last to desire you to look out for a
Purchasor for the house in Grub Lane, but have not heard from
you since. I should not have given you the trouble of this letter
for that only, but I desire to know how many sons you have &
the Christian names of them as they be in seniority of age. I suppose you have heard of Mr Ralph Porter's Transactions in this
countrey as well as in Lincolnshire, & of the £40 reward to
apprehend him, & wee hear hee has mortgaged my Estate & got
an woman to personate my mother to carry the cheat on more
speciously; it has done mee no hurt, but the poor Gentleman is
entirely bitt of his money. Your speedy answer will oblidge

Your affect: Kinsman
& humble servant
H. P.

P.S. Wee both join in our Respects & Service

ffor /
  M^r ffish...
      London

No. 389. E. P. *to* THOMAS ROBOTHAM

Shalstone
March the 31ᵗʰ 1742

I have this day sent M^r & Mrs Robotham...Hog puddings &
a neck chine & a couple of pulletts, which I hope will prove young
for such are very hard to get here; pray let mee know how they be.
My son has been so ill of a fit of the Cholick that I thought I
should have lost him, I thank God the fit is now gone of[f], but his
purging & bleeding makes him so chilly wee are afraid of an ague.
My son has received a letter, part of it in the following words:

S^r /   *March the 23ᵈ*

It is said here that a Lincolnshire gentleman has advertized a
reward of forty pounds for apprehending Mr Porter. This is certainly true & I am persuaded that you have heard it at Shalstone,
but whether the following reports have been made known to you
or not I am uncertain. It is said that the particular ffact of
fforgery which occasioned ye Advertizement relates to your estate;
that Mr Porter has prevailed upon the Advertizer to advance
money upon a counterfeit security. It is added that to carry
on the cheat better a well dressed woman passed for Mrs Purefoy
& joined with him in the Deed. /

I think Mr Porter is a very wicked man to use his best ffreinds
in this manner, for so wee should have been to him had hee been
like ourselves. The postmaster of Greenwich has sent a letter to
the postmaster of Brackley to know if one Mr Robinson had any
considerable Estate at Brackley, for that the said Robinson told
him hee had, & that hee (the postmaster) had trusted him for
an horse & eight pounds, & since hee read the Advertizements
of Mr Cant's against Mr Porter hee had great reason to beleive
it was Ralph Porter, wch made him give the Brackley postmaster
that trouble. If it lies in your way pray enquire after this &
Mr Cant. In the London Evening Post Mr Porter has advertized
to desire the Publick to suspend all judgment on either side between
him & Mr Cant till hee publishes his case, & I hope when M^r
Porter publishes this case hee will publish his actions in this

countrey. Wee wish you & Mrs Robotham your healths & with
our respects & service am   Your humble servant
                                                           E. P.

P.S. Pray don't forget the charger for the Blunderbusse & the
Swan shot.¹

ffor /
  Mr Robotham...
            London

No. 390. E. P. *to* THOMAS ROBOTHAM
Shalstone [*&c.*]
May 29th 1743

I rece͞d Mr Robotham's kind present of ffish for which wee
return you and Mrs Robotham many thanks, and have sent you
with your butter a brace of Hares; they are fresh killed, I hope
they will come sweet to you wch pray let mee know. I have heard
nothing from Mr Cant since I have seen you, but I hear hee has
put his case out in answer to Mr Porter's. They say there are but
few of them printed, but I desire you would get one of them if
possible & send it mee, & let me know if you hear anything of
Mr Porter or Mr Cant. This will oblidge   Your humble servant
                                                           E. P.

P.S. Our service & respect waits on yourself & Mrs Robotham.

ffor /
  Mr Robotham...
            London

No. 391. E. P. *to* THOMAS ROBOTHAM
Shalstone [*&c.*]
Aprill the 4th 1744

I hope Mr Robotham rece͞d the brace of hares, and I desire
you will send a yard & 3 quarters of superfine blue broad cloath,
the same colour to the pattern, and of blue ratteen the same colour
to the cloath, enough to line a coat & the skirts of the wastcoat.
Pray let the cloath & Ratteen be matched of a colour; & send

1 They were remembered, for they were acknowledged on 11 April. The
blunderbusses still hang on the gun-rack (see Plate 13).

half an ounce of blue silk twist for the wastcoat, and an ounce of grey silk twist, the same colour to the pattern of grey cloath sent, and send 4 yards & 3 quarters of good Shalloon[1] the same colour to the pattern sent.

It is strongly reported here that the attorney, that was hanged at Chelmsford in Essex for robbing a coach this last Assizes there, was our Kinsman.[2] I desire you will make it your Businesse to enquire & let mee know, wch will oblidge

Your humble servant
E. P.

P.S. Our respects & services are with yourself & Mrs Robotham.

ffor /
 Mr Robotham...
   London

No. 392. E. P. *to* THOMAS ROBOTHAM

Shalstone [&c.]
Aprill the 15th 1744

I rece^d Mr Robotham's letter of the 10th instant, the blue cloath will do very well, I desire you will send that & the rest of the things wrote for.

I thank you for enquiring after our Kinsman & heartily wish you may find the Truth of it out; wee have lost the paper wherein an account was given of the manner how hee was taken, I should be glad if you could procure it for mee, I think it was some time in ffebruary. Our respects & service attend yourself & Mrs Robotham & I am

Your humble servant
E. P.

ffor /
 Mr Robotham...
   London

The following letter to a niece upon the death of her mother, the writer's sister, is surely as strange a condolence as was ever written. Indignation soon overpowers sympathy.

1 A closely woven woollen material chiefly used for linings, from obsolete French *Chalon*. *O.E.D.*
2 Mrs Purefoy apparently did not know that Ralph Porter had been drowned nine months before this letter was written; see quotation at end of Letter No. 372.

No. 393. E. P. *to* SUSANNAH CLARKE

Shalstone [*&c.*]
ffebruary ye 16th 1745

I received Mrs Clarke's letter of the 4.th instant & am very sorry to hear of my sister's death, as I am that I could not have an account sooner that wee might have gone into mourning for her, but now the time is almost expired. I am glad you did not give yourself the Trouble of coming to Shalstone for since I received the barbarous usage from your Brother Ralph I made a Resolution never to see or have anything to do with any of the family of the Porters, & thereupon have settled my estate & what I have on my son Purefoy. Ralph was so great a favourite with my son & self that wee used him & intended him as a younger son in the family. His return was that hee made mee (as far as in him lay) a forgerer & a ffelon by bringing an woman down to Ailesbury & executing a counterfeit conveyance in my name for £4,946. 10s. on Lord Cobham's estate at Westbury, & when the Commissioners set on Ralph's affairs in Lincolnshire they sent up the deed by the Attorney who saw the woman sign it, to see if I was her, & when hee saw mee hee acknowledged I was not ye woman, but that she was taller & bigger than mee. This transcendent villany occasioned mee a great deall of trouble as well as charge. Ralph also took an house in our neighbourhood & cheated ye countrey of what Plate & Goods & Money hee could, & then made of[f] with it, which was a great Trouble & Disgrace also to us. The reason I did not acquaint my sister with this was I was not willing to add to her sorrow. I have not heard from her these 4 or 5 years,[1] then she said she had a son at sea & desired us to endeavour to get some preferment in ye navy for him; but I acquainted her it was not in my power. 'Tis well if Ralph is dead, otherwise as hee would have put an Halter about my neck, I fear 'twould have been his ffate. Adieu /

E. P.

ffor /
Mrs Susannah Clarke living
near Allbrough gates in
          Scarborough
               Yorkshire
By way of London

NB. My mother Purefoy set only the Initiall letters of her name to this Letter.

1 See Letter No. 379.

To face p. 260

Plate 17.   MRS. CHRISTOPHER HALES

Our next letter is the last from Mrs Purefoy to her niece: one is sorry for it. Letters Nos. 393 and 394 were apparently dictated by Mrs Purefoy.

No. 394. E. P. *to* SUSANNAH CLARKE

Shalstone [*&c.*]
July the 16ᵗʰ 1747

I received Mʳˢ Clarke's Letter & am sorry for your losse if it be so. 'Tis well you have something left to maintain you, if your mother would have been ruled by mee you would have had her fortune when my ffather died, which was £3.000, but nothing would satisfie her but to cancell her marriage settlement.

God blesse my Eyesight I desire never to see any of the Porter's ffamily any more. Direct what estate you have any where for I desire none of it.

Adieu

E. P.

ffor /
Mʳˢ Susannah Clarke...
         Yorkshire /
By way of London

NB. My mother subscribed only the Initiall Letters of her name to this Letter.

Thomas Jervoise, to whom the next letter is addressed, was Henry's first cousin once removed, his mother and Henry's grandfather having been sister and brother. He was born in 1667 and died in 1743; from 1691 to 1710 he represented various constituencies in Parliament. In 1704 he completed the building of his Herriard house of which Tollman was architect.[1] It was his grandson who was destined to be Henry Purefoy's heir, but a glance at the pedigree will most readily explain the Jervoise-Purefoy connection.

The Christian name of his second son was requested because the son by his first marriage was *non compos*. The son by the second marriage, Richard, died on 17 March 1762 and Henry Purefoy died on 28 April in the same year, so that Richard's son, who was in Holy Orders, actually came into the property, as was explained at the beginning of this chapter.

1 *The Ancestor*, No. 3, 1902, p. 7, in an article by F. H. T. Jervoise, F.S.A., the present owner of Herriard Park.

No. 395. H. P. *to* THOMAS JERVOISE

Shalstone [&c.]
January the 17ᵗʰ 1741

Sir! /

My mother & self designed ourselves the pleasure of waiting on you at Herriard last summer, but were disappointed. My present request is to let me know by the post your second son his Christian name & the Christian names of his four sons as they be in seniority of age. Wee hope to wait on you at Herriard some time next summer & in the mean time shall be glad to hear you enjoy good health, & with both our respects & good wishes for yourself & ffamily I am Sir!

Your affect: Kinsman
& very humble servant
H. P.

ffor /
Thomas Jervoise Esq.
at Herriard
near Basingstoke
in Hampshire
By way of London

No. 396. H. P. *to* THOMAS JERVOISE

Shalstone [&c.]
Septembʳ the 28ᵗʰ 1742

Sir! /

I am favoured with yours of the 9ᵗʰ of August & should certainly have waited on you at Herriard from Bath, but that Dʳ Rayner immediately after her drinking the Waters ordered my mother into a course of physick.

I thank you for your good wishes but I have received very little benefit by the waters myself, but wee hope my mother has & that wee shall be able to wait on you next spring. This is a Disappointment wee did not expect, but were much delighted with the Thoughts of coming to Herriard & had our Coach & horses all the while at Bath for that purpose. I would have done your message to Sʳ Hugh Clopton[1] myself but that hee came into his

1 Probably this is the owner of New Place, Stratford-on-Avon; the famous house had originally been built by a Clopton and returned to that family after the death of Shakespeare's grand-daughter. Hugh Clopton died in 1752, and the property was bought by the iconoclastic Rev. Francis Gastrell, who destroyed house, mulberry-tree and all. See Sir S. Lee, *Shakespeare's Life and Work*, ch. xv *ad finem*. Sir H. Clopton was made K.B. in February 1732 (W. A. Shaw, *Knights of England*, 1906, vol. II, p. 284).

Inne at Bath late at night & went out early in the morning fol-
lowing, I think by 6 a clock, so had no opportunity of seeing him.
My mother joins with mee in our best service and respects to you,
& I am Sir! /

Your affect: Kinsman
& very humble servant
H. P.

ffor /
   Thos Jervoise Esq...
         Hampshire
By way of London

No. 397. H. P. *to* THOMAS JERVOISE

Shalstone [&c.]
May the 8th 1743

Sir! /

I am favoured with yours of the 12th of last Aprill & hope this
will find you safe returned to Herriard. I wish you a good Journey
into Worcestershire[1] and at your Return I hope nothing will prevent our waiting on you at Herriard. Shall be glad to hear of
your health & your safe return home & with my mother's & my
service & Respects I am Sir! /

Your affect: Kinsman &
very humble servant
H. P.

ffor /
   Thomas Jervoise Esq...
         Hampshire
By way of London.

No. 398. H. P. *to* REV. WILLIAM PRETTY

Shalstone [&c.]
June the 15th 1743

Sir! /

I received yours of the 15th of May last & wee are heartily
concerned for the losse of our good kinsman Mr Jervoise & should
be glad to hear of the prosperity of the family.

---

1 The Jervoise family had owned Northfield and other manors in Worcestershire
since the middle of the sixteenth century; Thomas, the son, lived chiefly at
Northfield. (*Ancestor*, loc. cit. pp. 2 and 7.)

My late kinsman being deaf I could not have an opportunity of asking when his son Richard would return to Herriard agen & indeed I would have enquired more about ye affairs of the ffamily if I had had ye pleasure of waiting on him as I desired.

If 't is not a secret I should be glad to know where Mr Richard Jervoise is & if his children are all living, & when you think hee will be at Herriard. I suppose this is Mr Clarke of Chilcott & not the Gentleman who married Mr Jervoise's Daughter;[1] however, pray our compliments to him. My mother & self join in our service to you & I entreat your answer at your leisure wch will much oblidge

Your very humble servant
H. P.

P.S. I imagine you to be Rector of Herriard so direct to you as such.

ffor /
  The Revd Mr William Pretty, Rector of
Herriard near Basingstoke in
               Hampshire
By way of London

No. 399. H. P. *to* RICHARD JERVOISE

Shalstone [&c.]
July 12th 1743

Sir! /

I am favoured with both your letters & am glad to hear you & your ffamily are well. I had answered your first letter but thought to have been in Town before this, & so I shall still in a little time in case my mother is not ordered by ye Physicians to Holt[2] or Cheltenham for the waters. If I come to Town I will either wait on you at Mr Huddleston's or let you know where I am. If I should be disappointed in coming to London I had no other enquiry to make after your affairs[3] than to know of the welfare

1 A glance at the pedigree will show the two Clarke families; "the gentleman who married Mr Jervoise's daughter" assumed the name of Jervoise.

2 A spring at Holt, near Bradford in Wiltshire, is included amongst "nitrous waters" by Dr John Rutty: *A Methodical Synopsis of Mineral Waters*, 1757, p. 97: "It was first introduced into use in 1713, the occasion of which was an accidental cure of a child over-run and greatly emaciated with scrophulous sores".

3 See Letter No. 535.

of yourself & ffamily. My mother's & my compliments wait on you & your spouse & I am Sir!

Your affect: Kinsman &
very humble servant
H. P.

ffor /
    Richard Jervoise Esq
    at Mr Huddleston's¹ in
    Bedford Street in
    Covent Garden
        London

No. 400. H. P. *to* RICHARD JERVOISE

Shalstone [*&c.*]
January 11th 1743

Sir! /

I rece⃔ both your last ⅂res & in answer to your first wondred to hear that the Goods at Herriard house went to sale as you say for paymt. of debts, for as I understood by your late father when Amersden Hall² was sold hee should clear all his debts & if I had not rece⃔ your letter that you were gone abroad I should have endeavoured to have seen you when I was in Town.

Since my unhappy Kinsman³ is fallen into yours & Mr Clark's hands I question not but you will use him with Tendernesse & care.

I am at Times aflicted with the Gout so can't at present entertain Company here, but hope when I come to Town next summer to see you there.⁴ My mother & self desire to give you & Mrs Jervoise the compliments of the season & I am Sir!

Your affect: Kinsman &
very humble servant
H. P.

ffor /
    Richard Jervoise Esq...
        London

1 This was Richard Jervoise's father-in-law.

2 Richard's mother was dau. and heiress of Sir John Stonehouse, of Amberden Hall (as it should be spelled), Debden, Essex.

3 This was Richard's half-brother who has already been mentioned; he lived until 1776; "Mr Clark" was presumably his uncle or grandfather on his mother's side.

4 The Purefoys did not go to London that year; on 24 Apr. 1745 "my kinsman Mr Rich⃔ Jervoise of Hampshire" called at Shalstone.

Our next letter is not in the three letter-books and differs from all the rest as it is addressed to a Purefoy. The writer was no less a person than Browne Willis himself, and it serves to show him in a more courteous and kindly character than is usually allowed him.

The double-foolscap sheet consists of two letters, the first from the wife of the incumbent of Faringdon to Browne Willis, the other, transcribed below, is written by him on the fly-leaf; the letter has been folded again and directed, in Willis's writing.

To Henry Purefoy Esqre
at His Seat at Shalston near
the County Town
of
Bucks.

The insistence of "the County Town" here and in the text of the letter illustrates one of the great antiquary's little foibles. He has been called a bad writer, and some of his MS in the Bodleian justifies this, but this letter is perfectly legible and the writing and spelling are, on the whole, more "modern" than that of Mrs Purefoy or Henry, though Browne Willis was born in 1682, and lived until 1760.

No. 401. BROWNE WILLIS *to* H. P.

Plough Inne Carew Street near Lincolns Inne
March 10 1745

Sir,

I rec^d y^{rs} & am sorry I cannot give you so good an account as I would about y^r Family. I took all the notes & entry that any ways asisted us in y^r Pedigree at the Herald's office; & hoped to have had a better information from Faringdon Register in which parish Wadley is situate, which became y^r Ancestors' chief seat on their marriage with that Heiress. You see herein that all that is there entered is transcribed by the parson's wife (as I take it) in as particular manner as the Register furnishes it. I should have been glad of an acct. of the Burial of Sir Henry Purefoy, & the Lady Dame Katherine Purefoy.[1] I hope you will by these accts. form an exact & Regular Pedigree, which I shall be glad to receive & wait on you on my return at Whaddon in Easter Week. I dont value my Labour & pains to Friends of the County Town of Bucks; which that you may long continue to be, & see a numerous encrease of from all the world, & particularly in y^r Family &

---

1 Henry's great-uncle George married a widow, Catherine, Lady Bellingham, who is apparently alluded to here.

descendants is most heartily wished by him who is with tender of best respects to y.ʳ mother & self, Sir, y.ʳ most obedient humble Serv.ᵗ

Bro: Willis

You can best ascertain the Pedigree & distinguish the respective descendants. I am allways glad to put my notes into the Hands of the Heirs of Familys on whose exactness & regulation persons of my Trade must rely & referr themselves to for correction. I hope you will improve these accts which I cannot here transcribe & so send them away as I receive them. Pray pardon hasty scrall. I met with a charter for a Tuesday Market at Tingwick at the Tower Records.

The following letter is the first of several addressed to Browne Willis: it is expressly referred to on p. 262 of the *History of Buckingham*. "I stand indebted to Henry Purefoy Esq, who has very kindly imparted to me what his writings furnished of his ancient family." Such an acknowledgment by the learned but eccentric historian is fame, and after nearly two centuries we may now read the letter which gave rise to it.

No. 402. H. P. *to* BROWNE WILLIS

Shalstone
October the 12ᵗʰ 1745

Sir! /

I am favoured with your Łre of the 23ᵈ of last month & what I entreated of you was to know who were the severall possessors of the mannor of Shalstone from the Conquest down to this time, who were the severall Rectors of Shalstone from that time to this, & the names of the severall Patrons who presented those Rectors; as also what small quantity of Church lands were in Shalstone & in what part of the Parish they lay, & who were yᵉ Donors of them, & to inform mee of anything else relating thereto that might be worthy of notice. As to anything remarkable in Shalstone parish there is nothing that I know on, saving Potford, a little Brook at the bottom of Waterstratford hills in the road from Shalstone to Buckingham, where was drowned in a flood in K. James 1ˢᵗ his time young Master Purefoy, son to the Lady Glover, a young gentleman of great Hopes & Expectation. My grandfather Knightley Purefoy's fifth brother Valentine Purefoy was also drowned at this Potford in a flood. When there is no flood Potford is so shallow of water you may walk over it & not be wetshod, & the fford is supposed to derive its name from these two unfortunate accidents. I beg you would observe this Lady Glover was a Warwickshire Lady[1] & her 2ᵈ husband was a Purefoy, by whom she had the unhappy young gentleman who was drowned as above, & if hee had lived would have been heir to the Mannor of Shalstone in Com̄ Bucks, & the Mannor of Stockton in Com̄ Warwick. Lady Glover had the whole Mannor of Shalstone for her jointure, & as the antient men of Shalstone inform mee lived at yᵉ Mannor House there many years with notable hospitality, & it makes mee wonder you take no notice of her in yᵉ Pedigree of the ffamily. As to the Pedigree of the Purefoys of that part of yᵉ family I am on I can trace it no higher (of my own knowledge) than that wᶜʰ is inclosed, & beg you will accept of the few following remarks on it.

Mary Knightley, who married George Purefoy the father, was 3ᵈ & youngest Dauʳ & Coheir to Sʳ Valentine Knightley of ffausley & with her the 3ᵈ George Purefoy had in portion the mannors of Wadley[2] & Wickensam in Com̄ Berks.

Sʳ Samuel Luke,[3] of Woodend in Com̄ Bedford, married Elizabeth the eldest daughter, & Richᵈ Chetwood, of Chetwood in Com̄ Bucks, married the 2ᵈ Daughter of this Sʳ Valentine Knightley whose[4] mother was Anne, daughter to Sʳ Edward Umpton of Wadley in Com̄. Berks.

My great grandfather George Purefoy's first wife was Mʳ Rouse's wife's sister of Polsdon, in Com̄ Essex, whose maiden name I

1 For further particulars of Lady Glover see note on next page.

2 In a turret on the roof of the house at Shalstone hangs a bell inscribed: "G. Purefoy, de Wadley, Armiger, me possidet. 1656". (Both the *Hist. Monts. Commrs. Report* and the *Victoria County History* print the last word "placet" without comment.)

3 According to the long biographical account of Sir Samuel Luke in *Gentleman's Magazine*, 1823, pt. ii, p. 28, it was Sir Oliver Luke, father of Sir Samuel (generally considered to be the "original" of *Hudibras*), who married Elizabeth Knightley. See also J. G. Nichols, *Unton Inventories*, 1841, p. lxix.

4 Refers to the daughter, Ann; her mother was Anne, daughter of Sir Edward Unton. See Tucker, *Pedigree of Chetwode*, 1884, p. 29. Pedigree No. 24 in the *History of the Croke Family* (vol. 1, p. 450) is confused and misleading. J. G. Nichols (*loc. cit.*) is clear.

To face p. 268

Plate 18. KNIGHTLEY PUREFOY

know not,[1] & his 2ᵈ wife was Dame Anne Wynne whose first husband was Sʳ Henry Willoughby[2] of Risley in Com Derby, her 2ᵈ husband Sʳ — Wynne, & her 3ᵈ husband my great grandfather George Purefoy as above who, by his 1ˢᵗ wife Mʳˢ Rouse's sister, had five sons: viz⁵ George, Henry, Knightley, Wᵐ, & Valentine, & 7 daurs.

1ˢᵗ George the eldest married Lady Bellingham, wido. of Sʳ James Bellingham of Westmoreland, & daughter to this Dame Anne Wynne by her 1ˢᵗ husband, & Sʳ — Aston, of Aston hall in Coɱ. Chester, married Sʳ Henry Willoughby's other dauʳ from whom the present Sʳ Willoughby Aston of Wadley is descended. By Lady

1 This ignorance is surprising as the lady in question was daughter of the Lady Glover already mentioned by her first husband; in fact a widower and his son married a widow and her daughter, as the following entries from the register of St Anne's, Blackfriars (very kindly given to the editor by Mr Arthur Cochrane, Clarenceux King of Arms) clearly prove:

1626/7 Feb. 27 Mʳ George Purifie, Pater and Lady Jane Glover, mater. Hic.
1626/7 Feb. 28. Mʳ George Purifie, filius and Mʳˢ Anne Glover, filia. Hic.

"Polsdon" is Polesden Lacey, in the parish of Great Bookham, Surrey (not Essex); Anthony Rous lived there and married a daughter of Sir Thomas and Lady Glover; Manning and Bray (vol. II, p. 689) give her name as Anne, but this is clearly an error; several daughters are mentioned by Lysons, but Anthony Rous's marriage has not been traced. Lady Glover was the daughter of Francis Roberts, of Willesden, Middlesex, and married Sir Thos. Glover, described as "of Wilsdon, in Com. Midd.", who owned the manor of Ansley, Warwickshire (Dugdale, *Warwickshire*, 1656, p. 747), but sold it in 1609. This makes her a "Warwickshire widow", but the mention of Stockton, Co. Warwick (see this Letter *supra*), is less clear; according to Dugdale (*op. cit.* p. 227) that manor passed into the Purefoy family in 1547, and descended to Geo. Purefoy, of Drayton, Co. Leicester.

Our Ambassador at Constantinople, 1604–10, was Sir Thos. Glover; passages in *Calendar of State Papers (Domestic Series)* refer to his later career, and his sudden death is mentioned in a letter of 6 May 1625 (*op. cit.* 1625–6, p. 19). On the other hand, there was published in 1616 *A Sermon preached at Constantinople* by Wm. Forde, upon the death of "Lady Anne Glover", wife of the Ambassador, on 2 Nov. 1608. Her maiden name was Lambe, and she had lived five years in the East. Presumably, therefore, the ambassador was not the same as the Sir Thomas of Hayes Park, who married Jane Roberts in 1605.

Shalstone Church register records the death of "William Glover Esq the onlly sonne of Sʳ Tho: Glover of Hayes Parke in the county of Middl'x and dame Jane his wiffe deceased the 9ᵗʰ and was buried the 10ᵗʰ January Anno dɱ 1640 Decimo sixto Caroli Regis. The said William married Elizabeth Nevill the daughter of Sʳ Henry Nevill and Dame Anne his wiffe".

Thus Lady Glover long outlived both her husbands and both her children, her daughter dying in 1645 while she herself lived until 1664. (The editor is indebted to Mr C. White for extracting the references to Sir T. Glover.)

2 This is incorrect; Henry has confused Mrs George Purefoy II with III, Mrs George Purefoy III was daughter, not wife, of Sir H. Willoughby. See the pedigree.

Bellingham this George Purefoy had Sr Henry Purefoy, of Wadley, Barr^t, so created when a child in the cradle by King Charles the 2^d, his father then living.[1] Sr Henry died unmarried & gave away £5,000 a year to the late Sr Willoughby Aston & others from his name & family; so here the elder branch ends. I come now to

2^d Henry Purefoy, the 2^d son, who was a merchant & setled in Dublin in Ireland, but whether hee ever married or no I cannot tell.

3^d Knightley Purefoy,[2] the 3^d son, (& my Grandfather) who married as you will see in the Pedigree.

4th William Purefoy, the 4th son, of Drayton, in Com Leicester obiit sine prole.

5th Valentine Purefoy, the 5th son, drowned at Potford who also obiit sine prole.

For the rest I refer to the Pedigree enclosed.

You will find the Copy of the Ancient deed enclosed was no other than a surrender of the Mannor of Shalstone from Sr Richard Dammory to Laurence de Dete,[3] which the said de Dete had before granted to Dammory for life.

I shall be extreamly glad if you would favour mee wth your company to take a Commons with mee, either going or coming from Aynhoe, & let mee know the day. I have already looked up all my old writings & put them in two boxes & then you may read them over. My mother joins with mee in our respects & service to yourself & ffamily & I am, Sir! /

Your very humble serv^t

H. P.

ffor /
   Brown[4] Willis Esq at his Seat
   at Whaddon hall /
   To be left at Mr Ridghill's at the
   Crosskey's inne at
         Buckingham
           This

1 J. G. Nichols (*Unton Inventories*, p. lxxi) supposes that the father was "very probably afflicted with insanity, for it is otherwise difficult to account for his son, a boy of 9, being created a Baronet during his father's lifetime". The phrase "in the cradle" is exaggerated.

2 See Plate 18 for his portrait.

3 The spelling adopted by the *Victoria County History* (vol. IV, p. 224) is de Aëte; in 1324 (the date of the deed according to the note to the letter), Laurence is said "to have secured his right to the manor". (*Loc. cit.* quoting Place Rolls and Feet of Fines.) Browne Willis spells the name "Ayete".

4 Browne Willis himself used an "e" at the end of his first name.

To face p. 270

Plate 19. MRS. KNIGHTLEY PUREFOY

N.B. Sent enclosed in this letter to M.ʳ Brown Willis part of a Pedigree of the Purefoy's family & a copy of a very ancient deed from S.ʳ Rich.ᵈ Dammory to Laurence De Dete, date 17.ᵗʰ Edwardi Secundi.

It is interesting to note how Browne Willis adapted Henry's letter; thus of Lady Glover he says: "who being joyntured here, resided at Shalston, and kept Hospitality, as is by Tradition still remembred". Of the baronet he says: "having his Estate in his Power, of upwards of £4,000 per annum, by Will gave it profusely away to his Mother's Relations, from his own Family and Name". *History of Buckingham*, 1755, p. 263.

No. 403. H. P. *to* BROWNE WILLIS

Shalstone
Sir! /   *Octob.ʳ the 19ᵗʰ 1745*

I have sent you enclosed the Pedigree of my ffamily & when you have finished Shalstone affair I beg you'll let mee have a copy of it. If your amanuensis, or any writing master or such sort of a person, would transcribe it for mee from your manuscript as to what relates to Shalstone—I would satisfie them for so doing. My mother joins with mee in our humble services & I am Sir!

Your very humble servant
ffor /   H. P.
  Brown Willis Esq...
  Whaddon hall...
      This

No. 404. H. P. *to* BROWNE WILLIS

Shalstone
Sir! /   *November yᵉ 2ᵈ 1745*

Inclosed you will find extracted from Shalstone Register the names of such of my family as are born, married, or buried at Shalstone, together with the ffish's & Sandford's[1] arms. My mother's & my respects & service attend yourself & ffamily & I am Sir!
Your oblidged humble serv.ᵗ
ffor /   H. P.
  Brown Willis Esq....

[1] Henry's grandfather, Knightley, married Mary, daughter of Capt. Henry Sandford, of Bobbing, Kent. Her portrait appears on Plate 19.

No. 405. H. P. *to* BROWNE WILLIS

Shalstone [&c.]
March the 2ᵈ 1745

Sir! /

I am favoured with yours of the 27ᵗʰ instant as likewise with another letter before that containing the Eccl'i'ał History of Shalstone, both which are very perfect accoᵗˢ of what they contain. As to the ffee in the Herald's Office I will pay it you when I have yᵉ favour of seeing you. I have nothing more to request of you now but to have the Civill history of Shalstone from yᵉ Conquest down to this present time, wᶜʰ I hope I shall have an opportunity to accomplish when I have yᵉ Pleasure of waiting on you at Shalstone. If I could have yᵉ favour of you to dictate to mee I think verily I could take it down in an hour or an hour & an half's time; if I could have yᵉ satisfaction of having your Company one night wee have a little bedchamber for your man to lie in next to your bedchamber. With thanks for all favours I am Sir! /

Your oblidged hle servᵗ

ffor /   H. P.
Brown Willis Esq at the
Plough inne in Carey street near Lincoln's inne /
          London

P.S. My mother's & my Service & respects wait on you.

CHAPTER XI

BOOKS, NEWSPAPERS, ETC.

T HE phrase in Henry's epitaph which makes him "converse more with books than with men" was fairly earned: there is plenty of evidence to show that at every period of his life he was acquiring books, and that he read them, for many contain notes on the fly-leaves indicating where particular passages which interested him are to be found.

There is a roughly-made book of parchment with the heading: "A Catalogue of my Books made the 4ᵗʰ Aprill 1728 In an Alphabeticall order". The system which dictated this order is not obvious, since it is not by authors, subjects, or titles: a specimen page taken at random will illustrate very well the library (there are 376 titles¹ in the catalogue), and its owner's tastes:

Cabinet opened

Country Dances, a Book thereof by Playford.

Campden's Britannia in 2 vol. large folio

Compendious method of raising yᵉ Italian Brocoli

Chronologicall historian by Salmon.

Collection of Precedents for Justices of the Peace by—Harvey Esq

Culpeper's Herberess and Dispensatory in 2 Vollumes

Cornaro, his method to attain long life

Compleat measurer by Hawney

Curious & profitable gardiner by Jno. Cowell.

Countrey Builder's Estimator by Mʳ Salmon

Compleat ffamily Peice

Cap of gray Hairs &c.

Cowel Law Dictionary

Collectiones Theologicæ.

Compleat Angler

Compleat Servant Maid

Cluverius's geography in Latin.

Not much above a twentieth of these books remain at Shalstone.² The Account-books give us the names of several additional books and pamphlets; thus on 26 Mar. 1746 *The Fatall Effects of yᵉ present Rebellion*³ was bought for 1s. 6d. and on 25 May 1748 "the book about the Earthquake at Lima" for 5s. The last-named was no doubt *A True and Particular Relation of the Dreadful Earthquake at Lima 1746, with a description of Callao.*—1748.

1 As this includes some long runs such as Salmon's *Modern History* (eventually 31 volumes) this may represent a total of 500 volumes.

2 A note by Mrs FitzGerald (see Pedigree) says that on the death of Mrs Jervoise (Mary Hawes), in 1842, Mr G. P. Jervoise allowed many volumes to be removed by his brother-in-law, the Rev. F. Ellis (afterwards Jervoise); possibly they are still at Herriard.

3 This is still at Shalstone, bound up with other pamphlets. It purports to be by J[oh]n L[auren]ce, and is really a kind of tragic domestic story in which "The '45" is an incident. It consists of 115 pages in 8vo, printed for M. Cooper, and dated 4 Jan. 1745.

On 29 Apr. 1737 Henry paid for "Sir Josiah Child's Discourse on Trade & the book entitled ye Golden ffleece" 4s.: and on 22 Oct. 1739 for "Plautus his Comedies" 1s. 6d. One may not envy him "Dr Henry Moor's works in full" for 3s. 6d., but one would certainly like to see the "2 little books & 4 Ballads" purchased from "a Stranger man at the Door" for 4d. The "Adventures of Charles Cartwright M.D." and "The Memoirs of M^rs A—a W—t" cannot now be found at Shalstone. The *Gentleman's Magazine* causes a regular monthly payment of 6d. and a complete run of that extraordinary publication exists at Shalstone today.[1]

The later Diaries, after 1755, often refer to "Mr Seely (the bookseller)" when Henry went to Buckingham,—this must have been the "B. Seeley, Writing-master, Bookseller, and Stationer", who published many of the Descriptions of Stowe Gardens from 1744 onwards.[2]

The letters dealing with newspapers and stationery have some interest, and a few miscellaneous letters of a personal character have been thrown into this chapter.

No. 406. H. P. *to* MR COOPER

Shalstone
Wensday, ffebruary 18th 1735

Mr Cooper /

I send you by ye bearer fifteen of the Gentleman's Magazines for the year 1735. I desire you'l bind 'em in calf against next Wensday. Voll. 5. 1735 must be done on the back when bound. As to the colour of ye Leather it must be a speckled brown in the same colour the Salmon's history is bound in.

This will oblidge

Your freind to serve you
H. P.

ffor /
Mr Cooper a
Schoolmaster at
    Brackley &c.

No. 407. H. P. *to* MR COOPER

Shalstone
Wensday, March ye 2^d 1736

Mr Cooper /

I send you by ye bearer Dr Cheyne's Essay on the gout, Sr Walter Raleigh's Remains, Lillie's Book, & Cornaro, Rosse's View of all Religions, Balzac's Letters, & the 12 monthly Gentleman's Magazine for 1736 with the Supplement thereto, all which I desire may

1 See Letters Nos. 406–408.

2 By 1797 this had become J. Seeley, and an edition of the *Description* dated 1832 bears the name L. B. Seeley and Sons, Fleet St., London.

be bound in Calf. On the back of the magazines let there be 1736 in gilt figures & let the binding of that be a brown colour & smooth leather, let some of the other books be a smooth black leather for variety, & pray send word by ye bearer when I may send for 'em again wch will oblidge

Your freind & serv^t
H. P.

ffor /
  Mr Cooper...

No. 408. H. P. *to* MR COOPER

Shalstone
March ye 2^d 1737

Mr Cooper /

I send you by ye bearer the following Books to bind (to wit)

The 12 Gentleman's Magazines for 1737, & ye supplem^t thereto to be bound in brown smooth calf & 1737 to be done in gilt figures on ye back.

The Golden fleece
Every Body's Business &c.
And the Voyage to Georgia
To be bound together in black smooth calf

The 6 Numbers of the 30th vollume of Salmon's Modern History with the map of Chili, Patagonia, &c. to be bound as the Salmon's history sent, & the map of the Netherlands to be fastned in as well as you can. Pray get them bound as soon as you can conveniently which will oblidge

Your humble serv^t
H. P.

ffor /
  Mr Cooper...

Whilst Mr Jemmy Payne may have no other memorial than that afforded by these pages, his brother Ollive, and still more his other brother Thomas, have had something like immortality conferred upon them by appearance in John Nichols's *Literary Anecdotes*, Dibdin's *Bibliographical Decameron*, and Mathias's *Pursuits of Literature*, to say nothing of a long article in the *Dictionary of National Biography* by Mr W. P. Courtney. Apparently Ollive set up in the Strand as a bookseller in Round Court, the site of which is now occupied by Charing Cross Hospital, and Thomas at first assisted him, but afterwards ventured on his own account in Castle Street, now merged in the Charing Cross Road, his shop was near to the present entrance of the National Portrait Gallery.[1] He earned the gratitude of all bibliophils

1 The editor is indebted to Mr C. White for identifying the sites of these shops.

by issuing a fine catalogue of books for sale in 1740: for 35 years from 1755 a catalogue of nearly 200 pages was issued annually. These are in the British Museum, but there must have been a still earlier issue by the elder brother because in Henry's Account-book, under 11 July 1735, the following entry appears:

Paid Mr Jemmy Paine then for the 2 Gent. Magazines} 00 : 01 : 00
for May & Aprill

NB. I gave Mr Ollive Paine the Bookseller (myself) the
Catalogue of the Books agen.

Two years later brother Ollive (called Oliver in most of the biographical notices, though not by Timperley, *Encyclopaedia of Literary and Typographical Anecdote*, 1842) fell into disgrace with Henry because he omitted the title-page and table of contents belonging to the 29th volume of Salmon's *Modern History*. In a (cancelled) letter to Mr James Payne Henry is amazed at his brother's neglect, and tells his sad story concluding: "Thus you see what trouble this Carelessenesse creates".

Thomas Payne's shop was the resort of the literati of the day, and Thomas Beloe has preserved[1] for us a list of their names: Cracherode, George Steevens, Malone, Windham, Lord Stormont, Sir John Hawkins, Lord Spencer, Porson, Burney, T. Grenville, Wakefield, Bishop (then Dean) Dampier, Townly, Col. Stanley, and various other bookish men.

"Honest Tom Payne!" continues Beloe, "and well indeed did he deserve the name so universally bestowed upon him, and happily and effectually has he entailed it on his successor, than whom a worthier character does not exist."

The last reference is to his son who, in partnership with Foss, carried on business in Pall Mall. His daughter Sally married Admiral James Burney, brother of Fanny. Thomas Payne was buried at Finchley, with a curious epitaph in verse written by Hayley.

The three brothers were the sons of the Ollive Payne to whom Letter No. 71 is addressed.

No. 409. H. P. *to* JAMES PAYNE

Shalstone
Mr Paine /   *May ye 3^d 1738*

I desire you will send for Dr Bowles's Fundamentall Rules of the Latin Grammar and the 31st vollume of Salmon's Modern history (with the maps & cuts thereto) wch I am sure is come out because I saw it advertized.

This will oblidge   Your humble serv^t

ffor /   H. P.
   Mr Jemmy Paine a Baker
   at Brackley
      This

1 *Sexagenarian*, 1818, vol. 1, p. 197.

No. 410. H. P. *to* MR COOPER

Shalstone
June ye 14th 1738

Mr Cooper /

I send by the bearer ye six numbers of the last vollume of Salmon's Modern History & the map of the British Plantations wch I desire may be bound & lettered as the 30th vollume of Salmon, which you will find with them. Be as expeditious as you can & let mee know when I must send for 'em wch will oblidge

Your humble serv^t

ffor /
  Mr Cooper...

H. P.

No. 411. H. P. *to* JAMES PAYNE

Shalstone
September the [blank] *1746*

Mr Paine /

The book you sent mee instead of pursueing the Title & being a further History of the unfortunate young Nobleman &c is only the Triall between the Earl of Anglesey & Mr Annesley which I had of you long ago in folio & of consequence have no occasion for this, so must entreat you to return it to your brother & acquaint him of the Occasion, & to get mee ye book whose Title is enclosed. I hope you don't forget Abstract of ye Acts &c., & excuse ye trouble of returning ye book wch will oblidge

Your humble servant

ffor /
  Mr James Paine at Brackley
        This

H. P.

One hopes that the book was procured, but the Account-book does not prove it; on 8 November Mr Paine received 8s. 6d.: "for the Gentleman's Magazine for October last 6^d, for the Geography of Children 1^s 6^d, for the Attorney's Practice Epitomized 1^s 6^d, for the Art of Cookery made plain and easy 5^s".

For a convenient summary of the case in which James Annesley successfully sued Richard Earl of Anglesey in 1743 see F. W. Bull, *History of Newport Pagnell*, p. 278.

No. 412. H. P. *to* SAMUEL PASSELOW [PASHLER]

Shalstone
ffebruary ye 14th 1746

Sir! /

I send you enclosed the Proposalls for Printing by subscription Mrs Leapor's Poeticall works; if you like to subscribe thereto I will either bring or send you a receipt next Saturday for the money. My mother desires you'll buy a Surloin of Beef with ye Sewet on of 20 or 25 or 30 pounds weight, if you can't have it without you may buy a boiling peice with it. The Bearer has orders to pay you for it. Wee both join in Compliments to you all & I am Sir! /

Your very humble servant

ffor /   H. P.
  Mr Passelow at
        Buckingham
            This

Mr Passelow (or Pashler, as it is sometimes spelt) figures often in the Diaries; apparently his mother was a widow who married Mr Wall-bank, the Surgeon, and the young man followed his stepfather's profession. The name of Pashler occurs as Vicar (1672–1724). The Bailiff (or Mayor) of Buckingham in 1761 was Samuel Pashler, probably this was Henry's friend.

The "Mrs Leapor" of the letter was an interesting person who might, if she had lived, have joined the band of peasant poets. Her biographers[1] agree that she was born at Marston St Lawrence, a village to the N.W. of Brackley, 26 Feb. 1722,[2] and tell us that her father was gardener to Judge Blencowe; they further say that she died of measles at Brackley on 12 Nov. 1746.[3] It is fairly certain that "Mr Leapor, the Brackley gardiner", to whom Henry addressed several letters (Nos. 149 et seqq.) and whose name occurs constantly in the Diaries from 1735 onwards, was her father; thus the Account-book under 2 May 1748 has the entry "Paid Mr Leapor (the Brackley Gardiner) on receipt of his Book of Poems...2^s 6^d". As was mentioned at Letter No. 149, Henry's diary records a visit to the Leapors when he spoke to "Mr Leapor the Brackley gardiner's Daughter & the young Woman who showed us Mr Leapor's Garden".

1 In *Gentleman's Magazine*, 1784, vol. LIV, pp. 806–7, and *Dict. Nat. Biog.*
2 The registers of this parish were destroyed by fire last century.
3 This is an error, the date was 14 Nov., she "was Buried in woollen, as appears by an affidavit of ye 17th". (Entry in Brackley Register.) Baker (*Northants*, vol. I, p. 579), gives her epitaph on a stone (no longer to be found), in Brackley church-yard: "In Memory of Mary Leapor daughter of Philip and Ann Leapor: who departed this life Nov. ye 26. 1746 Aged 24".

Mary, or Molly, Leapor (in the earlier years Henry spelled it Lepper) had little education but sought knowledge at an early age and somehow managed, though only a "cook-maid in a gentleman's family in the neighbourhood", to acquire a few books, including the works of Dryden and Pope; it was the last whom "she most admired and chiefly endeavoured to imitate", says the address to the reader prefixed to her poems. Apparently there had been some attempt to publish a selection of her poems during her lifetime but the "Proposalls" which Henry sent to Mr Passelow were dated 1 Jan. 1746–7,[1] they offered a "handsome volume in octavo" for 5s., so perhaps Henry's 2s. 6d. already mentioned was the second moiety due on delivery, since the Proposals give the father's name as collector of the subscriptions. The volume actually appeared in 1748;[2] the D.N.B. says that Isaac Hawkins Browne, the elder, was editor, the Gentleman's Magazine makes him only responsible for a second selection issued in 1751. The issue of 1748 contains an imposing list of subscribers, Mr Passelow's name is not there, but Mrs Purefoy's and Henry's names appear together with the names of many of their friends—the Prices of Whitfield, Campbell Price of Westbury, the Lisles of Imley, John Pollard, Mr Trotman, Lady Willes, Archdeacon Trimnell, etc. It is likely therefore that Henry was able to secure some of the subscribers.

The Poems certainly show the influence of Pope, the wonder is that a self-educated girl could rouse the echo so successfully; take this couplet:

> "Then she is happy, tho' beneath the sky,
> Hold, not so hasty—let her husband die".

Or to take a longer passage from the *Advice to Myrtillo*:

> "The Herald's office you must search with care,
> And look you find no pimps nor taylors there;
> Bring none to light but honourable knaves;
> Shut up the peasants in their mouldy graves.
> If knights are wanting in the dusky breed
> Arthur's round table will supply your need".

One must not expect the master's technique; one finds weak rhymes like these:

> "With judgment sound and touch'd by no extreme,
> Speech gently flowing and a soul serene,
> For ever pleasing and for ever true
> By all admir'd, envy'd by a few".

Essay on Happiness.

1 A copy is in the Bodleian Library.

2 This is in the Bodleian Library (shelf mark 280. j. 611). No copy is noted in the catalogue of the British Museum Library, but selections may be found there included in *Poems by the Most Eminent Ladies of Gt. Britain*, 2 vols. 12mo, 1755, reprinted 1773 and 1780.

Some lines upon *Winter* certainly anticipate Bloomfield, and show a realism such as Swift might have used:

> "Poor daggled[1] Urs'la stalks from cow to cow,
> Who to her sighs returns a mournful low;
> While their full udders her broad hands assail
> And her sharp nose hangs dropping o'er the pail.
> With garments trickling like a shallow spring,
> And his wet locks all twisted in a string
> Afflicted Cymon waddles thro' the mire
> And rails at Win'fred creeping o'er the fire".

A poem entitled *Crumble Hall* suggests in part that very pleasant *Posthumous Tale* of Crabbe, called *Silford Hall, or the Happy Day*. Molly was able to turn her experience in the scullery to account and tell in this poem (what all do not know), how pewter plates were washed:

> "but now her dish-kettle[2] began
> To boil and blubber with the foaming bran.
> The greasy apron round her hips she ties
> And to each plate the scalding clout applies.
> The purging bath each glowing dish refines,
> And once again the polish'd pewter shines".

Had Fate allowed Molly Leapor a longer span of life one feels that she might have produced verse which would have gained her a fame equal to that of Bloomfield, and superior to that of "The Revd Mr Stephen Duck", whose name occurs in the list of subscribers to her posthumously published works.

No. 413. H. P. *to* JAMES PAYNE

Shalstone
Decemb^r ye 9th 1747

Mr Paine /

I have got severall old Books that I would change away with you for new ones, I dare say wee shall not differ about the Price of them so when you come here (wch I hope will be soon) pray bring a flag Basket or Wallet to take them away with you. This will oblidge

Your humble serv^t
H. P.

ffor /
   Mr James Paine at
      Brackley
      This

1 "Wet or dirtied by mud" is the definition given in the *English Dialect Dictionary*.
2 The *English Dialect Dictionary* defines this as "a large open iron pot suspended over the fire and used to wash up kitchen utensils, etc."; only West Country usage is cited for the phrase.

No. 414. H. P. *to* JAMES PAYNE

Shalstone
Mʳ Paine /   *January yᵉ 6ᵗʰ 1747*

The Plautus you sent mee[1] has only three of the Comedies translated whereas I hoped Echard had translated all his Comedies,
if hee has let mee have the rest of them. Hobb's Thucidides was
very lately to be had at one Samuell Birt's in Ave-Mary-Lane.
I return yᵉ Terence again it is so badly bound I don't care to
let it have a place in my study but desire you to get mee one that
is better bound. I have received yᵉ Quintus Curtius wᶜʰ I like
very well & desiring you to accept of the compliments of the
Season am

Your humble servant
ffor /   H. P.
 Mʳ James Paine
     at Brackley /
          This

No. 415. H. P. *to* JAMES PAYNE

Shalstone
Mʳ Paine /   *March the 9ᵗʰ 1747*

I received yours on Sunday night last by John Cowell. I wonder
you should so soon forget yᵉ contents of the last Łre I sent you
about the middle of last month, which were for you to send mee
the new edition of Quincy's Dispensatory, the Title whereof at
large I send you underneath. I hope Hobbs's Thucidides will
come with this. I want yᵉ Dispensatory so don't faill letting mee
have it as soon as it comes out, wᶜʰ will oblidge

Your humble servant
H. P.

In the Presse & soon will be published
a new Edition of

Pharmacopœia Officinalis & Extemporanea, or Quincy's English
Dispensatory in two parts—Theoreticall & Practicall.

N.B. In order to render this worke more extensively usefull the

1 Possibly this was the reprint in 1716 of the translation of three Comedies by
Laurence Echard, first published in 1694. Lowndes calls it "a coarse and
indelicate translation".

whole matter of the London & Edinburgh Dispensatories will be therein comprehended.

Printed for T. Longman & I. Shewell in Pater noster Row

ffor /
 Mr James Paine
  at Brackley
   This

No. 416. H. P. *to* JOHN WENTWORTH [CRESSWELL]

Shalstone
Saturday March 10th 1749

Sir!

According to promise I send you herewith Dr Profily's Treatise,[1] if you please to look on Page 35 you may see the dangerous effects of Mercury Sublimate, in Page 40 the good effects of Quicksilver Pills, in Page 100, and some succeeding that, you will find the Wonderfull Discovery of the Worms &c. In page 222 Curious Observations on Deafnesse. In page 252 the Doctors Notions of Inoculation of the Small Pox. As for other Parts of this Book 't is not worth your looking over. My mother joins with mee in our Compliments to Mrs Mussendine, yourself, & Mrs Wentworth & I am with all due esteem Sir! /

        Your very humble serv^t
         H. P.
ffor /
 John Wentworth Esq at
 Lillingston Lovell
   This

The following letter is ruled through and was presumably not sent; it is far too good to omit, however, and has in it the germ of humour, whether intentional or not.

No. 417. H. P. *to* JAMES PAYNE

Shalstone
Sunday March the 11th 1749

Mr Paine,

On 28th of ffebruary last I sent you a letter with an Advertizement inclosed on which was the Title of the following book (vizt)

1 The Account-book shows that Henry had bought it on 25 May 1748 for 6*s*. Presumably this refers to a work by John Profily, with a lengthy title; it treated principally of venereal disease and a method of curing scurvy. The second edition appeared in 1741.

Plate 20. HENRY'S STUDY

The Disadvantages of the Married State or the Artifices & foibles of the fair sex such as in Musick Dancing Dresse Equipage Desire of Ofspring &c considered, & the Single Life plainly proved preferable to that of Marriage.

> Art thou loosed from a Wife, seek not a Wife.
> Who can find a virtuous Woman?

This I say is the Title of the Book I desired you to send for mee & instead thereof you (by mistake I suppose) have sent mee a book entitled: A serious Proposall for promoting marriage &c, which I send you again by the bearer & desire you will return it to your bookseller. Your Behaviour to mee in this affair really puts mee in mind of the Confusion of Languages at Babell, when one asked for an Hammer they gave him a Trowell. What I desire of you now is to write for yᵉ book as I ordered. I can't say the title of the book is verbatim but I send you yᵉ substance of it so as to render it intelligible, & hope you won't use mee so any more nor give mee any other reason than to be

Your assured freind
H. P.

ffor /
  Mʳ James Paine at
   Brackley /
     This
     With a book

Mr R. F. Sharp, late Keeper of Printed Books at the British Museum, very kindly suggests that the book which Henry sought was *Essays on Marriage, in an Epistle to a Young Gentleman; wherein the Artifices and the Foibles of the Fair, and the Disadvantages and Difficulties of the Married State, are particularly inquired into.* London, Corbet, 1749, 8ᵛᵒ.

No. 418. E. P. *to* THOMAS ROBOTHAM

Shalstone [&c.]
March the 23ᵗʰ 1745

I received Mʳ Robotham's kind present of Salmon and Lobster for which wee return you thanks. Wee have killed an Hog & desire your acceptance of a neck chine & a couple of Pullets sent with your butter carriage paid; pray let mee know if the Pulletts are young. Our cook fell sick or otherwise you would have had

some hog puddings. I have lost a cow on calving & dare not buy
any more these perillous Times, so cannot pretend to serve you
with 6 pounds of butter a week in winter, but if it will be of any
service to you I can serve you this summer with it. Pray, if you
see Harry ffish ask him if he received my son's letter & desire him
to answer it. Pray tell M.ʳ Potts every now & then his people send
my son the Whitehall instead of the London Evening Post, & to
send it right for yᵉ future. Pray pay M.ʳ Curtis for 3 barrells of
Oysters 9.ˢ & for 2 codlin fish, & place it to account. The oysters
were very good, but now the time of yᵉ year grows too warm for
them. I will send the butter till I hear from you, our respects
are with yourself & Nelly & I am

Your humble servant
E. P.

ffor /
M.ʳ Robotham...
      London

No. 419. H. P. *to* SAMUEL POTTS

Shalstone [&c.]
August 2ᵈ 1747

I thought M.ʳ Potts had been paid before now for I ordered
M.ʳˢ Mason who now keeps the late M.ʳ Robotham's house at
Islington to pay you some time ago, & for fear she should not
I ordered another Gentleman to pay you; but since hee has not
I am glad of the opportunity to pay it to M.ʳ Shem Baxter, the
Postmaster[1] of Buckingham, & will for the future pay it him as
soon as it becomes due. I thank you for the book & am

Your humble serv.ᵗ
H. P.

ffor /
M.ʳ Sam.ˡ Potts[2] at the Generall
Post Office in Lombard Street
      London

1 The present post office at Buckingham occupies part of the premises which
were Mr Baxter's inn; see Letter No. 598.
2 Mr Potts was appointed "Clerk of the Road" on 2 May 1740; holders
of that office enjoyed the sole privilege of sending newspapers, free of postage,
in the mail bags. Eventually Mr Potts became Deputy Comptroller, and
ultimately Comptroller of the Inland Office. (Information kindly supplied by
the Secretary of the General Post Office in a letter dated 9 April 1930.)

No. 420. H. P. *to* SAMUEL POTTS

Shalstone [&c.]
January the 17ᵗʰ 1747

I have paid the Postmaster of Buckingham £1. 1s. according to Mͬ Potts's order, but I am informed by a neighbouring clergyman that Mͬ Eyres[1] of Cotsford & the Rev. Mͬ Halford[2] of Ratley pay you but 17s. 9d. a year for the news you send them; I think I should not pay more[3] than my neighbours so desire you would favour mee with a line or two ℔ post to clear up this Affair wᶜ.ʰ will oblidge

Your humble servant
ffor /   H. P.
  Mͬ Samuell Potts...
          London

No. 421. H. P. *to* MR COOPER

Mͬ Cooper /   *Shalstone Aprill 20ᵗʰ 1737*

I desire you will make mee 2 accoᵗ Books ruled with red Lines of about two quire of paper in each & to be bound in smooth calf leather. I desire they may be done this day fortnight at farthest wᶜʰ will oblidge

Your freind & servᵗ
ffor /   * H. P.
  Mͬ Cooper
  a schoolmaster at
      Brackley.
          This

* NB. Mͬ Cooper sent mee this letter again with an answer at the bottom thereof, to which answer of his I wrote at the bottom Thereof:—"To be of a quarto size & a single line only on each side. Cam's Treatise to be bound in black calf," and I sent Mͬ Cooper yᵉ said letter again.

1 Mr Richard Eyre was a lessee of Cottisford from 1739 till 1760. He had been a judge in India and exercised such power in the village life that he was thought to haunt it, and the legend was current that he had been buried in a cask in a pond, etc. (See J. C. Blomfield, *History of Cottisford*, 1888, p. 22.)

2 Charles Halford was presented to Radclive in 1730, he was also rector of Lillingstone Dayrell. New rectors were appointed in both parishes in 1754–5 "by reason of lapse" (Lipscomb, vol. iii, pp. 35 and 69).

3 As late as 1751 Mr Dunney Baxter received £1. 1s. 0d. "on account of Mͬ Saml Potts".

No. 422. H. P. *to* RICHARD BUDD

Shalstone [&c.]
ffebruary the 27ᵗʰ 1739

M.ʳ Budd /

I desire you will send mee the ffollowing things (to wit)

2 quarts of the best Ink in a stone Bottle tied down & sealed on yᵉ cork.

12 large sized wooden Pencills

ffour Diary books in Quarto printed according to the paper sent & bound in smooth black Calf and to be double leathered or made stronger on the edge of the Lids next the binding, because the lids always wear out & crack next the binding.

Some peices or slipes of parchment.

Three quarts of sand, to sand writing done up in strong paper so as not to spill.

2 dozen quire of small brown paper.

2 dozen quire of Issue paper.

Two dozen quire of cutt paper at 8.ᵈ a Quire.

12 sticks of superfine red sealing wax.

12 quire of largish sized Gilt paper.

2 quire of blue paper.

Half an hundred of the best Dutch pens.

Pray send these things in 3 weeks time at farthest by M.ʳ Eagles the Buckingham carrier... & give the Carrier a charge they come to no wet. I suppose you had as good send the things to the carrier on Monday night by reason they set out so early on Tuesday morning, & let mee have a Letter by the Post with your Bill of what they come to, that I may send to the carrier for them & order you payment.

I am

Your hĩe serv.ᵗ

H. P.

ffor /
    M.ʳ Budd   a stationer
    near the Pump in Chancery Lane /
                London

These things were paid for on 5 April; the bill came to £3. 14s. 9d. (see Letter No. 192).

No. 423. H. P. *to* MR REEVES

Shalstone [&c.]
October the 12th 1751

Mr Reeves /

I desire you will send mee the following things (to witt)

Two quarts of ink in the stone bottle I send
Two reams of small brown paper
One ream of the best Issue paper
Thirty quires of Cutt writing paper with the P marke, & it is such as they write the Councell's Briefs on.
ffour Quires of large brown paper
ffour Quires of large blue paper
One hundred of the best pens
A few slips of Parchment
Three dozen of Pencills the same size & sort to the Pencill I send inclosed in the stone bottle.
Six quires of large Quarto Gilt paper
Twelve quires of Copy paper.
Three Diary Books in Quarto printed according to the paper sent & bound in smooth black calf, and to be double leathered or made stronger in the Lids next the binding, because the Lids allways wear out & crack next ye binding.

The little nests in my Burow are six in number & each of the nests is 3 inches & a quarter wide, 4 inches & an half high, & 7 inches & an half deep. Now I want six little black boxes made of pasteboard covered with leather (to hold notes & receipts) to be made of these Dimensions, so as to go each black box into one of these nests. If you have no such thing by you must desire you will get mee some made & send them with the things above by ye Buckingham carrier...You need not be in an hurry on sending 'em but charge the carrier they don't come to any Wett, & let mee have a letter by the post with your bill enclosed & what time you send that I may send to ye carrier for them in due time & will order you payment & am

Your humble servant
H. P.

ffor /
Mr Reeves a
Stationer near the Pump in Chancery lane
London
With a stone bottle & a pencill therein

On 16 November the sum of £5. 12s. 9d. was paid for these. It is a matter of great grief to the editor that although there are many bureaux at Shalstone of the right date none can be found with the six "nests" of which such exact dimensions are given.

No. 424. H. P. *to* MR COOPER

Shalstone
Aprill 7ᵗʰ 1742

Mʳ Cooper /

I desire you will come over here on Saturday or any other day you shall appoint to write my will for mee in two parts. I have two skins of parchment ready ruled by mee, bring some skuttle bone[1] with you. I am afraid you won't finish it under 2 days. Send word by the bearer what day you will come over on & I will be in yᵉ way, & am in hast

Your humble servant

H. P.

Subscribed only the initiall Letters of my name

ffor /
 Mʳ Cooper a schooll master at
  Brackley /
   This

P.S. Pray don't come in any cloaths that you have had on when you have been with ffolks who may have had yᵉ small pox.

No. 425. H. P. *to* JOHN WELCHMAN

Shalstone
Tuesday 13ᵗʰ Aprill 1742

Sir! /

My Will is wrote out in two Parts & I never executed a will of two parts in my Life. Pray send mee Directions how it must be done. I should take it as a favour, by reason the small pox is so much at Brackley, if you could spare time to come over here & bring Mʳ John Watts the plummer & Mʳ Thomas Yates the shop-

---

1 This is the bone of the cuttle-fish; Addison in the 476th *Spectator* speaks of the "Scuttle-fish that blackens all the water about him".

According to the *Encyclopaedia Britannica*, the pounce made from powdered cuttlefish bone was used for drying ink on parchment after an erasure had been made. Henry's own pounce was made of sand, for the pages of the Diaries still retain a good deal.

keeper with you to be witnesses to it, & to take a dinner with us & to send word the day by John Boorten who will call too morrow for an answer. But if you can't favour mee with your company & that of your two neighbours as above I will, with your directions, get it done at Buckingham. I entreat your answer & am in hast

Your humble serv.ᵗ

ffor /
   Mͬ Welchman senior
   Attorney at Law at
        Brackley
            This

H. P.

This will followed Ralph Porter's disgrace, and was made three months after Letter No. 395 to Thomas Jervoise. It was not Henry's last will and testament, as that was dated 13 Sept. 1758, and proved 19 May 1762.

No. 426. H. P. *to* GEORGE DANCER

Shalstone
June the 27ᵗʰ 1747

Sir /

I received your Letter & intend with God's Leave to be at Buckingham on Wensday next to appeall, I entreat you will be in the way then to attend yᵉ Comͬˢ & Job Burman shall bring his Duplicate along with him to be set to rights.

I am

Your humble servant
H. P.

P.S. My mother's & my compliments
       attend yourself & Mͬˢ Dancer.

ffor /
   Mͬ George Dancer at Buckingham
            This

Who the Commissioners were we do not know; Mr George Dancer was presumably descended from him who was Bailiff (or Mayor) of Buckingham in 1679. He figures in a scurrilous ballad by Charles Blount, which was reprinted in *Records of Bucks*, vol. XI, pp. 233–241. At the end of the ballad, which was a No-Popery manifesto, is the list of "Those who voted for the L(ord) L(atimer), for the E(arl) of D(anby), for Popery, and for their Town-hall",—and the name of

"George Dancer, Tanner and Bayliff" comes first. There were twelve burgesses to return two members to Parliament and as six voted each way it is presumed that Dancer had a casting vote which he gave for Lord Latimer and Sir Richard Temple.

The Diary of 30 July 1748 refers to "Mr George Dancer, Alderman of Buckingham".

<h3 align="center">No. 427. H. P. to PETER MOULSON</h3>

Shalstone [&c.]
December y^e 27th 1752

Sir! /

I am favoured with both your letters & the wine & other things came safe to hand. Wee have just now tierced the red wine & drew out one pint, my mother thinks it rougher than it used to be & more flatt; it may be the cold weather may occasion it to be so, I beleive wee shan't draw it of[f] this month. I hope its standing in our Vault in the hogshead will not hurt it. The white wine continues to frett notwithstanding wee leave the Peg out. The last red port wine of yours wch remains in Bottles—the corks faill & some of it is worsted, I should be glad to know what quantity of rosin & other stuff is used to make a Liquid to dip the head of the Bottles in after they are corked to prevent the Evaporating. Most people who come here drink white wine so I would endeavour to keep the red port good in the Bottle, because of its being kept a good while.

Wee thank you for the Oysters & Raisins wch were very good, but I am afraid the Jarr was opened by the carrier's people, for the Jarr was not so full as usuall nor so hard squeezed down. Poor Mr Tooley ye carrier has all his Effects seized & on Wensday last was sent to Northampton Jayll for Debt, for wch it is thought Brackley people are to blame, hee being worth about £800, they advised him to set up the carriers Businesse against a wealthy carrier there & then let him have no back carriage which ruined him. Wee desire your acceptance of a Turkey & a chine sent this day by one Zachary Meads the Buckingham carrier, I don't know where he inns but hee will bring it as directed. Wee have not yet fixed on a carrier but when wee have will let you know, the things now sent are carriage paid. Wee give you & M^r & Mrs Vaughan joy of their Dau^r & my mother sais if Mrs Vaughan will dispense

with suckling the Dau.ʳ she will engage it will prove as healthy &
strong as George the second, for she sais it was her suckling after
she had so many children that made him so peevish, & that the
next she suckles will not have that disagreeable effect.

I desire when you go that way you will call on M.ʳ Cecill a
Lawyer of the Temple & ask him if anybody has paid 2 Guineas
into his hands for my subscription & if I be accepted & Registred
as one of the Associators to prosecute offenders against the Game
Laws &c. When you have received the Christmas Dividends pray
favour mee with your account by the Post; my eyesight is bad &
it will save mee the trouble of looking over your letters. My
mother desires to join with mee in entreating you to accept of
the Compliments of the Season, & I am with due Esteem Sir!

Your very humble servant
H. P.

P.S. The gamekeeper having failed to bring mee an Hare have
put up a couple of Barn Door ffowlls to fill up the Baskett.

ffor /
  M.ʳ Moulson
      in London

No. 428. H. P. *to* PETER MOULSON

Shalstone [*&c.*]
ffebruary the 7.ᵗʰ 1753

Sir! /

M.ʳ Greenvill never paid the two Guineas to M.ʳ Cecill but hee
has paid them mee here agen, so I thank you for paying M.ʳ Cecill
& am sorry to give this trouble, but desire your acceptance of an
hare & three woodcocks sent by M.ʳ Jones yᵉ Buckingham carrier,
carriage paid. Wee both join in our compliments to you & am
in hast to save yᵉ carrier, Sir!

Your very hᵗᵉ servant
H. P.

ffor /
  M.ʳ Moulson...
     London
  with a basket Carriage paid

No. 429. H. P. *to* JAMES CECILL

Shalstone [&c.]
August ye 23th 1753

Sir! /

I am favoured with yours dated 16th of this August & the gentleman who recommended your association to mee told mee the Subscription was two Guineas only, but I have since found it is an Annuall Subscription wch was the occasion I did not write to you, as I intend not to subscribe any more to it & am with due esteem Sir!

Your humble serv^t
H. P.

ffor /
   James Cecill Esq at his Chambers
   in the Temple
       London

No. 430. H. P. *to* PETER MOULSON

Shalstone [&c.]
August ye 10th 1736

Sir! /

I am favoured with yours of the 3rd instant. As to Mr Price the Clergyman's Daughters wee will let them alone. My mother has a God daughter who was partly bred up under her care, I may fairly say she is a Girl of as sharp sense as any in England & as stirring & housewifely as may be, & can sow well & understands to do everything in an house—if she had no fortune, if she was to be sold she is worth five hundred pound. As to her Person it is agreeable enough, & her fortune is £200 down & £200 at the death of her mother who is upwards of 60 years of age. This nobody can hinder her of & she has a chance to have more. Whether this takes or no Wee shall however be glad to see you here in your return from Wiltshire & wishing you a good Journey wee both join in service & respect to you & I am with reall esteem

Your very humble serv^t
H. P.

ffor /
   Mr Moulson...
       London

No. 431. H. P. *to* MR HOLTON

Shalstone
Aprill the 2ᵈ 1737

Mʳ Holton /

I desire you will send me by the bearer two of your best razors[1] & send sheaths with them & the price. If I like them I will send you yᵉ money for 'em next market day & am

Your freind & servᵗ

ffor /   H. P.
  Mʳ Holton
      at Buckingham /
         This

No. 432. H. P. *to* THOMAS GARRETT

Shalstone
Sunday Septembʳ yᵉ 16ᵗʰ 1753

Mʳ Garrett /

I have altered my mind as to my Perriwigg & instead of a Grizzell one I desire you will make mee a dark brown Periwigg of fifteen shillings price, in hast

Your freind & servᵗ

ffor /   H. P.
  Mʳ Garrett a
  Perriwig maker at
      Buckingham
        This

Haste apart, it is interesting to notice that so exact a writer as Henry manages to spell "periwig" three different ways in one letter—all different from the modern method.

On 2 Aug. 1752 the Diary records a visit from "Mʳ Thoˢ Garrett (the Barber) who brought my Periwigg but carried it away again because it did not fit".

No. 433. H. P. *to* THOMAS GARRETT

Shalstone
May the 23ᵗʰ 1747

Mʳ Garrett /

The new Periwigg you made mee has some Hair on the top of the Crown that don't curl & when I put on my Hat or the

1 In his early years Henry had a contract with the barber; 29 Apr. 1727. "Agreed then with Mʳ Markham the barber to shave for a year for Thirty shillings".

wind blows it stares & rises all up. I have minded other folk's periwigs & I think it should have another row of Curls higher towards ye Crown. Pray don't make my other wigg so, ffor you must alter this that I have. I hope I shall see you here soon which will oblidge

Your ffreind to serve you

H. P.

ffor /
  Mr Thomas Garrett junior a
  Barber at Buckingham
        This

CHAPTER XII

CLOTHING

OUR matter here is very abundant, in spite of careful selection.
Both Mrs Purefoy and her son had decided tastes, and Henry
evidently took trouble with his clothes.

It will be seen that he was afflicted with gout before he was 40 (Letter
No. 441), by the time he was 48 he was becoming bulky (Letter No. 467);
two years later he was still swelling (Letter No. 478 postscript).

One notices here how mother and son ordered each other's clothes.

No. 434. H. P. *to* MR PURCELL

Shalstone
January the 10ᵗʰ 1735

Mͬ Purcell /

Every place is now so deep in dirt where one walks that my
Galloshoes¹ are of no service to mee so I desire I may see you
here too morrow when I intend to consult with you to have something made instead of the Gallo shoes—which I now send you to
be mended & desire you will bring them with you wᶜʰ will oblidge

Your freind to serve you
H. P.

To Mͬ Purcell Senͬ
a shoemaker at Buckingham
This

No. 435. H. P. *to* JOHN BOYCE

Shalstone [&c.]
May the 5ᵗʰ 1736

This desires Mͬ Boyce to let mee have a letter of what Cloaths
are most fashionable together with some patterns of superfine
cloath, & whether they button their Cloaths with Silver or Gold
Buttons, or continue to wear laced wastcoats of silk or cloath, &
whether dressed coats or undressed coats. My mother desires if

1 This phonetic rendering of "galoshes" does not accord with its French origin,
and possibly Greek source.

The Account-book of 8 May 1741 has this entry:

"Paid Mͬ Purcell senͬ (the Buckingham Shoemaker)
for making my Galloshoes into Slippers   oo : oi : oo"

you have any of the white Indian Peeling[1] which she had a peice
of from you—she desires you will send her 3 or 4 yards with the
patterns of cloath by Webster the carrier who inns at the Oxford
Arms in Warwick Lane by Ludgate Hill & sets out of London
every Wensday morning. My mother joins with mee in our service
& respect to yourself & Mrs Boyce   Your ħħe serv^t
                                                              H. P.

To Mr Boyce at the
    Golden Ball in
        Surry Street in ye Strand
                London /

P.S. if you should see Mr Baxter pray tell him have rece͞d the
Bedstead[2] & will return ye money for it as soon as possible.

No. 436. E. P. *to* MRS WHITE

Shalstone [*&c.*]
May ye 5th 1736

This desires Mrs White to send mee a long Alamode Hood with
a very good black lace round it (as wide as anybody wears) to
wear when I am dressed or a Manteell hood if they be most wore.

I understand you have a son a mercer, I am sorry I did not
know it when in Town that I might have bought my silks of him.
Pray let mee know where hee lives & I desire hee will send me
4 yards of Shagreen the same colour to ye pattern if to be matched.
Pray send these by the Buckingham carrier. . ., let mee know what
they come to that I may order you payment wch will oblidge

Your humble serv^t
E. P.

ffor /
    Mrs White a milliner
    in the Old Bailey
        London

No. 437. H. P. *to* JOHN BOYCE

Shalstone [*&c.*]
May the 11th 1736

I rece͞d Mr Boys's letter of ye 6th instant & have sent you enclosed
the pattern of cloath that I will have my coat & Breetches of, with

1 A thin fabric used as a dress material; *O.E.D.* quotes use in 1769.
2 This may refer to the "new fashioned low bed" referred to in Letters Nos.
162–164.

Buttons & Trimming of the same colour, the coat to be lined wth a shagreen silk & to be half trimmed & but one pair of Breetches wch I desire may be made the same size as ye Breetches sent with pockets on each side, but no flap to the codpeice. The wastcoat to be a very good unwatered Tabby the same green to ye pattern trimmed with silver buttons & a silver lace about the breadth of the gold lace I had last year on my wastcoat, & to have pockets to it. I would not bestow anything extraordinary in the ounce for the making the lace, but let it be a showy lace of the common price by the ounce.

The Gold laced wastcoat you made mee last year has done you no credit in the making, it gapes so intolerably before at the bottom, when I button it at ye wastbone of my breetches & stand upright it gapes at the bottom beyond my breetches & everybody takes notice of it. As to my size I am partly the same bignesse as I was when in Town last, but you made the last cloaths a little too streight.

Pray let this be all done perfectly well & send mee some coat & wastcoat & breetches buttons & mohair & a naill of cloath the same to ye coat & a quarter of a yard of silk the same to ye wastcoat for I han't a bitt left to my last wastcoat—if I had ye gaping might be rectified.

My mother would have 3 yards of the white peeling if you can get it. The Breetches are sent this week by Webster.... My mother's & my service & respect waits on you & Mrs Boyce & I am

Your humble serv^t

H. P.

P.S. /

I desire I may have my cloaths as soon as possible & send your Bill with them & a letter by the post that they may not lie at ye Carriers.

ffor Mr John Bays[1]...
      London

[1] This is the same as the Mr Boyce of Letter No. 435; it is noticeable that this letter begins by calling him "Boys", concludes with "Boyce", and is addressed to "Bays".

No. 438. H. P. *to* JOHN BOYCE

Shalstone [&c.]
June the 6ᵗʰ 1736

I receᵈ Mʳ Boys's letter & the sute of cloaths wᶜʰ fit tolerable but I was forced to have an inch cut of[f] the coat before at yᵉ bottom & the breetches are too short at the knee, But wee must see & alter them; the green wastcoat is a very poor silk & my mother has bought a better for 4ˢ. I doubt your man did something to it for sure you yourself would not put such a silk in any wastcoat. I have sent you a bit of my wastcoat & a peice of the 4ˢ. silk. The Sattin won't match with the other so shall have no occasion for it. The sleeves of the coat come quite down to my wrist & are a great deall longer than yᵉ coat you made last year & a great deall longer than the wastcoat sleeve, let mee know if they wear their coat sleeves longer than they did last year, then I shall know how to alter it. Wee thank you for the mustard seed & the list & the book, & I have ordered Mʳ Webster yᵉ Bucks carrier to pay you £13. 15s. Pray date & sign the recᵗ underneath & leave it out if you should not be in yᵉ way it will [be] ready for Webster who will pay you either this week or the next. My mother & my service & respect is with yourself & Mʳˢ Boys & I am

Your humble servᵗ
H. P.

June yᵉ 8 1736

Received of Mʳ Henry Purefoy by the hands of Mʳ Webster thirteen pounds fifteen shillings in full for a suitt of cloaths & all other demands, I say received by mee

ffor /
  Mʳ John Boys...
        London

No. 439. E. P. *to* THOMAS ROBOTHAM

Shalstone [&c.]
Decembʳ 2ᵈ 1736

I received Mʳ Robotham's łre of the 29ᵗʰ of last month & therein inclosed the case with Mʳ Serjeant Draper's opinion thereon. My

son desires you will buy for him a fashionable pair of Russia
leather tops for half Jack boots & a pair of Russia leather spur
leathers & a pair of strong spurs for half Jack boots. The Russia
leather is red withinside. Wee shall kill an hog against X^{t}mas
pray let us know if you would have the chine sent a week before
X^{t}mas or on X^{t}mas Day, for the Carrier sets out then. Wee both
join in service & respect to yourself & Mrs Robotham & I am

Your humble serv^t

E. P.

P.S. Our parish Clerke John Gibbs is lately dead of the Small
pox, I thank God it has not yet spread any further, but it continues
still at Buckingham.

ffor /
   Mr Robotham...
      London

No. 440. H. P. *to* MR PURCELL

Shalstone

December ye 18th 1736

Mr Purcell /

I have now rece^d the Russia leather Topps, So I desire you will
come over soon to take measure of mee for a pair of half Jack
Boots & for a pair of Shoes. Bring with you some leather to line
the straps of my shoes as likewise some strings to set on my Boots
wch will oblidge

Your freind to serve you

H. P.

ffor /
   Mr Purcell Senr...
      Buckingham
        This

No. 441. H. P. *to* MR PURCELL

Shalstone

January the 15th 1736

Mr Purcell /

On Thursday last the swelling returned on my gouty foot so
that it was with Difficulty I got on my shoe. I hope to see you
here soon with my shoes, let the soles to the Jack boots be thick

enough otherwise the stirrup will not be so easie to my foot when
I ride. This will oblidge

Your freind to serve you

ffor / H. P.
Mr Purcell Senr...
    Buckingham
    This

No. 442. E. P. *to* MR STRANKS

Mr Stranks / *May 4th 1737*

The blew Cloath won't do, there is but 9 yards of it, I must
have 10 yards & all of one peice. This being of 2 peices is of
2 colours. Wee stayed for the wastcoats stuffs so the Taylor did
not begin to cut out till yesterday, or otherwise you should have
had it sooner. If you don't send the ten yards of blue cloath
speedily I must procure it some where else. In hast

Your freind to serve you

ffor / E. P.
Mr Stranks
    at Brackley
    This

No. 443. E. P. *to* THOMAS ROBOTHAM

Shalstone [&c.]
May ye 8th 1737

I received Mr Robotham's letter of the 3.^d instant and all the
things you mention therein very safe. As to the Hatt it is too little
in the head & my son can't wear it & the Brim is but 4 inches
wide. The gentlemen here wear 'em with a larger Brim but I
desire you will enquire whether that is the fashionable size or No;
it is sent again this week by Webster, the Buckingham carrier. If M.^r
Gamull will not send one big enough in ye head & of a fashionable size, must desire you to buy one any where else. As to the
Gold Lace it will do well enough, but I would not have had it
from Mr Gamull, it might have been bought cheaper at the shops,
however pay him for it. It is very well you did not pay Mr Mulford, I will see how ye watch goes then you shall hear further.

As to ye iron Chest enquire for that at your leisure. Wee thank you for the Turbot, it came sweet & eat exceeding well. My son & self join in service & respect to you & Mrs Robotham & I am

Your humble servant
E. P.

ffor /
Mr Robotham...
London

No. 444. H. P. *to* MR JONES

Shalstone
Decemb^r the 6th 1737

Mr Jones /

I have sent you the following things (To wit)
2 yards ¾ grey cloath for the coat
2 yards ¼ of black cloath for the wastcoat & breetches
5 yards ½ of black shalloon
2 dozen ½ coat buttons
3 dozen ½ wastcoat buttons
½ an ounce of Twist
1 yard ¼ of Buckrom
2 yards & ½ of Dimmothy
¾ of an ounce of black sowing silk
2 ounces of black thread
3 peñoth of stay tape
Canvas
⅝ y^d of glazed linnen
3 shammy skins

I bought these things of Mr Joseph Harris & I have paid him besides for hair cloath & for a yard & half of wadding, which hee sais you have of his. The breetches must have pockets on ye sides, but the coat must have no buttons at ye pockets, nor at the bottom of the Pleets; & the coat & wastcoat to be buttoned no lower than ye wast. The Breetches must not have a flap at ye cod peice but only buttons & buttonholes. I have sent a pair of breetches for a pattern. Take care I have the buttons & cloath & what is not used. I hope you may save black cloath enough for a pair of shoes for my mother. If you can with any con-

venience get them ready against Sunday next, but pray don't
hurry them over, but let them be done very well if I stay longer,
which will oblidge

Your freind to serve you

ffor /
   M.ʳ Jones
    a Tayler at
         Brackley /
          This

H. P.

No. 445. H. P. *to* MR PIDENTON

Shalstone
May ye 31.st 1738

I reced̄ M.ʳ Pidenton's Ł̵re & my mother desires you would buy
cloath enough for 2 servants frocks y.ᵉ colour to y.ᵉ pattern; her
price is about 4 shillings a yard & if it be worth y.ᵉ money & will
wear well she don't care what countrey cloath it is, but it must
be sure not to shrink. She would also have 12 yards of serge
Padua soi¹ the same colour to the pattern you have & as many
fashionable brasse Livery buttons as 2 frocks & 2 wastcoats will
take up & 2 ounces of mohair the same colour to y.ᵉ pattern.
Thread & other things I suppose may be had of you when you
come home. I should have been glad of your grey cloath but have
one already of that colour. I wish you a good journey & am

Your humble serv.ᵗ

ffor /
   M.ʳ Pidenton
   at Brackley /
         This

H. P.

No. 446. H. P. *to* EDWARD FELL

Shalstone
Wensday June 5th 1738

M.ʳ ffell /

I have sent you the grey breetches again, your man prevailed
with mee to take them, but I can't wear them, so you must change

---

1 Paduasoy, strictly speaking, is a strong corded silk fabric; originally serge was
a silk fabric. In Letter No. 461 we shall find the spelling paduaSa (capital S);
the association with Padua is perhaps imaginary. The French have it *pont-de-
soie*, *pou-de-soie*, and *poult-de-soie*. See also Letter No. 453.

'em. I have sent you a pair to make them by, pray let them be exactly as they are. I despair of your altering them, they are so unfit as you'll see by them I send, so fancy you must make another pair. Pray send word by the servant if I may send for them on Sunday next, if you can't convey them to mee by any other hand by that time, pray dont faill letting mee have them then. Let there be a button hole at the ffob to put ye chain of the watch through. Send mee 4 of the black coat buttons & 6 wastcoat black buttons & a naill of the grey cloath & will pay you for them. I paid your man 5 guineas which I hope you had. In hast

Your humble serv^t
H. P.

ffor /
  M^r ffell Senr a Tayler
  at Chipping Norton
        This

No. 447. H. P. *to* ANTHONY BAXTER

Shalstone [*&c.*]
July the 15th 1739

Mr Baxter /

I desire you will send mee a dozen printed cambrick pocket handkerchiefs or something like that, about two shillings a peice for common use. Send also fine thick printed Cotton enough to make two wrappers for my mother, they must be of 2 different handsome patterns. You must remember the last cotton you sent for the window curtains was too dear. You must also send a neat white quilted Callicoe petticoat for my mother which must be a yard & 4 inches long. Send also 10 or 12 yards of Irish Holland of ab^t 3^s. a yard & it must be a good close Holland, if I like it & the price of it I shall want a good deall more. Send also a yard of Cambrick of about 10s. ye yard, if what you send is not liked it shall be returned you again. Let mee have your Bill & I will order you payment. Send these things at your leisure by the Buckingham carrier.... This will oblidge

Your humble serv^t
H. P.

ffor /
  Mr Anthony Thomas Baxter...
      London.

No. 448. H. P. *to* ANTHONY BAXTER

Shalstone [&c.]
August ye 5th 1739

Mr Baxter /

I rece^d all the things in the Box & have returned you the Marseilles Quilt petticoat by Mr Eagles ye Carrier. It is so heavy my mother cannot wear it. Wee will have the rest of the things, but our neighbours have bought Cottons 6.^d in a yard cheaper & as good which I hope you will 'bate. Mr Eagles the carrier... comes into Town on Monday morning about 4 a clock, so then you may send for them if you please. As soon as I can get a return I will order you payment,[1] I hope it will be in about a fortnight, & am

Your humble serv.^t
H. P.

ffor /
Mr Anthony Thos Baxter...
London

No. 449. H. P. *to* ANTHONY BAXTER

Shalstone [&c.]
March the 26th 1740

Mr Baxter /

I desire you will send mee ffive and thirty yards of Irish holland of about three Shillings a yard to make mee night shirts, it must be yard wide cloath & very good of the price. Pray send with it seven ells[1] of Irish Holland at 6s. 6d. a yard, or thereabouts, if as fine and as white as Dutch Holland, if not send Dutch Holland of about 7s. an ell. And send two yards of Cambrick for shirt Rufles; the Last you sent was too thin. Send these by the Buckingham carrier....

I am
Your humble servant
H. P.

ffor /
Mr Anthony Thos Baxter...
London

P.S. Pray send your Bill with the things.

1 Mr Baxter was paid £9. 16s. 6d. on 18 August.
2 The English ell was 45 inches, so that presumably 8¾ yards were wanted and the Irish was more expensive than the Dutch holland. The bill came to £8. 17s. 6d. and was paid on 19 April.

No. 450. H. P. *to* CHARLES MEREDITH

Shalstone [&c.]
Sunday March ye 30th 1740

Mr Meredith /

I have sent you a woman's silk stocking for a pattern & desire you to send down half a dozen pair of fine white thread stockings of 3 Threads of 5 or 6 shillings a pair, & 2 pair of fine white thread gloves that are open fingured, but the fingers must come to the Top of the fingers. The stockings & gloves are both for my mother, I desire you will let them be good at the price. I desire you will send 'em by the Buckingham carrier...with your bill[1] & if they are approved on I will order Mr Eagles to pay you for them. The gloves must be for a small hand and arm. Pray take care the silk stocking sent is not soiled.

                              I am
                                    Your humble servant
ffor /   H. P.
    Mr C. Meredith[2] at the golden
    ffleece against St Dunstan's
    Church in ffleet street
              London

No. 451. H. P. *to* MR JOHNSON

Shalstone
May 14th 1740

Mr Johnson /

I have a red wastcoat & Breetches to be faced with silver lace for you to make up, & desire you will call here some time on Sunday next to tell me what Tackle will be wanting for it, wch will oblidge

                    Your freind to serve you
ffor /   H. P.
    Mr Johnson jun^r a Taylor
    at the Barber's Pole at
         Tingwick /
              This

1 The bill came to £2. 7s. 0d. and was paid on 19 April.
2 Mr Ambrose Heal kindly says that he has seen the bill-head of Meredith and Reynolds, hosiers and hatters, of this address, dated 1759.

No. 452. E. P. *to* THOMAS ROBOTHAM

Shalstone [&c.]
July the 13th 1740

I receď Mr Robotham's of the 10th of last month, with the red Cloath, Lace, Buttons &c as also the Turbatt wch was fresh & exceeding good, wee return you many thanks for it & are sorry wee have nothing in our Countrey at present to make a return.

I desire you will enquire at the White Bear in ffleet Street near the Bridge, the price of the new ffrench Gold & silver Hatts sold there for women & what they be made on, some say here they be made of Leather. I entreat you will send 20/- Silver Buttons for my son's Breetches, the same sort and size you sent last, wch if the man that sells 'em has forgot I must send up a Button for a pattern; & send also red shagreen silk enough for puffs for the Breetches ye same colour to the red pattern sent. Wee know the Tiles are allways of seuall ffigures but all of a bignesse so I entreat when you have an opportunity to send 6 dozen of them in a Box; & send 4 pullies to go on swivells every way to put on the bottom of an easy chair; they are to be had at Mr Parkins & Sitwell at White Lion in ffoster lane, Cheapside, pray see they be strong enough.

Wee hope by this time you have got better health & shall be glad if you will come soon to Shalstone and tell us so, & with our best services & respects to yourself & Mrs Robotham I am

Your humble servant
E. P.

P.S. I think verily Astrop Waters would do you good, this is the season to drink them. However consult your physician.

ffor /
  Mr Robotham...
      London /

No. 453. E. P. *to* MR WOODFIELD

Shalstone
July the 30th 1740

Mr Woodfeild /

I have sent you the pattern of Cloath & desire you to send me eight yards of it, I hope 4s a yard will do for it; and send twelve yards of the yellow Padua serge and brasse Buttons enough for the 2 wastcoats & frocks, & stay tape & thread & silk & all materialls for them except Buckrom. So soon as you have got the Padua serge send them & let it be as soon as possibly you can wch will oblidge

Your humble serv^t
E. P.

ffor /
Mr Woodfeild a mercer
at Bircester /
This
Carriage paid two pence

No. 454. E. P. *to* MR WOODFIELD

Shalstone
August 26th 1740

Mr Woodfeild /

When you send the stuff for the servants wastcoats pray send with it ffive yards of 3 quarter camlett, I don't care much what colour so it is but strong, 'tis for a Charity coat for a girl. This will oblidge

Your humble serv^t
E. P.

ffor /
Mr Woodfeild a mercer
at Bircester /
This

No. 455. H. P. *to* CHARLES MEREDITH

Shalstone [&c.]
March 14th 1740

This desires Mr Meredith to send mee a fashionable sized Beavor hatt of the very best sort, it must be 26 inches and an half round the outside of the Crown. The last you sent they tell mee was not all Beavor. Send it with your bill by the Buckingham carrier..., & I will order you payment for it forthwith, & am

Your hle serv^t
H. P.

ffor /
Mr C. Meredith...
London

No. 456. E. P. *to* MR WOODFIELD

Shalstone
June the 3ᵈ 1741

Mʳ Woodfeild /

I desire you will send mee in some time this week the following things (To wit) 4 yards of cloath the same to the pattern, wᶜʰ is what I had on you for the last frocks. The footman who went away took his frock & wastcoat with him. I have stuf enough for the wastcoat that I had of you; send also mohair thread & frock & wastcoat brasse buttons, canvas, & stay tape for the frock & wastcoat the same to the patterns, & a yard of fustian for the pocketts, & send your bill with them. This will oblidge

Your humble servant
E. P.

ffor /
   Mʳ Woodfeild a mercer at
     Bircester /
       This /
   Carriage paid 2 pence

No. 457. E. P. *to* HENRY LLOYD

Shalstone [&c.]
June the 11ᵗʰ 1741

Mʳ Lloyd /

I desire you will send mee a very good whale bone hoop Petticoat of the newest fashion. It must be 3 yards & a quarter round at yᵉ bottom, & it must draw in a Top for a wast half a yard & a naill round,¹ and the length upon the hip to yᵉ bottom a yard & half a quarter. The last hoop you sent mee was so big a top it would not draw in to my wast by half a quarter of a yard. Send this by Mʳˢ Eagles the Buckingham carrier with your bill of what it comes to. She inns at the George inne in Smithfeild & sets out of London on Tuesday morning about 4 a clock, & send with it one of your printed Bills. This will oblidge

Your humble servᵗ
E. P.

ffor /
   Mʳ Henry Lloyd at Long's
   Warehouse the Corner of
   Tavistock Street in Covent
   Garden /
      London.

1 Mrs Purefoy was 68 at this time, and her waist was 20¼ inches round. The letter had to be repeated on 2 July; the garment came on 26 July, but there was no "printed bill" with it.

No. 458. E. P. *to* CHARLES MEREDITH

Shalstone [&*c.*]

Mr Meredith /   *Aprill 18ᵗʰ 1742*

I desire you will send mee two Caroline Hatts[1] of a fashionable
size for the Servants. Let them be so good as to be serviceable.
The bignesse of the head on the outside of the crown of the hatts
is twenty three inches round each; let each of them be laced with
a gold lace of an inch & half a quarter of an inch wide & to have
gold Loops & gold Buttons. It must be gold of both sides & not
a gaws lace. Send them by next Saturday's return of the Buckingham carrier...& send your bill with them, & will order you
payment by Mrs Eagles & am

Your hle servant

ffor /   E. P.
  Mr C. Meredith...
        London

No. 459. H. P. *to* ANTHONY BAXTER

Shalstone [&*c.*]

Mr Baxter /   *Septembʳ the 21ᵗʰ 1742*

I desire you will send mee 8 yards of the same vermilion or
Dimmothy that you sent mee before for night capps,[2] and send my
mother for under petticoats 16 yards of tufted Dimmothy to wear
under an Hoop, & 3 or 4 yards of very fine cambrick. If one
Mrs Wentworth should come to you for any goods pray use her
well, in doing wᶜʰ you will obledge

Your humble servant

H. P.

P.S. Pray send down some patterns of fine striped Cotton &
the price for washing gowns, & send the things by the Buckingham
carrier....When I receive the things will order you payment on
sending your Bill.

ffor /
  Mr Anthony Thoˢ Baxter...
        London

1 "Caroline" was applied at the end of the 17th century to a fashion of hats.
These cost £1. 15*s. 8d.*
2 Two of Henry's nightcaps are still at Shalstone; the present Mrs Purefoy
kindly writes that they "have a kind of embossed material groundwork with
embroidery superimposed, but I think one is of linen, and the cotton one is
most like dimity; neither answers to our idea of vermilion".

No. 460. H. P. *to* EDWARD FELL

Shalstone [&c.]
May the 19th 1743

M^r ffell /

I desire you will come over here as soon as possible and bring some patterns of cloath to make a suit of mourning for mee; 't is for a Distant Relation,[1] I mention this that you may the better know what colour to bring & am

Your humble serv^t
H. P.

ffor /
   M^r ffell senior at
      Chipping Norton
         in Oxfordshire
By way of London

No. 461. E. P. *to* EDWARD FELL

Shalstone
July the 10th 1743

M^r ffell /

I desire you will make the coachman a ffrock the same coloured cloath to the pattern as near as you can & a gold coloured serge paduaSa[2] wastcoat. Pray let the serge paduaSa be better than the last was. It must not be a lemon colour but a gold colour, & the lining of the frock must be of the same colour; & let mee have it within a week or as soon as you can. I desire you will tell Jo: Sheppard's mother that hee is very slight but I will try him for a year upon these terms: his wages shall be 40 shillings, I will make such cloaths, as frock & wastcoat as I like hee shall wear & a pair of boots, & if hee should be visited with the small pox hee must quitt his service & his mother must engage to provide for him. I have cloaths by mee that will serve him. If Mrs Sheppard don't approve of this the boy may go home when the Coachman's ffrock comes.

Your freind to serve you
E. P.

ffor /
   M^r ffell senior at Chippingnorton
         This

1 This clearly refers to the death of Thomas Jervoise (see Letter No. 398).
2 See Letter No. 445, note upon paduasoy.

No. 462. H. P. *to* GEORGE VAUGHAN

Shalstone [&c.]
Aprill the 4ᵗʰ 1744

Sir! /

I desire you will send mee 5 yards of silver Lace to bind a wastcoat as good & fashionable as any is worn; as also two dozen & four silver twist buttons for the wastcoat,[1] and enough of fashionable Silver Lace to lace four pair of shoes for my mother, & a yard of narrow silver lace to go up the seam behind the shoes. Send these by the Buckingham carrier.... Send your bill with them & will order you payment, & with our compliments to yourself & Mʳˢ Vaughan am, Sir!

Your humble servant
H. P.

ffor /
 Mʳ George Vaughan at the Golden
 Ball[2] near Arundell Street
 in the Strand
  London

No. 463. E. P. *to* THOMAS ROBOTHAM

Shalstone [&c.]
Novembʳ the 27ᵗʰ 1743

Wee reced Mʳ Robotham's kind present of a Barrell of Oysters for which wee return thanks. The trouble wee give you is worth all the hares wee send, therefore pray don't trouble yourself to send any ffish for wee have plenty in our own Countrey at present. I desire you to accept of a brace of Hares fresh catched wᶜʰ are sent with your butter & a box with my son's half Jack Boots therein wᶜʰ are too little, for tho' hee did them with soap withinside as hee ordered him yet hee can't possibly draw 'em on; for it is true as our shoemaker sais—when you come to draw them on they come to the same littlenesse as they were before they were stretched; so that Mʳ Creach, since hee beleived they were not too little, must change them for another pair which must be at least an inch bigger in the leg. So pray, when you give him these, measure them how big round they be in the leg, & then

1 One of Henry's waistcoats, still preserved at Shalstone, has silver-spangled edging half an inch wide, and made buttons with silver spangles worked onto them (information kindly given by the present Mrs Purefoy).
2 Mr Ambrose Heal has a bill of George Vaughan, laceman, at this address dated 1750.

you will know that they be an inch bigger. If hee must have anything for the change of them you must allow it him, tho' I do assure you they have never been upon no leg since wee had them, for my son could not get them on. The worke is liked by every body that sees them so I hope hee will get Businesse by making them. I hope you don't forget where M.ʳ Creach lives, it is on yᵉ corner of Great Turnstile next Lincolns-inne ffeilds, & hee used to make Mʳˢ Robotham's shoes; pray place the portridge of yᵉ boots to account. Underneath you will find the receipt for D.ʳ Lower's Tincture. Wee both join in our service & respects to yourself & Mʳˢ Robotham & I am

Your humble servant
E. P.

P.S. I shall kill an hog against X.ᵗ'mas & desire to know whether you would have the chine & Turkey sent on yᵉ Saturday before X.ᵗ'mas day or yᵉ Wensday after.

To make D.ʳ Lower's Tincture[1]

Take of Guiacum chips the smallest you can get, leaves of Senna, Liquorish, Anniseed, Coriander Seed, Elicompane Roots dryed,— of each two ounces, one pound of Stoned Raisins of the Sun, three quarts of Aqua Vitæ. It must be infused a fortnight before it be drawn of[f].

P.S. Pray don't let the Shoemaker offer to let the half Jack Boots out, for my son won't submit to that.

ffor /
   M.ʳ Robotham...
      London

1 This is the first recipe in *Dr Lower's and Several other Eminent Physicians' Receipts*, 4th edn., 1716; it is commonly called Daffy's Elixir. The weights are one quarter of those quoted by Mrs Purefoy, and one quart of aqua vitae is named; but on p. 106 "D.ʳ Lower's Elixir" is given with much the same ingredients while 3 quarts of aqua vitae are required. (Information kindly supplied by Mr J. Bishop of the Royal College of Physicians.) Dr Richard Lower (1631–1691) was the most noted physician of his time in London; a life appears in the *D.N.B.* and other works of reference.

No. 464. E. P. *to* THOMAS ROBOTHAM

Shalstone [&c.]
June 16ᵗʰ 1744

I this day heard by Mʳ Zachary Meads that Mʳ Robotham was well. Hee tells mee yᵉ butter did not prove good, 't is allways strong about a fortnight or 3 weeks at this time of the year; but last week & this week 't is good again & will continue so. I desire you will send mee a short flourished black hood, such an one as Mʳˢ Robotham saw that I sent for from Turnstile, I was to give half a guinea for it; & pray buy half a dozen gilt breast buttons same to the button sent, & half a dozen gilt coat buttons same to the button sent, And 2 dozen & an half of silvered coat buttons with cat gutt stalks to them & 20 silvered breast buttons with catt gutt stalks, also the newest ffashion, & a yard of green silk the same to yᵉ pattern. My son joins with mee in our service & respect to yourself & Mʳˢ Robotham & hope wee shall see you here some time this summer, & I am

Your humble servant

ffor /
   Mʳ Robotham...
       London
   Carriage paid.
   Deliver this with yᵉ butter

E. P.

As a matter of fact Mr Robotham came on his visit on 14 July and stayed until 29 July. During that time he went "on coursing" twice, paid visits to the Rev. Mr Hawes at Syresham and to the Rev. Mr Price at Whitfield, besides a glorious day at Blenheim House which they went over, dining at the Wheat Sheaf Inn at Woodstock. Altogether they seem to have given Mr Robotham a very good time of it.

No. 465. E. P. *to* MR YATES

Shalstone
November the 30ᵗʰ 1744

Mʳ Yates /

I understand you have a son in law who has set up a Draper's shop in Brackley, with your interest & a prospect of a customer I make no question but you can prevaill with him to send mee ye following things, good of the kind & as cheap as hee can afford (vizt)

> 5 yards of narrow cloath of about 3s. a yard, that won't shrink to make a servant's surtout coat of the colour of the pattern sent, & rather lighter than darker, if not of that colour.
>
> 2 dozen large brasse round coat buttons.
>
> 6 round brasse breast buttons.
>
> a quarter of a yard of shalloon.
>
> a quarter of an ounce of silk twist.
>
> an ounce of 3 penny thread.
>
> a quarter of an ounce of sowing silk.
>
> All of them the same colour to ye cloath.
>
> A pennorth of stay tape, a pennorth of canvas, & half a quarter of a yard of ffustian.

Send your bill with them by ye bearer wch will oblidge

> Your ffreind to serve you
>
> E. P.

P.S. I thank you that you got the road mended for mee; but there is since that a quick sand in the lane that goes up from Bandilands near where the 2 ways meet, that my coachman with his coach horse was like to be mired in it as hee will tell you, & that prevents mee from coming to Brackley.

ffor /
> Mr Yates sen^r a Grocer at
> Brackley
> > This

No. 466. H. P. *to* MR JOHNSON

Shalstone
25th Aprill 1745

Mr Johnson /

I have had the misfortune to burn the sleeve of my great coat in a sorrowfull manner, so entreat you will not faill to come over

too morrow morning to mend it, for if I had businesse of the utmost consequence I can't ride out till it is done. This will oblidge

Your freind to serve you
H. P.

ffor /
   Mr Johnson junior a
   Taylor at Tingwick
      This

It is hoped that no business of consequence arose, for the tailor did not
arrive until 29 April. Except to go to church on the 28th Henry did
not leave the house from the 25th to the 30th.

No. 467. H. P. to EDWARD FELL

Shalstone [&c.]
Tuesday May ye 14th 1745

M.^r ffell /

I admire you never took measure of mee when you was here;
my cloaths are all too little about the belly, I am grown much
fatter than I was. If you bring them and they don't fit mee I
won't have them; so I desire next Sunday when you come to
Tusmore,[1] instead of bringing the cloaths come & take measure
on mee. I beg you would not come in such an hurry another time
so as to forget to take measure; I can't help taking it amiss of you

Yours in hast
H. P.

ffor /
   M.^r ffell senior...

No. 468. H. P. to EDWARD FELL

Shalstone
Sunday June ye 9th 1745

M.^r ffell /

I hoped to have seen you here before now, and my mother
having a new footman you may now take measure of him as well
as ye coachman, & the Revd Mr Haws our Rector would have a

1 On 23 May at 2.30 there arrived "the young man who brought my cloaths
from M.^r ffell senior ye Taylor". Tusmore was the home of the Catholic and
Jacobite family of Fermor; a note upon them will be found on p. 372.

suit of cloaths of you, & stayed at home on purpose on the Thursday I desired you to come on. I entreat I may see you here next Wensday or next ffriday[1] & I will desire M.r Haws to be at home then; if you don't come by that time wee shall think you neglect us. My new Breetches fit very well, but I wear a Buckle behind & you have made Eye lid holes for strings only & no cloath straps at all for y.e Buckle. As to the coat it is much too bigg about the stomach & must be altered, so I desire you will bring some thread & silk of the colour to it, as also some scraps of cloath the same to the coat & breetches, & 10 coat buttons & 10 breast buttons & an hank of mohair the same colour to them. I asked for them of the man you sent with the cloaths but hee told mee you did not give him any. Let mee have your bill also. My mother has got a maid so you need be in no case about that. I am

Your freind to serve you
H. P.

ffor /
  M.r ffell senior at
  Chipping Norton
       This

No. 469. E. P. *to* GEORGE VAUGHAN

Shalstone [&c.]
June the 13.th 1745

Sir! /

I desire you will send mee by...the Buckingham carrier,... three yards & half a quarter of a yard of gold Lace an inch & a quarter wide & two gold Buttons & two gold Loops for y.e Livery hats, & a quire of paper to paper laced cloaths, & your bill with them, & will order you payment. My sons & my compliments wait on M.rs Vaughan & yourself & I am

Your humble servant
E. P.

ffor /
  M.r Vaughan...
    London

1 Mr Fell did not come until Monday, 17 June.

No. 470. H. P. *to* CHARLES MEREDITH

Shalstone [&c.]
June 13ʰ 1745

This desires Mᵣ Meredith to send mee a fashionable sized Beavor Hat of the very best sort. It must be 27 inches round the outside of the Crown. Send it with what convenient speed you can by yᵉ Buckingham carrier...& send a bill & will order you payment for it forthwith & am

Your humble servant
H. P.

ffor /
Mᵣ C. Meredith...
London

No. 471. E. P. *to* THOMAS ROBOTHAM

Shalstone [&c.]
May yᵉ 17ʰ 1746

I received Mᵣ Robotham's letter of the 8ᵗʰ instant but wee have such dreadfull accounts of the small pox that wee have no thoughts of coming to Town at present, but return you many thanks for your kind proffer to meet us. I have sent a blue Damask gown & must desire Nelly to get it cleaned or dyed of any colour it will take best. I have sent some of the same that was cleaned before to be done with this, that it may be all of a colour if it is required to be cleaned or Dyed with it.

They say Sattins are much worn, I desire to know if they be; if they are pray send mee some patterns of a beautifull green Sattin, and some patterns of a fine pretty deep-blue Lutestring, & the prices of them wᶜʰ will oblidge

Your humble servant
E. P.

P.S. There are 7 breadths of the gown & 4 peices of the new. Our respects attend you & Nelly. Yesterday William Baker yᵉ Coachman left my service, if you should chance to hear of ever a coachman who can have a good character[1] & is a sober, honest fellow, & can drive a coach well and has been used to ploughing & other Husbandry businesse, if you let mee know what wages

[1] On 28th May Mrs Purefoy gave Wm Baker "a certificate that hee lived with her as Coachman seven years & that during that Time hee behaved Soberly and Honestly".

hee expects I will let you have my answer. I have no farming only a few closes on my hands at present. Hee must look after ye cow pasture & must not be idly inclined.

I have also sent more Ten breadths of white slight silk, wch I desire may be dyed yellow.

ffor /
  Mr Robotham...
        London
    Carriage paid

The rising anger in the three next letters produced Mr Fell,—late in the evening of 26 July.

No. 472. H. P. *to* EDWARD FELL

Shalstone
June the 26th. 1746

M^r ffell /

I desire you will come over here yourself to take measure on mee on Monday or Tuesday next & amongst other patterns bring some of red cloath for a wastcoat & Breetches for mee, & some patterns of cloath for the Servants' frocks. This will oblidge

Your humble servant
H. P.

ffor /
  M^r ffell sen^r at
      Chippingnorton
      in Oxfordshire
By way of London

No. 473. H. P. *to* EDWARD FELL

Shalstone
July the 20th 1746

M^r ffell /

I admire you disappoint mee so,—I shall go a journey very soon & should have gone before this if wee could have got in the Hay sooner. I desire you will bring my cloaths soon & bring the Coachman a linnen frock to put over his cloaths when hee rubs his horses down. If you can't get any shalloon of the colour of my coat bring some blue shalloon the colour of the pattern enclosed instead thereof. I am

Your humble servant
H. P.

ffor /
  M^r ffell senior at Chippingnorton
        This

No. 474. H. P. *to* EDWARD FELL

Shalstone
July the 23ʳᵈ 1746

I am amazed you don't bring my Cloaths according to your word; I have thoughts of going a journey so am forced to send a messenger whom I have ordered to see you or your man set out with the Cloaths. You said in your last I should have them last Tuesday or Wensday se'nnight. I suppose you han't my letter I sent to Mʳ ffarmer's,—you may bring a ffrock over for the Coachman to do his horses in.

Yours in hast

ffor /   H. P.
　Mʳ ffell senʳ at Chippingnorton
　　　　　　This

NB. I sent this letter by Bruce Smith.

No. 475. H. P. *to* HARRY FISH

Shalstone [*&c.*]
ffebruary the 18ᵗʰ 1746

Sir! /

I am favoured with yours of the 14ᵗʰ instant & since the Lottery Tickets fetch no higher a price I will let them lie as they are at present. My mother desires you will buy her a Genteell fashionable Capuchin of about three pounds price & an handsome Ermine Tippett, & send them by yᵉ Buckingham carrier.... When you have sent these things with the receipt for them you may call on Mʳ Moulson in Wood street & hee will pay you the money for them if you show him this Letter. My mother joins with mee in our Respects & good wishes for yourself & ffamily, & shall be glad to hear of your healths & I am

Your affectionate kinsman
& humble servant

ffor /   H. P.
　Mʳ ffish...
　　　London

P.S. You may call on Mʳ Moulson for the money & then send the receipts with the things.

No. 476. H. P. *to* HARRY FISH

Shalstone [&c.]
March y 22*ᵗʰ* 1746

Sir! /

I received yours of the 14ᵗʰ instant together with the Capuchin & Tippett which is very well liked of, & desire you will go to Mʳ Moulson in Woodstreet in Cheapside & receive of him four pounds and fourteen shillings & desire him to place it to my mother's account.[1]

Wee have had the Small Pox here in this parish ever since August last & six folks have died of it, but I thank God ourselves & our ffamily have escaped it & the Parish is now clear of it.

Wee are both pretty well in health only my mother has got a cold & wee desire our respects to yourself & ffamily & I am Sir! /

Your affectionate kinsman
& humble servant
H. P.

ffor /
    Mʳ ffish...
        London

No. 477. H. P. *to* ANTHONY BAXTER

Shalstone [&c.]
June the 8ᵗʰ 1746

Mʳ Baxter /

I desire you will send mee six ells of such Gulick Holland[2] as you sent last time for my shirt sleeves, six shillings & sixpence an ell; & one dozen of fine Cambrick red and white Handkercheifs of about half a crown a peice; and ten ells of Holland of about a Crown an ell (ell wide, or what you call so,) let it be any sort of Holland so it be a penñoth of the sort for a pair of sheets. I want a pretty many more but I will see how I like these first. Send these by the Buckingham carrier....And if you have any such thing as a Chintz with a brown ground or anything that is very fine that imitates it—send it with these & your bill, & if I don't

---

1 See Letter No. 331.
2 A very fine, white linen named from Dutch "Gulik", the town of Juliers. Perhaps it is the same as the "Dutch Holland" referred to in Letter No. 449.

like it and the Price I will send it up again; it is for a wrapper for my mother. This will oblidge

Your humble servant

H. P.

ffor /

Mᵣ Anthony Thomas Baxter...
London

No. 478. H. P. *to* EDWARD FELL

Shalstone [&c.]
May the 7ᵗʰ 1747

I received Mᵣ ffell's letter dated the 2ᵈ of this May together with the Patterns, but there are none of them but what are too like what I have already, so I would have somewhat of a Cinnamon colour or very light colour, if they are worn lined with a shagreen silk of the same colour. I shall want only a coat & a pair of Breetches, I have so many Wastcoats by mee.[1]

I hope you'll be in the Countrey soon & over here at Shalstone because the Servants Liveries are also wanting, & am

Your humble servant

H. P.

You must come here & measure mee yourself for I am grown fatter.

Mᵣ Edward ffell senior at Mᵣ Lane's in Craven buildings near yᵉ New Church in the Strand /
London

No. 479. H. P. *to* EDWARD FELL

Shalstone [&c.]
June the 4ᵗʰ 1747

Mᵣ ffell /

My mother desires you will bring 3 Linnen washing frocks for the 3 men servants such as you used to bring; let them be big enough, the last were too tite upon 'em, & I entreat you'll make mee some straps on my Breetches behind, because I wear a Buckle there. Wee really forgot to tell you of yᵉ frocks or else you should not have had this trouble from

Your hite servant

H. P.

ffor /

Mᵣ Fell senᵣ at Chippingnorton
in Oxfordshire
By way of London

1 Six of Henry's waistcoats, handsomely embroidered, are still preserved at Shalstone.

No. 480. H. P. *to* CHARLES MEREDITH

Shalstone [&c.]
May the 25ᵗʰ 1748

This desires Mᵣ Meredith to send mee a fashionable sized stout Beavor hat of the best sort. It must be 26 inches & 3 quarters of an inch round the outside of the Crown. Send it, with what convenient speed you can by yᵉ Buckingham carrier. .& send what it comes to & will order you payment. Your last Beavor Hat you sent mee cracked sadly at the edges & I was forced to have it pared of[f]; I hope I shall have no reason to complain of anything of that sort in the Hat you now send & am

Your humble servant
H. P.

ffor /
Mᵣ C. Meredith...
　　　London

Mr Meredith sent the hat but no bill, and was chidden on 22 June in the words "you did not use to be so negligent". This produced the bill (£1. 4s. 0d.) which was paid on 2 July.

No. 481. H. P. *to* ANTHONY BAXTER

Shalstone [&c.]
October 29ᵗʰ 1749

Mᵣ Baxter /

I desire you will send mee nine yards of flowered Cotton with a brown ground & coloured flowers yard wide; it is for my own morning gown so that if half of it be of one sort & half of another it will do, but both of them must have brown Grounds. Send also twenty Ells of broad Sheet Holland, of about four or five Shillings an Ell, by yᵉ Buckingham carrier...& send your bill[1] with them & will order you payment, & am

Your humble servant
H. P.

ffor /
Mᵣ Anthony Thoˢ Baxter...
　　　London

1 It came to £7. 5s. 0d. and was paid on 2 December.

No. 482. H. P. *to* FRANCIS FELL

Shalstone
July the 7ᵗʰ 1751

Mʳ ffell /

I desire you will come over here as soon as may be to take measure on mee for a suitt of second mourning & to bring patterns of Cloath with you. I must have them made and brought for mee to wear on next Monday come sennight at night, being the 15ᵗʰ of this instant July, for next morning early being the 16ᵗʰ I am warned to be on the Grand Jury. You should have known sooner but I did not know myself till last night that I was to be at the Assize. Pray let the Patterns be fine fast cloath. The grey Breetches you made mee are too shallow in the Seatt & must be let out, so desire you will bring with you a naill of grey cloath the same to the pattern enclosed to enlarge them. This will oblidge

Your freind to serve you
H. P.

ffor /
   Mʳ ffrancis ffell
   a Tayler at
         Chipping-norton
             in Oxfordshire
By London

No. 483. E. P. *to* MISS BARRETT

Shalstone
Decʳ the 6ᵗʰ 1748

This acquaints Miss Barrett I have sent the lace again and money to pay for two yards of the wide Lace, which two yards of the wide lace I desire you will send mee again by the Bearer. Pray let Mʳ Wallbank know that my leg is closed up and that my foot on the Instep as far as my Toes is swelled bigger than my other foot by three quarters of an inch, but no Pain.[1] Wee both join in our Compliments to you all and I am

Your humble servant
E. P.

ffor /
   Mʳˢ Barrett at Mʳ
   Wallbank's at Buckingham
         This

1 This had troubled Mrs Purefoy for years; see Letter No. 486 et seq.

No. 484. E. P. *to* ANNE BAXTER

Shalstone [*&c.*]
September y^e *2*^d *1753*

I had a letter from Mrs Baxter some time ago that she would use mee as well as Brother did in her way. I desire you will send mee 3 quarters of a yard of black silk for an Handkercheif for my neck, three quarters of a yard every way or wider if any,—it must be square. And send mee a fine Cotton for a Gown with a Cinnamon or yellowish ground flowered very handsomely with shades of Colours, & enough for another gown of fashionable cotton with a white Ground flowered wth colours, of a crown a yard. I have black lace to put about ye Handkercheif. If I don't like ye Gowns I will return them you again. Pray send them as soon as you can by ye Buckingham carrier....You had best send them to ye carrier over night & send your bill with 'em. This will oblidge

Your freind to serve you
E. P.

P.S. Pray send one of your printed papers. The black silk for ye handkercheif must be a yard square every way, or near upon it.

ffor /
    Mrs Anne Baxter
    a Linnen Draper in Dartmouth
    Streett near the Cockpitt
    Westminster London

CHAPTER XIII

MEDICAL, DENTAL, OPTICAL: VISITS TO BATH AND LONDON

THE editor hesitated considerably about the inclusion of this group of letters, which seemed somewhat too intimate for publication. On the other hand, no true picture of human life can ignore the ills that flesh is heir to, and, however much the ailments of our acquaintances bore us in the repetition, after two centuries "nous avons tous assez de force pour supporter les maux d'autrui", as De La Rochefoucald says.

The letters dealing with dental matters have some historic interest, and the whole set illustrates the way in which people who are not very busy become assiduous in attention to their health.

There have been added some letters which deal with a visit to Bath (first referred to in No. 496), since the visit was paid in search of health.

A few letters dealing with visits to London conclude the chapter, although they have no direct reference to the main subject-matter. Some diary extracts are included which give very precise information about the difficulties of reaching London from Shalstone in 1749.

No. 485. H. P. *to* DR CHARLES KIMBERLEY

Shalstone near Buckingham
Thursday June y^e *17*th *1736*

Sir! /

My mother has an ill state of health & would be glad to advise with you. She will be at home on Sunday, Monday, & Tuesday next if it suits with your conveniency to give us your Company on either of those days, if not let us know what day you can come by the return of Mr Palmer the Northampton carrier. My mother joins with mee in our service to you & I am

Your very humble serv^t
H. P.

ffor /
Dr Kimberley at
Northampton
Carriage p^d 2^d

Dr Charles Kimberley was born at Coventry in 1691; he matriculated at Christ Church College, Oxford, in 1707 and died at Northampton in 1754 (Foster, *Alumni Oxonienses*, 1891, vol. II, p. 850). Apparently Dr Kimberley had been consulted before, presumably by Henry, for an entry in the Account-books tells us:

1729

Sep. 23th. Paid my mother also then Dr Kimberley's ffees: 04 : 14 : 6.

No. 486. H. P. *to* DR CHARLES KIMBERLEY

Shalstone near Buckingham
Wensday, July ye 7th 1736

Sir! /

I had answered your kind request to know how my mother's leg did before this but she was not willing till she had took all her physick & saw some little alteration in her Leg. Mr Wallbank has attended her every day since but one to ffoment & dresse her leg, but yesterday my mother told him that she thought she could dresse it herself so hee sais now hee will come every other day.

He dressed it for a week & what he put in it that time made very little alteration but my mother told him she imagined that stuff would not do wch she supposed to be white Basilicon.[1] Then hee put some brown & green stuff in a spoon & did some lint in it & put it as hot as she could bear it into the hole & laid white basilicon upon lint upon that, & then a plaister over that & he has swathed her leg pretty tight ever since hee has dressed it. This last stuff he dresses it with torments it much at the first laying on but this day hee sais hee has moderated it, but it smarts pretty much still. The wound now is full as broad as a shilling, it looks fresh & clean at the bottom & my mother is of the mind it might be healed up. 't would be a favour if you would let mee know, by the return of Palmer the carrier if you can, whether it need

1 This presumably means basilicon ointment, made of yellow wax, resin, Burgundy pitch, and olive oil; to these, when melted, turpentine was added. Dr John Aydon, to whom the editor is indebted for this information, thinks that Mrs Purefoy was probably "suffering from a chronic (? varicose) ulcer"; he fears that the basilicon was likely to cause her some discomfort.

be fomented any longer. Her leg swells a little towards night & is always down again in a morning, it is very quiett on nights & my mother sleeps well & (thank God) is pretty well in health in other respects & don't question but she should have her health very well if she could walk about as she used to do. Mr Wallbank talks she must have more Physick which makes her very faint after it. Wee both join in our service to you & I am with reall esteem Sir!

Your very humble serv^t
H. P.

ffor /
   Dr Kimberley at
   Northampton This
      Carriage paid 2^d

No. 487. E. P. *to* MR COPPIN

Shalstone [&c.]
August the 29th 1736

Sir! /

   I am afflicted with a sore on my Ancle wch is thought to be somewhat of the scurvy settled there. I have been so unfortunate that tho' the sore is small they cannot heall it. I have heard so much of you that I have a great desire you should see it, so entreat you will give mee leave to wait on you. The cures you performed on Mrs Walls of Buckingham & Mrs Morgan, a wheelwright's wife, give mee great hopes I shall find releif in my Case. I did not know whether I should find you at home or no if I did not acquaint you on it ♗ letter. I desire the favour of an answer from you when I may wait on you, as soon as may be, directed to mee at Shalstone near Buckingham in Bucks by way of London wch will much oblidge. Sir! /

Your unknown hle serv^t
E. P.

ffor /
   Mr Coppin
   at Market street near
   Dunstable in
      Bedfordshire
         by way of London
   Postage paid /

No. 488. E. P. *to* HARRY WALLBANK

Shalstone
March ye 12th 1736

Mr Wallbank /

I admire you won't let mee know what I am in your Debt so often as I have sent to you about it,—if you don't think fit to come pray send my Bill that I may continue

Your freind to serve you
E. P.

ffor /
  Mr Wallbank
    a surgeon at
        Buckingham /
        This

This had the desired effect and eventually Mr Wallbank became a close friend as well as medical attendant. He was medical attendant at Claydon House, and was called in to the wife of the Ralph who eventually became the second Earl Verney. See *Verney Letters of the Eighteenth Century*, vol. II, pp. 191 and 242.

No. 489. H. P. *to* HARRY WALLBANK

Shalstone
September 24th 1737

Sir ! /

My mother desires you would send her word if she must take her wood drink fasting in a morning & at 4 a clock in the afternoon as she used to do, or whether she should take the wood drink (wch she used to take at 4 a clock) when she goes to Bed after her Electuary—Your answer hereto by the bearer will oblidge

Your humble serv^t
H. P.

ffor /
  Mr Wallbank
  a surgeon at Buckingham
    This

P.S. Wee both join in Service to you and Mrs Wallbank.

No. 490. E. P. *to* HARRY WALLBANK

Shalstone
Sir! /   *October 8ᵗʰ 1737*

I have drunk my wood drink up 2 days ago, the reason I was so long about it was I was on visiting last moon. My Æthiops¹ is not gone & will hold mee another week, I desire your Judgment whether the weather will not be too cold to go on with it, tho' I have no cold as yet. My leg is almost dryed up & I have no pain attends it. I have sent your bottles & flasks. What you think proper for mee to take pray send by the bearer if you can, if not hee shall fetch it. Wee both join in service to you & Mʳˢ Wallbank & I am

Your humble servᵗ
E. P.

ffor /
    Mʳ Wallbank
    a surgeon at
        Buckingham
            This

No. 491. E. P. *to* HARRY WALLBANK

Shalstone
Novemb: the 5ᵗʰ 1737

I have sent Mʳ Wallbank's bottles by yᵉ servant & thought you would have sent mee some wood drink by him, you thought I would take no more, you told him; but I am very willing to take it as long as you think proper for I have found great Benefit & the plaister has stuck on 3 weeks & is not come of[f] & I have neither found pain nor smart. The lower part where the plaister is loose, as I can see it, 't is scurfy, pray send mee some more wood drink by the bearer wᶜʰ will oblidge

Your humble servant
E. P.

P.S.
    Our service to Mʳˢ Wallbank. I want a maid for myself.
ffor /
    Mʳ Walbank a
    surgeon at Buckingham
        This

---

1 This still appears in the *British Pharmaceutical Codex* as "œthiops martialis"; it is magnetic iron oxide. Nowadays iron in a more assimilable form is more often used.

No. 492. H. P. *to* MR TURLAND

Shalstone
Aprill the 11ᵗʰ 1739

M.ʳ Thurland /

This acquaints you as you desired that my Knee is easie when I set still or when I lie in my bed, but when I walk about I still feell a sort of Tendernesse or little pain which I hope proceeds from the Bruise. The sear cloath¹ sticks on still. Pray let mee know by the bearer if I may venture to ride out about 7 miles from Home the latter end of this week or beginning of the next, & return the same day, & if you have any further directions for my knee, wᶜʰ will oblidge

Your hle serv.ᵗ
H. P.

ffor /
    M.ʳ Thurland Senior
    To be left at M.ʳ Owen's
    at the Post Office at
            Brackley /
                This

According to the Account-book, Mr Thurland (or Turland) was paid 5s. 6d. for coming from Charlton, about 5 miles west of Brackley, on this occasion. Mr Turland's aid was summoned years later; on 24 July 1756 the Diary tells us that "the Jenny mare threw me", next day "my shoulder bone was cracked & lamed by the ffall". On the 26th "M.ʳ Thurland senior (the Bonesetter) of Charlton & his son who lives with him, & his other son M.ʳ Thurland (the Bonesetter) of Addington" —all arrived to give the combined skill of the family. See also Letter No. 500.

When Lord Fermanagh's steward broke a bone in his leg "M.ʳ Turland of Addington" came to set it; "I advised him to send to Bicester for the other brother". On another occasion the victim of an accident "came to Winslow and Turland gave him ease immediately". *Verney Letters of the Eighteenth Century*, vol. II, pp. 185 and 212.

No. 493. H. P. *to* HARRY WALLBANK

Shalstone
January the 3ᵈ 1740

Sir! /

My mother had the misfortune to fall down stairs 2 steps backwards last Saturday. There stood a Buckett of milk behind, she

---

1 Presumably "cere cloth",—used as a plaster in surgery. Mr Pepys applied one after he sprained his foot near Epsom on 14 July 1667.

ffell just upon the iron staple that holds the Bale[1] thereof, & bruised her lower parts so that she bled very much & has been exceeding faint ever since, & her soreness encreases; I could not prevaill on her to give mee leave to send for you before this. When she lies all along she does not feell it so painfull, but when she goes to walk she feells a great deall of pain.† I entreat you will not faill to be here some time tooday wch will oblidge

Your humble serv^t in hast
H. P.

† I give you this Information that you may bring wth you something proper to apply.

ffor /
  Mr Wallbank a surgeon
  at Buckingham /
        This

No. 494. H. P. *to* THE POSTMASTER, CHELTENHAM

Shalstone [&c.]
Aprill 18th 1742

I having occasion to drink your waters at Cheltenham am oblidged to write to you, the Postmaster, to let mee know if the small pox be at Cheltenham, if not I shall be there soon after I have your answer, wch I desire you will oblidge mee with & am

Your unknown humble servant
H. P.

I have no other opportunity but writing by the post to you it being acrosse ye countrey.

ffor /
  The postmaster at the Post Office
      at Cheltenham
        in
      Gloucestershire

---

1 The curved handle; given by Wright under "bail"; the *E.D.D.* quotes Clare, as cited by Miss A. E. Baker, *Glossary of Northants:* "The rime e'en blisters on the bucket bale".

No. 495. H. P. *to* THE REV. RICHARD DALBY

Shalstone
Wensday May the 26th 1742

Sir! /

I am informed the small pox is at Chipping Norton, I entreat you will enquire of some of your neighbouring ffarmers how the small pox is there, & how long it has been there. I should not have troubled you about this affair, but wee must necessarily either bait or lie at Chipping Norton in our way to Cheltenham. I hope I shall have the favour of your company here soon to take a commons with us & then you may satisfie us in this particular. Wee both join in our hearty service & respects to yourself & family & I am Sir!

Your humble servant
H. P.

ffor /
  The Revd Mr Dalby
   at   Croton
        This
  Carriage paid two pence

In the end they went to Bath, not to Cheltenham; see Letters Nos. 529 to 534.

No. 496. E. P. *to* DR RAYNER

Shalstone [&c.]
October the 7th 1742

Sir! /

Since you was so kind to desire to know what effect your medicines had on mee I can now acquaint you I have done taking what you prescribed mee last ffriday and I hope they will perform a cure on my Leg, and then I shall think my Journey to Bath very fortunate. I have kept the Plaister to my leg as you ordered & it is quite dryed without any soreness or Tendernesse. I have not yet had an Issue made in my Leg & should be glad to know if it could be avoided without danger, if not I will be sure to have it done out of hand when I have your answer. The swelling in my Leg is in a manner quite gone. I bound on a binder higher on my leg besides that which you bound on, which I thought helped to lessen the swelling thereof. I desire your Directions whether I must take your last Prescriptions any more or if you would order mee anything else. I still continue your plaister on & to swath my Leg as usuall. My son's compliments wait on you

Shalstone

April the 16th 1743.

Madam /

I could get But 7 Bottles of Water this week
the Carrier brought twelve to Oxford But was forced to
part with 5 there — Hee hath promised to
procure more what Quantity I will have this
day fortnight if I let Him know Between
this & next Tuesday — This Water will not
Keep above 3 weeks, in a little time Hee will
bring It every Week — I wish mr Wentworth
may receive Benifit by drinking It

Madam I wish the Weather to be fine that
Wee may have the pleasure of waiting on you
& mr Wentworth at Shalstone & to acknowledge
how much I am oblidged to you for procuring
moo the wine — I wait for your farther
Commands about ye Waters My Sons & my
Compliments wait on mr Wentworth & yourself
I am Madam   Your oblidged humble servt

To mrs Wentworth   E. P.

April the 15th

Plate 21. FACSIMILE OF LETTER NO. 499

& these your successfull endeavours shall be allways acknowledged by

Your humble servant
E. P.

P.S. Pray direct for mee at Shalstone, near Buckingham, By
way of London, & pray favour mee with our best services to
Mrs Price when you see her.

ffor /
  Dr Rayner[1] in Queen Square
  in Bath /
      Somersetshire
  By way of London

No. 497. H. P. *to* HARRY WALLBANK

Shalstone
March the 29th 1743

Sir!

My mother has got a very bad cold so entreat you would send
her 2 ounces of Lintseed Oyll cold drawn, pray let it be fresh
done; & send an ounce of your best manna. Should be glad to
have your Bill as soon as may be; with our respects to you all
am in hast

Your very hle serv^t
H. P.

ffor /
  Mr Wallbank a Surgeon
  at Buckingham /
      This

No. 498. H. P. *to* JOHN WENTWORTH [CRESSWELL]

Shalstone
Aprill the 9th 1743

Sir! /

As you was wishing to tast Cheltenham waters upon enquiry
you may have what Quantity thereof you please every ffriday
in the afternoon if you send here for them then, or else send to the
red Lion Inne at Brackley. They are 9 pence a bottle, I have sent

1 Possibly this was Alexander Rayner, born at Barnstaple in 1698, matriculated
at Christ Church College, Oxford, in 1716, and M.D. in 1731. (See Foster,
Alumni Oxonienses, 1888, vol. III, p. 1181.) From Letter No. 503 we see that
Dr Rayner died in 1747.

you 2 bottles and my mother's opinion is you should drink one bottle in a morning at half a pint at a time betwixt every half hour, lukewarm. Wee heartily wish they may be of service to you; if they should be approved on should be glad of your further commands,[1] & with our compliments to yourself & Mrs Wentworth I am sir! with reall esteem

Your oblidged humble serv^t
H. P.

P.S. There is Cheltenham on the seall round the Cork. My mother is much afflicted with this new cold.

ffor /
    John Wentworth Cresswell Esq
        at Lillingston Lovell
                    This

No. 499. E. P. *to* MRS WENTWORTH [CRESSWELL]

Shalstone
Aprill the 16th 1743

Madam /

I could get but 7 Bottles of Water this week, the Carrier brought twelve to Oxford, but was forced to part with 5 there. Hee hath promised to procure mee what Quantity I will have this day fortnight if I let him know between this & next Tuesday. This water will not keep above 3 weeks. In a little time hee will bring it every week; I wish Mr Wentworth may receive benefit by drinking it. Madam, I wish the weather to be fine that wee may have the pleasure of waiting on you & Mr Wentworth at Shalstone, & to acknowledge how much I am oblidged to you for procuring mee the wine. I wait for your farther Commands about ye waters. My son's & my compliments wait on Mr Wentworth & yourself.

I am, Madam,

Your oblidged humble serv^t
E. P.

To Mrs Wentworth
Aprill the 15th

1 On 15 April "my mother Purefoy gave Daniell Hutchins an acquittance for five shillings & 3 pence as by order of Mrs Wentworth for six bottles of Cheltenham Water".

No. 500. H. P. *to* MR TURLAND

Mr Turland /

Shalstone
Novembr 5th 1743

This day se'nnight my horse stumbled with mee & as I had the Bridle in my hand hee pulled my hand so hard as hee fell that hee has either sprained or put out my wrist; so I desire you will come over too morrow morning[1] to see it & bring a sear cloth along with you which will oblidge

Your humble servt

ffor /
  Mr Turland a bone-Setter
    at Addington
           This
  Carriage paid
  two pence

H. P.

No. 501. H. P. *to* JOHN WENTWORTH [CRESSWELL]

Sir! /

Shalstone
May ye 4th 1747

Inclosed you'l find the receipt for the Sore Breast which wee heartily wish may have a good effect & successe; if you should want Rosemary wee abound with it here if you please but to send for some.

My mother joins with mee in our Respects & service to yourself & Mrs Wentworth & I am, Sr

Your oblidged hle servt

H. P.

P.S. Be pleased to take notice this Ointment is to be made in May.

ffor /
  John Wentworth Esqr at
    Lillingston Lovell
       This

No. 502. H. P. *to* REV. EDWARD TROUTBECK

Sir! /

Shalstone
July ye 4th 1747

Understanding wee have lost our good neighbour Mrs Price, I entreat ye favour of you to enquire of some person who attends

---

1 Mr Turland arrived during the afternoon next day. This is Mr Turland, junior, see Letter No. 492.

her ffunerall if D.ᴿ Rayner, a physician of Bath, be living & resident at Bath and if the small pox is much at Bath or no, and let mee know thereof which will oblidge   Your humble servant

ffor /   H. P.

 The Rev.ᵈ M.ᴿ Troutbeck[1]
  at Westbury
   This

No. 503. H. P. *to* JEREMIAH PEIRCE

Shalstone [&c.]
October the 18ᵗʰ 1747

Sir! /

I have had the misfortune to loose my very good ffreind D.ᴿ Rayner who cured my mother of a sore in her leg, w.ᶜʰ had been of some years Standing, with a red, stiff, dry Plaister w.ᶜʰ she was to lay to the sore & turn it & wipe it every day, w.ᶜʰ was the cure of her leg. But now the Plaister is all used up & her leg broke out again this autumn wee can't find any Remedy that has so good an effect as that Plaister had. When I was at Bath in 1742, which was the last time I saw D.ᴿ Rayner, hee told mee I might have it of you in case I wanted it, for that hee had given you the receipt how to make it. Which if it be so, if you please to send about 3 peices of it about as big as half a sheet of paper altogether by the Bath Carrier, directed to mee to be left at M.ᴿ Moulson's in Wood Street in Cheapside, and what you are to have for them, I will order the money for 'em to be paid you either at London or Bath. When wee were at Bath last wee lodged at Major Bolton's and had been there this autumn but that the small pox was with you; if you enquire of the Major hee will give you a character of us. I hope if it is in your power you will oblidge mee in this affair, especially as my mother's Health & Quiet are dependant, & it shall be ever gratefully acknowledged by Sir!

Your unknown humble serv.ᵗ
H. P.

P.S. I pray the favour of your answer by yᵉ post.

ffor /
 M.ᴿ Pearse a Surgeon
 in Bath
  Somersetshire
 By way of London

  1 Edward Troutbeck was vicar of Westbury 1744–53.

Mr Jeremiah Peirce, to whom this and other letters are directed, was a person of importance; "he was an intimate friend of the celebrated Dr Oliver, and on May 1st 1740 was appointed first surgeon to the Royal Mineral Water Hospital in Bath, where may be seen a portrait, by Wm Hoare of Bath, of Oliver and Peirce examining a patient; there is also, I believe, a bust of Peirce at this Hospital. He resigned on May 1st 1761. In 1738 John Wood, the eminent architect, built for Peirce a house called Lilliput Castle on the top of Lansdown. Twice the single chimney caught fire, endangering the roof. The house was later incorporated in the Battle Fields". For this information the editor is deeply indebted to Miss Russ, Deputy librarian of the Municipal Libraries, Bath.

No. 504. H. P. *to* JEREMIAH PEIRCE

Shalstone [&c.]
November the 15ᵗʰ 1747

Sir! /

I am favoured with yours of the 27ᵗʰ of last month with the Plaister enclosed, which has had an exceeding good effect on my mother's leg, for she has felt no smart nor Pain since she has laid it on her leg, and all the things that were laid on it before that came made her very uneasie. Her leg is Scorbutick & has a Scurf comes on it & then it breaks. I hope by this time you are perfectly recovered of your Indisposition and as the plaister you sent will soon be gone I must entreat the favour of you to convey some more to us by the Bath carrier, directed to be left for mee at Mᵣ Moulson's in Woodstreet in Cheapside, London, or if you would be so good to let us have the receipt how to make this Plaister wee should be glad to make you any Recompense you should think proper, & if required never to discover what it is made on. Your great condescension & goodnesse in this affair I can't but admire & hope to be at the Bath next year to make a farther acknowledgemᵗ how much I am

Your obligded humble servant
H. P.

ffor /
  Mᵣ Peirce
    Bath...

No. 505. H. P. *to* JEREMIAH PEIRCE

Shalstone [&c.]
January ye 10th 1747

Sir! /

I am favoured with yours of last month with the 2 peices of Plaister & the receipt to make the Sparadrop[1] ffor which wee return you our present hearty thanks till wee can have an Opportunity to make a further acknowledgment. I hope wee shall have no occasion to make it up till wee see you, for what you have sent has almost cured my mother's Leg already. Wee heartily wish you the Blessing of Health & that so much Goodnesse & Humanity as you have afforded us may long continue on this side the Grave, shall be glad to hear you are ꝑfectly recovered, & desiring you to accept of the compliments of the season I am Sir!

Your oblidged ħłe servant
H. P.

P.S. People here are very fond of this sparadrop & if any body should write to you in our names about it pray take no notice of it, wee shan't communicate y^r rec^t to any body.

ffor /
  Mr Peirce
    Bath...

No. 506. H. P. *to* HARRY WALLBANK

Shalstone
August the 23th 1747

Sir! /

I return you abundance of Thanks for your kind present of the Jack which wee had for dinner on Wensday & a great deall of good Company at the eating of it; it was exceeding good.

On Thursday morning when I got out of my bed I was taken Ill & at Dinner time had no appetite to my Victualls, neither indeed

---

1 Sparadrap, for that is the correct spelling, was used to denote "a piece of linen dipped in, or spread with some ointment, for use as a bandage or plaster"; thus the *O.E.D.* which quotes *Chambers' Cyclopaedia*, 1728, and Johnson, 1755. The word is still current in the official French Codex, which lists eight kinds of sparadrap. (Information kindly supplied by Mr W. J. Patey.)

have I any Stomach to my Victualls since that time, but am allover Pain from head to foot & very faint and restlesse a nights, & sick at stomach & inclined to wretch so must entreat ye favour of you to come over to mee too night or too morrow morning wch will much oblidge

Your humble servant
H. P.

ffor /
  Mr Wallbank at Buckingham
      This

No. 507. H. P. *to* HARRY WALLBANK

Shalstone
Septemb^r the 19th 1747

Sir! /

I took all your Pills about 4 or 5 days ago but not your bitter draft which would not set on my stomach as the first Bottle of Bitters did. I desire no Bitters but being very faint between break-fast and Dinner Time if you could order mee something to help mee I would take it. My water holds of a good colour. Wee both join in our service & respect to you all & I am

Your humble servant
H. P.

P.S. I will take either Drops or Pills

ffor /
  Mr Wallbank at
      Buckingham
          This

No. 508. H. P. *to* HARRY WALLBANK

Shalstone
Decemb^r the 12th 1747

Sir! /

My Pills are all gone but six, so if you think it proper I should take any more I desire you would send them. My mother con-tinues taking the mercury, but she has got a very bad pain in her side & I am afraid it makes her catch cold. She has enough to serve a week longer; pray let us know if she had not best leave it of[f]. I hope by this time M.ʳ Pashler is perfectly recovered of his Indisposition, pray our Compliments to him & Miss Barrett & accept the same from Sir!

Your humble serv.ᵗ
H. P.

ffor /
   M.ʳ Wallbank a surgeon
   at Buckingham
         This

No. 509. H. P. *to* DR [HUMPHREY?] PITTS

Shalstone near Buckingham
ffriday Octob.ʳ 28.ᵗʰ 1748

Sir! /

I must entreat the favour of you to come over here immediately on the Receipt hereof w.ᶜʰ will much oblidge

Your unknown humble serv.ᵗ
H. P.

ffor /
   D.ʳ Pitts at Oxford
         This

Dr Pitts came over on Saturday afternoon and the faithful Mr Wallbank was in attendance. The Doctor "& y.ᵉ Lad who came with him" stopped all night and left before noon on Sunday. The occasion of his visit is mentioned in the next letter. It is possible that D.ʳ Pitts was Humphrey Pitts, who was born in 1672, and matriculated at Wadham in 1689, graduating M.D. in 1702; he was also a student of the Inner Temple (Foster, *Alumni Oxonienses*, 1891, vol. III, p. 1170).

No. 510. H. P. *to* PETER MOULSON

Shalstone [&c.]
Novemb.ʳ the 9.ᵗʰ 1748

Sir! /

I am favoured with yours of the 29.ᵗʰ of last month together with the 2 Gallons of Brandy, 4 pounds of Grasse seed, 1 Quart of peas, together with my shirt sleeve Buttons,—all which pray place to my account. Wee have 3 twenty pounds prizes and 2 blanks in last Lottery, being the 5 Tickets you bought us; desire to know when you think 't will be the best Time to sell them. My mother desires you will send by M.ʳ Jones yᵉ Buckingham carrier an hogshead of your best red port wine, half an hogshead of your best white mountain wine, & three gallons of the best Sack in pint Bottles. Wee are very sorry for M.ʳˢ Vaughan's losse. My mother was taken on last Sunday fortnight very ill in her Stomach, and the Distemper has since fell into her left Leg. D.ʳ Pitt the Physician & the Surgeon hope the Danger is over. Pray put up a pound of Savoy biskets and six pounds of shavings of Hartshorn with the Sack and place 'em to account. M.ʳ Jones yᵉ Carrier sets out of London at 2 a'clock on Tuesday mornings and on Saturday mornings early, & inns at Oxford Arms in Warwick lane. Wee desire you would let us have a Letter with your account by the post when the wine comes, but don't send it in such weather as may damage it. Wee both join in our complim.ᵗˢ to you & I am Sir! /

Your very ħħe servant
H. P.

P.S. & pray buy my mother a pair of black silk ffrench Muftees¹ for the Hands & without Lace & send with yᵉ things. She thinks you & M.ʳˢ Vaughan can guesse at her arm; they must be with thumbs to them.

ffor /
  M.ʳ Moulson in
        London

No. 511. H. P. to HARRY WALLBANK

Shalstone [&c.]
December the 29ᵗʰ 1748

Sir! /

I desire you to enquire of Nan Woodcock (the bearer hereof) if she is able to pay you for the cure of her Breast, if she is not wee must give the parish notice of it,—for my mother will not bear

---

1 Muffetee is the modern spelling.

any Charge thereof. Pray accept the Complimts. of the Season, & I am

Your humble Servant

ffor /

H. P.

Mr Wallbank at
    Buckingham
            This

P.S. Pray your answer by the bearer.

No. 512. H. P. *to* SAMUEL PASHLER [PASSELOW]

Shalstone
January 1st 1748

Sir!

You said you would favour us with your Company to Dinner one day this Xt'mas. Wee should be glad to see you & Mr Wallbank any Day this week after Tuesday next; pray let us know ye Day by the bearer wch will much oblidge

Your humble servant

H. P.

P.S. Wee wish you all an happy new year.

ffor /

Mr Pashler at Buckingham
            This

Young Mr Pashler appeared on the Wednesday and the Thursday following this letter; but on neither occasion was he accompanied by other members of the Wallbank Household (see note to Letter No. 412).

No. 513. H. P. *to* MR TITCHBURN

Shalstone [&c.]
May the 3d 1747

Mr Titchburn /

Some time ago when I lodged in Cooks Court by Lincolns inne I had some Dimmothy trusses of you which proved very well & I gave you half a crown a peice for them. Now they have got into another method of making them with Tape to tie about the middle there may be a small matter more of stuff to make 'em, but not more workmanship, so shall be willing to give you three shillings a peice for them but no more, & if you are willing to take that price I will send you a Truss by ye Buckingham carrier to make them by, & will have half a dozen Trusses of you & if you make them to fit mee shall want more. Your answer by ye Post will oblidge

Your friend to serve you
H. P.

ffor /
   Mr Titchburn at the Golden Ball
   next door but one to ye Swan in
   Shoelane near Holborn bridge
          London
   post paid three pence

Mr E. M. Corner, F.R.C.S., has looked at this and following letters and says that the word "truss" was used popularly for almost any apparatus employed in the genital region. He thinks it probable that Henry had developed a hydrocele, for which, in those days, there was no operation.

No. 514. H. P. to MR TITCHBURN

Mr Titchburn /

Shalstone [&c.]
May the 10th 1747

I received yours of the 5th instant & I have sent you a Trusse in a little paper box by...ye Buckingham carrier.... 'Tis wrote on the direction Carriage and Porteridge paid, so you need not pay either. I desire you will make the bags of the new Trusses just the same as the bag of ye Trusse sent for a pattern, & be sure let the hole of the bag be full as low as that is, for I am corpulent & fat & can't bear the hole to be higher. The new trusses must be made of Dimothy & be bigger in the round about the wast by 2 inches than the trusse sent, & must have tapes & tags to them as the pattern is, only as that is a patched up concern you will easily see where there is no occasion for eyelet holes, and the Tapes that come up behind & so round the body must be 2 inches longer each than the tapes of the Truss sent. I think these Instructions are sufficient & you can't well err if you duely observe them. I entreat you will make mee half a dozen of these Trusses & send them in a fortnight's time by the aforesaid Mr Jones ye Carrier, & when I have them if they fit mee I will send you the money for them by this Mr Jones, & am

Your freind to serve you
H. P.

22-2

P.S. You must send mee the old Truss again; because then I may be satisfied if the new ones are made agreeable to my Instructions, & let mee have a letter by ye post when they come.

ffor /
   Mr Titchburn...
      London

No. 515. H. P. *to* THOMAS WILLETT

Shalstone [&c.]
July the 14th 1747

Sir! /

I received your Letter of the 6th instant & you are a stranger to mee but since you succeed Mr Titchburn in the Businesse I hope you have the same skill as Hee had. Hee was a very mannerly, civill man & always made my things to fit mee. I desire you will make the new Trusses and the Bags thereof just the same as the Trusse sent, only they must be made of Dimmity & be bigger in the round about the wast by 2 inches than the Trusse sent & must have Tapes & Tags to them; and the Tapes or things that come up behind & so round the body must be 2 inches longer each than those of the pattern. I am thus particular least you should have lost my letter.

Send half a dozen of them by ye Buckingham carrier... & when I have them I will order you the money for them. You must send mee the old Trusse with these that I may see the new ones are made like unto it & according to my Instructions. You must let them be worked up neat & made fit for mee as you expect a future Customer of mee, & let mee have a letter by the Post when they come that I may send to the carrier for them. This will oblidge

Your unknown humble servant

H. P.

ffor /
   Mr Thomas Willett at the Golden Ball next door
   but one to the Swan in Shoe lane near Holborn bridge,
      London
    Post paid 3 pence

No. 516. H. P. *to* THOMAS WILLETT

Shalstone [&c.]
March the 18ᵗʰ 1748

Mʳ Willett /

I send you by yᵉ Buckingham carrier...a Band Box with a Trusse therein for a pattern. I desire you will make mee half a dozen Trusses yᵉ same size to the Pattern sent, only bring the hither end of the loop hole as far as the Pin, for these you made mee were too narrow in the Back. Remember I give you a guinea for the half dozen. I expect them in a fortnight or three weeks at farthest by yᵉ Carrier as above & when I have them will order payment for 'em & am

Your ffreind to serve you

ffor /   H. P.
Mʳ Thomas Willett...
    London

The few letters which relate to dental matters have considerable interest apparently; Mrs Lindsay, of the British Dental Association, has kindly considered them and says that they "add another link in the chain of elucidation of the manner in which artificial teeth were constructed in those early days when methods of taking impressions of the mouth were in their infancy". After referring to the methods of Purmann, Pfaff, Fauchard, and Pilleau, Mrs Lindsay goes on to say: "Mrs Purefoy has apparently written to Mr Coryndon for a set of teeth (these were sent to people as samples). I gather from the letters that Mrs Purefoy has sent Coryndon a piece of wood on which were marked the places where the teeth were standing and the tape would be the length of her gums. In her letter of 24 December she probably has the set of teeth and the 'holes', i.e. spaces for the teeth standing in her mouth, do not correspond to the position of the teeth, also the bite is too high on 'the two hind teeth'".

No. 517. E. P. *to* WILLIAM CORYNDON

Shalstone Novʳ yᵉ 13ᵗʰ 1737

Sir! /

Some time ago it was advertised you were removed from Angell Court into yᵉ Strand. I have some businesse for you in yoʳ way,

if these should find you there pray let mee know by the Post &
I will give you orders. This will oblidge   Your humble servant
P.S. /   E. P.
   Direct for mee at
      Shalstone near
         Buckingham
ffor /
   Mr William Corindon Operator for ye Teeth
   near the new Church in ye Strand /
              London

No. 518. E. P. *to* WILLIAM CORYNDON

Shalstone [&c.]
Decemb^r the 4th 1737

I rece^d Mr Coryndon's 2 letters & I don't think there is any
Occasion for your coming here. My orders will do which will be
at Mr Webster the carrier's...next Tuesday come sennight, & I
desire you will call there for them & am   Your humble serv^t
ffor /   E. P.
   Mr William Coryndon...
      London

No. 519. E. P. *to* WILLIAM CORYNDON

Shalstone [&c.]
Decr ye 11th 1737

Mr Coryndon /
I have sent you a bit of wood for a pattern the shape of w^{ch}
I beleive will Direct you. It must be made a little longer, the
length of wch I have sent you on a Bit of Tape.
If you think you can compleat it by this Direction you may,
if you cant I will stay till I come to Town in ye Spring. I do beleive
the stick to be too thin at one end & too thick at t'other, but that
you must manage. I think if you send it down before you make
any holes in it I can send it up again for you to finish, & am

Your humble serv^t
E. P.
ffor /
   Mr Coryndon...
      London
P.S.
   You must divide it into six parts.

No. 520. E. P. *to* WILLIAM CORYNDON

Shalstone [&c.]
Decemb^r the 18th 1737

I received Mr Coryndon's letter & the box;[1] the carrier's return is so quick I could not return ye box this week, but next week you shan't faill of it with Directions from

Your humble serv^t
E. P.

ffor /
Mr Coryndon...
London

No. 521. E. P. *to* WILLIAM CORYNDON

Shalstone [&c.]
Decemb^r ye 24th 1737

I have sent Mr Coryndon ye Box & I have markt it at both ends for ye height. [I] desire you to make ye holes as they dont break out as ye last did, if you can, & take a bit of[f] from the 2 hind Teeth as I have marked, and I will order you payment[2] very speedily, & am

Your humble serv^t
E. P.

ffor /
Mr Coryndon...
London

No. 522. H. P. *to* PETER MOULSON

Shalstone [&c.]
March the 1st 1751

Sir! /

I send you this day by Jones ye Carrier an empty half hogshead wch I desire you to fill with the strongest white mountain wine, it is for my own drinking; & let mee have a Ɫre of advice by the post when it comes as also your account. My mother (I thank God) is better than she was but weak still. As to the soldier at Dublin our Law dos not admitt of any money in the affair, but if your ffreind could let us know when hee comes to England & if then hee declares ye truth concerning his wife having the Bastard during his absence,—hee will be rewarded after the thing is decided.[3]

1 Webster, the carrier, brought it on 17 Decr., charging 3d; it was returned on 24 Decr.
2 The sum paid was £3. 4s. 0d., see Letter No. 341.
3 This refers to a matter fully explained in Letters Nos. 15–17.

If it would not be too much trouble I desire you will buy for mee & send three bottles of the Tincture for preserving the Teeth & two Tooth Brushes[1] from M[r] Greenough's near S[t] Sepulchre's Church, on Snowhill; as also to send a quarter of a pound of gold coloured mohair the same colour to the Pattern sent for the Servants Liveries. My mother joins with mee in our Compliments to you & I am with all due esteem, Sir! Your very humble serv[t]

H. P.

P.S. The sack came safe.

ffor /
   M[r] Moulson
      in London

No. 523. E. P. *to* THOMAS ROBOTHAM

Shalstone [&c.]
Sunday, ffebruary y[e] 6th 1736

I rece[d] M[r] Robotham's letter of the 30th of Decemb[r] last with a quarter of lamb & oranges & lemons which were all very good, & for w[ch] wee return you thanks. I am sorry your fowls proved old & had answered your letter before this had not our hog been threatned often to be killed, but now hee is dispatched & desire you to accept of a spare rib and a couple of pulletts w[ch] I am promised are young, & that M[rs] Robotham will accept of five dozen of black hog puddings w[ch] I made myself, & hope she will like them. I have strove hard for an hare but could get none. I have sent a gold & silver watch in y[e] basket which pray carry to M[r] Mulford in Cursitors Alley to be mended, for they will not go. I have also sent 2 of my son's seeing-glasses, one of them w[ch] is cracked must have a new glasse put in, the number is on y[e] back of the case, w[ch] show the man, & the other only wants a new case to it. The man's name to whom you are to carry them is Ralph Sterrop at y[e] Archimedes & 3 pair of Spectacles in

1 How far were tooth-brushes in general use at this date? A century earlier they were a distinct novelty in Paris to Sir Ralph Verney (*Verney Memoirs*, vol. III, p. 39); he speaks of them as "inconsiderable Toyes". About 1755 Coles Child, a toyman on London Bridge, was selling tooth-brushes (see Ambrose Heal: *Tradesmen's Cards* attached to Gordon Home's *Old London Bridge*, 1931, p. 324). In a letter to the editor Mr Heal kindly says that he has advertisements of Mr Greenough's "Tincture for the Teeth" in various papers from 1749 to 1773; in 1749 the notice appeared in the *London Evening Post*, which we know Henry read. Later Mr Greenough moved to Ludgate Street, and to Ludgate Hill.

Ludgate Street. Mr Porter has sent mee a pretty mare enough,[1] but I han't rid her myself tho' they who have say she trips. But when the weather is a little finer I will mount her myself. When ye watches are done pray send 'em again with all convenient speed & pay Mr Mulford for doing them. My son's & my service & respect is with you & Mrs Robotham & I am   Your humble serv.^t

ffor /   E. P.
    Mr Robotham...
            London

P.S. Just now have received yours of the 1st instant. The gold watch is not sent. Pray let us know if the things come safe.

No. 524. E. P. *to* THOMAS ROBOTHAM

Shalstone [*&c.*]
November 6th 1737

I desire Mr Robotham's acceptance of a Brace of Hares wch I send you this day by Webster ye Carrier (carriage paid) & sealed at ye knot of the Direction with my coat of arms, Webster comes into Town on Tuesday. I hope by this time you have paid Mr Mulford & ye ffishmonger, as also that you have bought my son's Lottery tickets. I have also sent you 3 of my son's seeing glasses to be mended, the tortoise shell one wants ye silver Rimm round ye glasse to be mended, & the horn one to have a new Rimm made to it, & the Other to be made with an horn case to shove to & fro' as you will see the horn & tortoise shell one done. The man who dos them lives at the Archimedes in Ludgate Street. I desire you would send mee a dozen panes of London Crown glasse 12 inches & a quarter by ten inches & half a dozen panes 12 inches by ten inches, you buy these by the foot & wee used to buy them of a man in a street by Clare market, & I desire you will send me three yards of fine black lace two inches wide, & with my son's & my service & respect to you both I am   Your humble serv.^t

ffor /   E. P.
    Mr Robotham...
            London
        P.S.
    There are six Tea Canisters in ye Basket wch pray lay by to send tea in.

1 See Letter No. 374.

No. 525.   H. P. *to* MR HOLTON

Shalstone
ffebruary the 21ᵗʰ 1740

Mʳ Holton /

I have sent by the bearer a pair of spectacles & a glasse in a black cover wᶜʰ I desire you will take out & put in the spectacles if you can, & return it by the bearer. If you cannot do it now I hope you will get it done by your next Tuesday's fair; if it is not in your way to do it pray return it by the bearer wᶜʰ will oblige

Your humble servant
H. P.

ffor /
Mʳ Holton at
Buckingham /
                  This

No. 526.   H. P. *to* MR HOLTON

Shalstone
24ᵗʰ ffebrʸ 1740

Mʳ Holton /

Since you can't do them otherwise I desire you will put my 2 glasses into a new spectacle frame; let it be a silver one if you have any, but I beg you'll take care & not break the glasses because I can't get any such in the Countrey, & send them by the bearer wᶜʰ will oblidge

Your humble servant
H. P.

ffor /
Mʳ Holton at   Buckingham /
                  This

P.S.   Pray send word ℔ bearer what they come to.[1]

No. 527.   H. P. *to* JOSEPH HURT

Shalstone [&c.]
March the 4ᵗʰ 1748

Mʳ Hurt /

If you can't make a shorter Barometer than what you mention I shall not have occasion for any, for I have one by mee already

1 The Account-book, under 7 March, shows that Mr Holton was paid 6*d.* "for altering my spectacles".

just 3 foot long that I bought at your shop either from yourself or your Predecessor Mr Sterrop. But you have made an ugly mistake in Relation to my Glasses, for I sent to you for six concave glasses Number six for my spectacles, to repair ye same when they chance to break, & you have sent mee six Glasses in Horn cases which are of no use to mee for I have damaged one of my eyes already by using such as these are, & now use only those that are put in spectacles; so must desire you to change these six for as many concave glasses N°. 6 (without any cover or spectacles to 'em) as come to 12s. wch my freind Mr Land paid you for these I send you. When I have ye Glasses I put 'em into ye spectacles myself. I desire you will send them by ye Buckingham carrier.... You yourself fitted up severall spectacles of concave glasses N°. 6 for me in 1743 at my Lodgings in little Lincoln's inne ffeilds, so wonder you should make this mistake wch I desire you will rectifie, wch will oblidge

Your humble Servt
H. P.

ffor /
  Mr Joseph Hurt at the Archimedes
  & 3 golden Spectacles near Ave
  Mary Lane in Ludgate street
       London
  Carriage & portridge paid

From 1690 to 1695 John Yarwell carried on an optician's business at this sign, or under that of "Archimedes & 3 Golden Prospects"; in 1697 he was in partnership with Ralph Sterrop, whose name occurs in Letter No. 523, written in 1736-7. Letter No. 527 mentions Mr Sterrop as Mr Hurt's predecessor, and says "you yourself fitted up spectacles for mee"; this is confirmed by the Diary, for on 26 Aug. 1743 Henry spoke to "the man at the Archimedes head", and on 27 Aug. to "Mr Hurt (the spectacle man)".

Letters 184 and 185 were written in 1752 and addressed to Mr George Sterrop, whose address was then in St Paul's Churchyard.

Mr Ambrose Heal, who kindly supplied some of this information, adds that he has trade cards of Francis Morgan, at the Archimedes & Three Spectacles No. 27 Ludgate Street, and of Samuel Whitford at the same address, both opticians; perhaps they succeeded Mr Hurt.

No. 528. H. P. *to* JOSEPH HARRIS

Shalstone
July the 18ᵗʰ 1742

Mᵣ Harris /

I would have £50 of Mᵣ Whitten at first & £50 more or lesse as I shall have occasion; upon consideration I think this will be the best way & am

Your humble servᵗ

H. P.

ffor /
  Mᵣ Joseph Harris at
     Buckingham
          This

The "Instruments Executed" book shows that in 1730 Henry drew upon "Mᵣ Whitten of Bristoll" for £40, and upon a Bath carrier for £50; this was on 26 Aug. and 10 Oct. respectively; on 14 Jan. following he had returned home and paid Mr Harris £90, when "he gave mee agen these two Acquittances wᶜʰ I then cancelled".

This letter failed in its purpose, which was to finance a visit to Bath, and caused considerable trouble, as will appear in the following letters; the first would serve as a model letter from master to bailiff.

No. 529. H. P. *to* WILLIAM STRANGE

Bath
August the 3ᵈ 1742

Master Strange /

Wee got safe to Bath on Saturday about 2 a clock & I thank God are all well after our journey. Wee have very fine weather here as I hope you have at Shalstone & I desire you will see Master Walker makes all the hast hee can in cutting down the grasse in Dovehouse Close & carrying the Hay into yᵉ barn, but be sure it be not laid next yᵉ walls; if Sparks is come home hee may help him. I hope Master Walker will look after the ffruit & let Mary Blake have the Disposall of it, & give our love to her & hope to hear all things are well & go on Right, & that you all enjoy the blessing of Health.

Pray take care of the dogs & the two horses, for they are not able to take care of themselves.[1]

Wee shall be glad to hear Cloe is well. Pray when you write

1 On the fly-leaf of Henry's copy of *The Guardian* is a reference to No. 61 (by Pope), and the note: "Of yᵉ Tenderness due from Man to yᵉ inferiour Ranks of his fellow Creatures".

ask Mary Blake[1] if she has anything to write about, & let us hear from you as soon as may be wch will be acknowledged by

Your freind to serve you

H. P.

Direct your letter
 ffor /
 Mr Purefoy at Major Bolton's
 at Bath in   Somersetshire
 By way of London

ffor /
 Mr William Strange at Shalstone
  near Buckingham   in Bucks
 By way of London

No. 530. H. P. *to* THOMAS JERVOISE

Bath

Sir! /   *August the 3^d 1742*

I am favoured with both your Letters & thank you for your kind Invitation to Herriard & should have waited on you there before now had not all our servants fell ill of the Scarlet ffever & sore Throat, wch has been very rife & mortall in our parts. It detained us at home so long that I despair of waiting on you this Summer, for wee are ordered to drink these waters six weeks & by that time I am afraid the Roads will be bad, but wee hope next Spring, or the first fine Season, to do ourselves ye pleasure of visiting you at Herriard. My mother & self both join in our Love & Service to yourself & family, & I am Sir!

Your affect. Kinsman &

very humble servant

H. P.

P.S. Now the Season is so fine should be glad to see you here or else to hear of your health, & pray direct for mee at Major Bolton's at Bath, in Somersetshire, By way of London. Your kinsman & old acquaintance Sr Hugh Clapham[2] is here.

ffor /
 Thomas Jervoise Esq. at Herriard near
 Basingstoke in   Hampshire
 By way of London

1 One of the maids at the Manor House.

2 Presumably in error for Sir Hugh Clopton, as to whom see note to Letter No. 396 which was written to T. Jervoise after Henry returned home from Bath.

No. 531. H. P. *to* JOHN LAND

Bath
August the 7ᵗʰ 1742

Sir ! /

I went to Bristoll last Thursday to receive the £50 of Mʳ Whitten where Mʳ Jo. Harris directed mee & promised I should be paid that summe there, but to my surprize Mʳ Whitten would not pay it.

I doubt Mʳ Harris's credit is but low or else hee would not have served mee such a slippery trick. I desire you will return & pay fifty pounds to Mʳ Thomas Robotham, at the King's head Tavern at Islington on my account with all speed, & when you have his receipt for it keep it by you till I come home. I desire you will enquire if you can get any Return from Buckingham hither in case I should want more money. I lodge at Major Bolton's in Cheap street, Bath. Mʳ Walls of your town used to want returns. I beg you will not faill mee in this affair for our Purse here is almost empty, & it shall be acknowledged by

Your very humble servant

H. P.

ffor /
  Mʳ John Land Attorney
  at Law at Buckingham
              in Bucks
  By way of London

No. 532. E. P. *to* THOMAS ROBOTHAM

Bath
August the 7ᵗʰ 1742

This acquaints Mʳ Robotham wee got well to Bath the 31ˢᵗ of this last month & I thank God wee are pretty well after our Journey. Here is very little Company here as yet,—wee are disappointed in our Returns of money to this place, so this post have ordered Mʳ John Land, the Attorney of Buckingham, to remitt £50 to you which I desire you will receive & give a Receipt for it on account of my son. As soon as ever you have received this fifty pounds pay it to Mʳ Henry Crabb, paymaster at the East India House, & take a receipt for it of him & send the receipt down in a letter by yᵉ post. Major Bolton of Bath is to pay this fifty pounds here to my son when hee has advice that Mʳ Crabb has received it of you. If Mr Land don't send you the £50 write a letter to him by the next post after you receive this that you have orders to receive £50 of him for my son's use, for Mr Land has a good deall of money more than this of ours in his hands. M^r Jo: Harris the mercer of Buckingham promised to remitt £100 for us to Bristoll to one Mr Whitten there, & when wee came to Bristoll Mr Whitten would not pay it, wch is the occasion of our present Disappointm^t With both our hearty Service & respects to yourself & Mrs Robotham, wishing you both your healths—am in hast

Your humble servant
E. P.

P.S. Direct yours for mee at Major Bolton's at Bath in Somersetshire

ffor /
  Mr Robotham...
        London

No. 533. H. P. *to* WILLIAM STRANGE

Bath
August the 11th 1742

Master Strange /

I received yours & wee are glad to hear that you & Mary Blake & Cloe & all the Things are well & that you have ended some of the Hay, & hope in your next to hear that you have near ended the rest in case the weather serves.

I desire you will go over to Mr Land, Attorney at Buckingham, to know if hee has returned the £50 to Mr Robotham as I directed him in a letter from hence of the 7th of this August, for M^r Jo: Harris of Buckingham served mee a scurvy trick in giving mee orders to receive £50 at Bristoll of one Mr Whitten & when I came there hee refused to pay mee any. If Mr Land has not, desire him to return it with all speed to Mr Robotham. Tell Mary Blake that when my mother came to open her Band box she had but six yards of the Lace she bought of her brother, to make her a double mobb & a double handkercheif & let her send word in your next if she knowns anything of the other two yards, for my mother bought eight yards of her brother. I hope to hear you and Mary Blake & all the Things are well. Your speedy answer will much oblidge

Your freind to serve you

ffor /

Mr William Strange...Shalstone

H. P.

No. 534. E. P. *to* THOMAS ROBOTHAM

Bath
August y^e *19*th *1742*

I received Mr Robotham's letter of the 17th instant with Mr Crabb's receipt for the fifty pounds; wee thank you for this favour & all others. I am sorry wee were not at Shalstone to entertain you but shall hope to see you there as soon as wee return home. As you go for your Butter on Saturday I desire you will buy mee a pound of the best Bohea Tea, of Mr Cossins at the 3 Sugar loaves in St Paull's Church yard, & let them know 't is for mee & to be such as I used to have & I used to pay fourteen shillings a pound, & send it by the Bath Stage coach wch Inns at the 3 Cupps in Bread Street & at the Belle Savage Inne on Ludgate Hill. They set out for Bath on Mondays, Wensdays, Thursdays, & ffridays; pray send it as soon as possible. The waters, wee thank God, agree with us very well at present. I hope you had the two shoulders of venison sweet. With both our hearty service & respects to yourself & Mrs Robotham I am in hast

Your humble servant

ffor /

Mr Robotham...
London

E. P.

This is the last letter from Bath; the Account-book, under 14 Septr 1742, records a payment of £4. 10s. 0d. to "my mother Purefoy for my Lodging at Bath".

No. 535. E. P. *to* PETER MOULSON

Shalstone [*&c.*]
*July the 31*th *1743*

Sir! /

Yours I rece^d of the 18th of last month with the half Hogshead of Mountain wch was good. I should have answered yours before now only wee had thoughts of coming to Town every week since & design to come to Town the week after this that comes in, but desire it may be a Secrett[1] for reasons that I will acquaint you of when I see you. If anything has happened in your family you should not have conveniency for us to be at your house, pray let mee know by the next post that wee may write for Lodgings, for our stay in London will be short. My son has ordered Mr Murcott of Buckingham to pay you one hundred & forty pounds on his account. It won't be paid all at a time, so pray give a note for it as you receive it payable to my son or order after 4 days sight. Wee both join in our service & respects to yourself & Miss Moulson & I am, Sir,

Your humble servant

E. P.

ffor /
Mr Moulson...
London

No. 536. E. P. *to* PETER MOULSON

Shalstone...
August the 11th 1743

Sir! /

I am favoured with yours of the 9th instant, and you having such an affair in agitation as you mention wee shall be troublesome in your House, so desire to be excused. The reason I accepted your kind proffer was our acquaintance in Town being pretty much worn out I thought I should be safest in your House. I wish you all imaginable Successe in this affair & will wait upon Miss Moulson when I come to Town, with whom I desire you will leave the money payable to mee or my son.

I do write by this Post to have Lodgings taken. Wee both join in our hearty service & respects & I am, Sir!

Your humble servt

E. P.

P.S. The affair you mention will remain a secret.[2] Wee wish you a good Journey & safe return.

ffor /
Mr Moulson...
London

1 It clearly had reference to the ultimate disposal of Shalstone; see the ingenuous Letter No. 399 to Henry's second cousin Richard Jervoise.

2 In the following January Miss Moulson married Mr Vaughan.

No. 537. H. P. *to* PETER MOULSON

Shalstone
May the 7ᵗʰ 1749

Sir ! /

You was so kind some time ago to give my mother & self an Invitation to be at your house in Town. If it now suitts with your conveniency wee should gladly accept of the favour. Wee are fearfull of the small pox, so if it is near you & you are otherwise engaged I entreat you to let mee know, & when I have your answer I will beg the favour of you to take Lodgings for us. My mother joins with mee in our compliments to you and I am Sir ! with due esteem

Your very humble servant
H. P.

ffor /
Mᵣ Moulson in
London

No. 538. H. P. *to* PETER MOULSON

Shalstone [&c.]
May the 22ᵗʰ 1749

Sir ! /

I am favoured with yours of the 9ᵗʰ instant & wee thankfully accept of your kind invitation & design to set out for London on Monday next, & if you please to procure standing for 5 horses & a coach wᶜʰ I was forced to Register on my being appointed Sherriff & shall be glad to change it for one that is light & fit to travell with, & second hand but not very much the worse for wearing; if it lies in your way to enquire after one against wee come to Town. Wee both join in our compliments to you & I am with due esteem Sir !

Your very humble servant
H. P.

P.S. Pray our compliments to Mᵣ and Mᵣˢ Vaughan. I have receᵈ the favour of your last letter, but was disappointed in answering it by reason wee could not get returns for money. If any body should offer to pay you money on my account, or on Mᵣ Harry Wallbank's account, pray take it & give a proper rec't for it.

ffor /
Mᵣ Moulson

The opportunity seems fitting for examining this journey to London as shown by the Diary. They left Shalstone at 8.40 on 29 May, called on Mr Wallbank at Buckingham, and reached the George at Aylesbury at 1.50. There they dined and stayed until 4.20, when they went on to Missenden, reaching the White Hart at 6.20; here they stopped for the night and took leave of "M.ʳ Blackwell, landlord of the White Hart inne and his hostler and two maid servants" at 8.20 on 30 May. At 12.40 they reached the Red Lion at Southam (Southall) where three hours were needed for dinner; finally Mr Moulson's house in Wood Street was reached at 6.15. The total time on the road therefore was 14 hours, and if we put the mileage at 61 we have an average speed of something like 4⅓ miles per hour.

The morning of 31 May was a very busy one as a lot of shopping had to be done: Mr Belchier, the cabinet-maker, Mrs Ward, at the china-shop, Mr Deard at the Toy shop, Mr Stratton, the cane-shop, Mr Emon, the turner, Mr Lake, the coachmaker, young Dr Tayler, the oculist, and Mr Overton, the map-seller—all these were visited before 1.45, and the afternoon was taken less strenuously, though a little shopping in or near Wood Street was managed—visits were made to a pewterer, a barber, and to "the inne where the coach stands".

The 1st, 2nd and 3rd of June also saw a good deal of shopping; the 4th was a Sunday, and the afternoon was devoted to a visit to the White Lion at Putney. On the Monday there was a goldsmith in Cheapside, Mr Thornborrow, to see in the morning, after-dinner calls were made on "the man and woman who sold Sedan chairs in Coventry Street, and the man and woman at the glove shop in Turnstile Alley". Tuesday, 6 June, was a very busy day again; in the morning there were a saddler, an upholsterer, and a silversmith to visit. Mr and Mrs Wentworth, from Lillingstone Lovell, dined with them at the Moulsons', and they afterwards went to St Stephen's Church, Walbrook, the Bank, Southsea House, the Guildhall, and Moorfields. They then went westwards to Westminster where they went into the Abbey and saw "the new bridge at Westminster".

On the 7th there was more shopping, and on the afternoon of the 8th they called upon Mr and Mrs Wentworth at their "lodgings in the Pallmall", afterwards going on to Ranelagh House. The 9th was the great day, for they went to the Tower, "where I saw yᵉ Armory & Lions", and conversed with the "Beefeater who showed us the Armory, and the woman who showed us the Lions, and sundry other persons whom I spoke to at the Tower whose names I know not". Then they went down the river to Greenwich "and to the Ship inne there by the Thames side"; altogether a wonderful day, and one's only regret is that one does not know how Henry reacted to this strange environment.

The following day cleared up a few more visits to tradesmen, and on Sunday, 11 June, they set out for home at 10.20, reaching Missenden at 6.30; there was a stop at Chalfont St Giles where Henry "spoke to sundry people when the Coach was greasing whose names I know not". They left Missenden at 10.0 the next morning and reached Buckingham at 4.0, leaving "Lord Cobham's Arms inne" at 6.45 and finally getting home an hour later. The travelling time of the return journey seems to have been about the same as on the way up to London; probably it could only have been done at that time of year.

Presumably Mrs Purefoy, who was then 76 years of age, accompanied her son in his travels about London, so that she had evidently made a good recovery.

No. 539. H. P. *to* MRS GOOD

Shalstone [&c.]
June the 7ᵗʰ 1753

Mʳˢ Good /

When I was in Town I set my horses up at your spouse's where they had very good usage wᶜʰ I hope I may have still. I am sorry to hear your husband is dead, and desire you will let mee know if Mʳˢ Langley be living still, and if I may have a two pair of stairs room backward & a Dining room & Bed Chamber one pair of stairs; or if she is dead or don't let lodgings, if you know of any sober honest ffamily near your Inne, where I may have such Lodgings as above, excepting a Lawyer's because once I had ill usage from one of them,—pray let mee know by yᵉ Post & direct yours for Mʳ Henry Purefoy at Shalstone near Buckingham in Bucks, wch. will oblidge

Your freind to serve you
H. P.

ffor /
   Mʳˢ Good at the
Grange inne in Carey
Street near Lincoln's Inne
        London

No. 540. H. P. *to* PETER MOULSON

Shalstone [&c.]
July the 1ˢᵗ 1753

Sir! /

I have ordered £25 on my account & my mother £40 on her account to your hands by Jones yᵉ Carrier wᶜʰ I find you have received. I beg leave to order £15 more to you on my account by him, & entreat you will buy mee four Tickets in the present

Lottery at Dobson & Cockle's Office in Pope's head alley, Corn-hill, from whom I had a letter to proffer their service & to have the said Tickets registred there & send them mee ℔ post. Wee purpose to come to London as soon as wee have got our Hay in & entreat to know if you will give leave that my Trunk may have a place in your house, & be under your care till I come to Town. My mother desires to join with mee in our Compliments to you & hope you will be so good as to excuse this trouble from, Sir!

Your oblidged h'le servant
H. P.

P.S. If you think the Lottery Ticketts will be cheaper you may delay buying them for the present.

ffor /
  Mr Moulson...
    London

The following letter should be compared with No. 256, which gives Mrs Purefoy's version of the same calamities in the household.

No. 541. H. P. *to* PETER MOULSON

Shalstone [&c.]
August the 16th 1753

Sir! /

I am favoured with yours dated ye 3^d of July last & am much oblidged to you for your kind Invitation, I should be glad to accept it & should endeavour to make a suitable return, but at present my coachman is run away from mee for fear of a great Belly a Girl lays to him, & our Cookmaid was forced to go to Oxford Assize[1] to be evidence against a felon there, & when she came home she said she was married, & our Gardiner has married my mother's maid, & wee have had a very valluable mare lamed with a fforke but now in a fair way of Recovery; so our little ffamily is in a state of Confusion at present. However if wee can't come to Town I hope wee shall see you & M^r & Mrs Vaughan & George the Second here. The Birmingham Coach runs thro' in a Day from London to Buckingham & the fair is Ten shillings

1 See Letter No. 586.

each passenger, & if you let us know when you will come our Charriott shall meet you at Buckingham. Our mountain wine is out so desire you will send half an hogshead of your best white mountain wine as soon as may be by Mr Jones ye Buckingham Carrier....I should not have let the wine run out so near but I really expected to have been in Town.[1] My mother joins with mee in our Compliments to you & I am with all due esteem, Sir!

Your very humble serv.^t
H. P.

P.S. Pray let mee know what the wine comes to that I may keep the account even, & let mee have a łre of advice of the wine's coming that I may send for it.

ffor /
  Mr Moulson in
    London /
       This

1 See Letter No. 539.

Plate 22. FINMERE HOUSE

CHAPTER XIV

THE SHRIEVALTY

IN an uneventful life the year during which Henry exercised the chief office of the Crown in the county must necessarily be memorable. As it happens, we are able to learn some interesting facts about his year of office; the letters make several allusions to a subscription list which would be obscure had not a very interesting paper come to light at Shalstone. It is now clear that those in the county who considered themselves at all liable to serve subscribed five guineas each to a fund which was devoted to "regulating and reducing the expenses attending the office of Sherriff of the County of Bucks". The paper gives us various amendments to the Articles, and lists sixty-five subscribers; how benefits were paid under this scheme of insurance we do not learn, but to join such a fund was a natural act in one so prudent as Henry.

The letters tell us a good deal about his assumption of office, and one is a particular gem (No. 550), without parallel in the Letter-books, as it is addressed to his mother from Aylesbury on the occasion of attending the Assizes at Aylesbury. In a letter to Grenville, afterwards Earl Temple, he speaks of the office as "this troublesome Jobb", but one suspects that it was not altogether distasteful to him, and it is certainly interesting to us, to meet all the "Gentlemen of ffigure" in the county in 1748–9.

The paper mentioned above has on the outside: "A List of the Gentlemen who subscribed five Guineas each for Regulating and Reducing the Expenses attending the office of Sherriff of the County of Bucks. Taken 27th July 1749", and is given in full in Appendix C. p. 441.

No. 542. H. P. *to* JOHN POLLARD

Shalstone
January ye 8th 1747

Sir! /

I have received a Łre from Mr Sheppard of Lidcot by the Bayliff Mr Hall in which hee informs mee that at the Quarter Sessions at Aylesbury the 14th January next will be a meeting of the Gentlemen & Subscribers to the Sheriff's articles to nominate a Committee & to make some necessary additions to & alterations in ye same. As I am very bad with a cold I can't possibly go to

Ailesbury, so if you go yourself please to make my excuse to the Gentlemen or otherwise do it by Letter if you write. When you have paid the five guineas for mee be so good as to let mee know & I will either bring or send them to you. My mother & self desire you & Mrs Pollard to accept of the Compliments of the Season & I am Sir!

Your very humble serv^t

H. P.

ffor /
   John Pollard Esq at
     ffinmere /
       This

Lipscomb tells us[1] that John Pollard was a native of Dorsetshire who held lands at Leckhampstead; this seems rather an inadequate way of describing his connection with the parish, since the Register[2] shows a succession of Pollards since the early seventeenth century; one of them was buried 14 Oct. 1696 and is described as "citizen and grocer in ye county of Middlesex". A John Pollard was buried in 1718, probably our John Pollard was his heir; he was made Sheriff of Bucks in 1735 and is then described as of Leckhampstead. Mr J. C. Blomfield[3] says that Mr Pollard was present at the Finmere Vestry of 1740, but he must have owned land there earlier as Henry Purefoy's Diary mentions "Mr Pollard's grounds at Finmere" on 4 Sept. 1738; six months earlier he had called upon Mrs James whose property John Pollard purchased.

The illustration (Plate 22) shows the large wing built by Mr Pollard and the rain-water heads bear his crest (a stag tripping) and the date 1739; this wing retains its panelling and staircase, and the principal bedrooms have powdering-closets attached to them. The northern wing of the house is apparently of the late sixteenth century.

John Pollard's altar-tomb is in Finmere church-yard; the sides bear entwined ciphers reversed, and the ends the stag crest. The inscription on the top is nearly illegible, but his name can be made out; the arms are plain: A cheveron between 3 mullets.

The Purefoys became very friendly with the Pollards, and the Diaries record frequent visits; on 30 Aug. 1744 is an entry of such a call when Henry noted that he "conversed with Mrs Pollard & her maid & her servant man (a fat one)".

On 18 Sept. 1740 Henry went to "Mrs Chaplin's at Finmere on visiting Mrs Pollard". Mrs Chaplin was the rector's wife, presumably the Pollards were staying with her whilst their house was being finished, as Henry spoke to "the Joiner man at Worke at Mr Pollard's House".

1 *History of Bucks*, vol. III, p. 26.
2 *Leckhampstead Parish Register*, printed 1912, pp. 8–28.
3 *History of Finmere*, 1887, p. 16.

No. 543. H. P. *to* JOHN POLLARD

Sir! /

Shalstone
January ye 22th 1747

I have received advice from a ffreind in London that the three Gentlemen who were prickt down for Sherifs for the County of Bucks have all got of[f], and that Mr Campbell Price of Westbury or myself will certainly be the Pocket Sheriff.[1] I must beg the favour of you to let mee know whether or no I shall have the Benefit of the Articles for Regulating the Expences attending our Sheriff's Office by reason I have not paid the five Guineas. If I am within the articles and shall have ye benefit of them I will not endeavour to prevent being prickt down Sheriff; but if you imagine I am not I must write immediately to my ffreinds in Town to use their Endeavours to get mee of[f]. Our best compliments attend Mrs Pollard & yourself & I am Sir!

Your very hĩe servant
H. P.

P.S. Pray favour mee with your answer ℈ bearer.

ffor /
John Pollard Esq at
ffinmere /
This

No. 544. H. P. *to* THOMAS SHEPPARD

Sir! /

Shalstone
January the 23th 1747

I received your Letter by Mr Hall of Gawcott & would have waited on you & the other Gent. at Aylesbury but was ill of a cold. Mr Pollard told mee hee would pay you the five Guineas for mee which I did not understand till yesterday but that hee had paid it. I having an opportunity have sent you the five Guineas by the bearer & desire you would give a proper Receipt for the same, wch will oblidge

Your humble servant
H. P.

ffor /
Mr Thomas Sheppard Attorney
at Law at Lidcot /
This

1 According to Christian's edn. of Blackstone: *Commentaries*, a pocket sheriff is one appointed by the King, and is not one of the three nominated in the exchequer. "It is probable that no compulsory instance of the appointment of a pocket sheriff ever occurred."

The Sheppard family had held Lidcot since the sixteenth century. Lidcot is a hamlet of Stewkley, Bucks, now called Littlecote. Lipscomb says that the estate continued in 1760 "in possession of a descendant of the same family, who followed the profession of the Law, and acted as Deputy Sheriff for many years, and from whom it devolved to his descendant Sir Thomas Cotton Sheppard, Bart. the present (1847) possessor" (vol. III, p. 478).

No. 545. H. P. *to* JOHN POLLARD

Shalstone
Monday ffeb^{ry} 6th 1748

Sir! /

I last night rece$\bar{d}$ a Łre from Mr Sheppard of Lidcot wherein hee acquaints mee that I am appointed Sherriff of our County of Bucks. As I am a perfect stranger to this affair & you thoroughly acquainted therewith I beg I may wait on you some time to Day[1] to have what information you can give mee therein. I am to answer Mr Sheppard's letter too morrow wch makes mee the more earnest to confer with you soon about it. My mother joins with mee in our Compliments to yourself & Mrs Pollard & I am Sir!

Your very hſe servant
H. P.

ffor /
   John Pollard Esq at
      ffinmere /
         This

No. 546. H. P. *to* THOMAS SHEPPARD

Shalstone [&*c.*]
ffebruary the 7th 1748

Sir! /

I rece$\bar{d}$ yours dated the 4th instant &, as you think it proper I should soon be sworn into my Office of Sherriff, the persons in my Dedimus I would have to be John Pollard Esq. of ffinmere in the County of Oxon, the Revd Mr Wright Haws, Rector of Shalstone in our County of Bucks, the Rev^d M^r ffrancis Edmunds,

---

1 The Diary shows that he called upon Mr Pollard in the afternoon and saw "M^r & Mrs Pollard, & their two servant men who 'tended, the Rev. Mr Edmunds of Tingwick, & a young Lady with him whom I suppose to be Mrs Marlow".

Rector of Tingwick in the said County, M.r Harry Wallbank of Buckingham in the said County, Surgeon, & as to the Bar.t you may chuse him yourself for now S.r Charles Tyrrell is dead[1] I don't know of any one of that Rank near us. I desire you will sue out my Patent & Dedimus & shall be glad to see you here on Monday next at 1 a' clock to take a dinner with mee. All whom [sic] are my ffreinds I expect should set up their horses at M.r Shem Baxter's an Inn holder at Buckingham, & in particular that you & my men should be there during the short continuance[2] of the future Summer Assizes at Buckingham. I am Sir!

Your humble servant
H. P.

ffor /
  M.r Thomas Sheppard Attorney
  at Law at M.r Howard's in
  Crane Court in ffleetstreet
          London

No. 547. H. P. *to* JAMES GIBBS

Shalstone
ffebruary the 8.th 1748

M.r Gibbs /

Since I saw you last I am appointed High Sherriff of our County of Bucks & shall want to use y.e Coach at our next Assizes at Ailesbury, w.ch are 28.th of ffeb.ry next; but one of our wheell mares is so broken winded she can't perform a Journey; So must entreat you to get a new Coachmare for the wheell which must be about 16 hands high & a strong one. This will oblidge

Your humble servant
H. P.

ffor /
  M.r James Gibbs at Souldern
        This
  Carriage paid two pence

1 Lipscomb shows him as dying in 1755, but Thornton Registers have been printed and it appears that he was buried on 28 Jan. 1748 (p. 38).

2 Lord Cobham procured the Act for fixing the Summer Assizes at Buckingham in 1748; there are three folio pamphlets concerning this highly controversial question, all dated 1748 (vide *Bibliotheca Buckinghamiensis*, by H. Gough, p. 26). The Midsummer Assizes were not transferred to Aylesbury again until 1849. The Diary of 18 Feb. 1747 shows that a "stranger man" called with a "Petition against the Bill to have y.e Assizes held at Buckingham in summer, which I refused to sign". On 24 Feb. "young M.r Pashler & another gentleman" brought a Petition in favour of the Bill, "which I signed".

No. 548. H. P. *to* RICHARD GRENVILLE M.P.

Shalstone [*&c.*]
ffeb^ry 12th 1748

Sir! /

I am favoured with both your Łres but did not trouble you with an answer to ye first by reason I rece͞d a Łre from a freind in Town with the Gazett inclosed by wch I found I was appointed Sherriff of our County of Bucks & that last Monday was the last day the King had power to nominate Sherriffs for this year, saving vacancies &c., On wch I wrote to Town to my under-Sherriff to sue out my Patent & Dedimus to take my Oath of Office in the Countrey. It is not disagreeable to mee in any other Respects than ye short-nesse of time allowed mee to enter on the Discharge of the Duty of my office, for I don't know that I have deserved such usage from anybody having always bore a sincere good affection for my present gracious sovereign & those in Authority under him; besides it has been very unlucky in another circumstance, my mother was taken ill on 23^d of October last with a mortification in her leg as Dr Pitt & the surgeon thought was for some time incurable, but has weakened her to that Degree she has been confined to her Chamber ever since, & now I have so ill a state of health that I have not been out of doors for a considerable time. Had I not engaged in the 5 guinea subscription it would have been impossible for mee to have got my cloaths & equipage & affairs with my under sherriff in Readinesse by ye next Assize on so short a warning; so there now remains no more for mee than to return thanks to you & my other ffreinds for their kind endeavours to rescue mee from this troublesome Jobb, wch tho' they were not successfull I beleive were sincere, & I am, Sir! with due esteem

Your humble servant

ffor /
Richard Greenville[1] Esq. member
of Parliam^t in Pall=mall
    London
ffrank /

H. P.

[1] At this time he was M.P. for Buckingham; he succeeded his mother as Earl Temple and Viscount and Baron Cobham in 1752, died 1779. Macaulay's character of him in his Essay on *The Earl of Chatham* will be remembered: "It was his nature to grub underground. Whenever a heap of dirt was flung up, it might well be suspected that he was at work in some foul crooked labyrinth below".

To face p. 368

Plate 23. HENRY WHEN HIGH SHERIFF

No. 549. H. P. *to* HARRY WALLBANK

Shalstone
ffebruary 23ᵗʰ 1748

Sir /

I understand the small pox is not at Ailesbury to do any harm, therefore desire you not to speak to M.ᵣ Sheppard to give himself the trouble of coming over here, for I design to go to Ailesbury myself if I can't get anybody to supply my Place. I yesterday went to Aynhoe after M.ᵣ Brown Willis to personate mee, but could not meet with him; I should be glad to procure him or any body else to do mee that favour. Pray let the bearer have some scions from of[f] your summer Jenneting apple tree to graft with. Shall be glad to see you or M.ᵣ Pashler here. Our compliments attend you all & I am

Your humble servant

ffor /
  M.ᵣ Wallbank at
      Buckingham
          This

H. P.

The next letter appears in the book *after* five letters dated 18 to 22 March, so that, odd as it may seem, it is almost certain that it was copied out when Henry had been home some days; it has no alterations or corrections in it.

No. 550. H. P. *to* E. P.

Ailesbury
Wensday March yᵉ 8ᵗʰ 1748

Honoured Madam /

After my thanks returned for your kind Desire to know how I concluded my Journey, I can now acquaint you that yᵉ day I left you I got to Buckingham exactly at 3 a'clock where I deliũed your box to M.ᵣ Wallbank himself who promised mee to take particular Care of it. I came to yᵉ George inne here 40 minutes after 7 a clock at night, so guesse I was 7 hours at least on my Journey, but sure I am I never made a more unked or solitary one in my life, & the roads were bad enough; but I thank God I have got into a good warm Bed chamber where I rest well. The Judge came in here about five a 'clock last Monday night; wee have seventeen gentlemen on the grand Jury, of whom S.ᵣ W.ᵐ

Stanhope[1] is foreman, & 2 Barr[ts] (To witt) S[r] W[m] Bowyer[2] & S[r] Charles Palmer,[3] & the rest most of 'em Gentlemen of ffigure. The Judge leaves this Town on ffriday morning abt. 8 a'clock, so desire you will let Goodm[n] Strange come here on Thursday night. I long to be at home with you & desire my compliments to M[rs] Mary Price & any other ffreinds who may chance to enquire after, Madam

Your most oblidged & Dutifull son
H. P.

ffor /
    M[rs] Purefoy at Shalstone near
    Buckingham in Bucks
        post paid twopence
    To be sent away immediately

No. 551. H. P. *to* THOMAS SHEPPARD

Shalstone
July the 3[d] 1749

Sir ! /

I expected to have seen you here before this time & hope to see you before you give the Grand Jury notice to attend &c. because the Grand Jury must be served with notice in due time & I expect to have y[e] naming the fforeman and the rest of them. Also I would speak to you about other matters, pray don't faill to let mee see you w[ch] will oblidge Sir !

Your humble servant
H. P.

ffor /
    M[r] Sheppard Attorney at
    Law at Lidcott
        This

No. 552. H. P. *to* THOMAS SHEPPARD

Shalstone
August the 5th 1749

Sir ! /

According to promise I send you seven Hare-Scutts w[ch] I desire your acceptance of & wish they may clear your Pen to your satisfaction & am

Your very humble servant
H. P.

1 Younger brother of the great (fourth) Earl of Chesterfield; he lived at Eythrope and was M.P. for the county at this time; he was one of the fraternity of Medmenham "monks", commonly called "The Hell Fire Club".

2 This is the third Bart. who succeeded his grandfather in 1721, when he was himself only 11 years old. (See Lathbury, *History of Denham*, p. 309.)

3 Of Dorney Court, bart. (1706–1773). Portraits of himself and of Anne, his wife, by Bardwell, hang above the daïs in the Great Hall at Dorney.

P.S.

When you do mee ye favour to come here ab^t settling the £95 I am to receive,[1] let mee have a line when you come for I am pretty much from home this Astrop season.

ffor /
Mr Sheppard Attorney at
Law to be left at Mrs Smith's
at Padbury
    This

No. 553. H. P. *to* THOMAS SHEPPARD

Shalstone

Sir! /

Monday Aprill the 9th 1750

One Goodman William Strange, my late Tennant, I fear has been guilty of an act of Indiscretion, on going from Shalstone with his Goods, corn & hay, to Blagrove where hee now lives hee tells mee hee had 6 teams to draw ye same & the Act of Parliam^t declaring that a Team laden with Corn is to pay but 6^d was the occasion of this mistake & I suppose hee might have some goods jointly loaded with the Corn, wch might irritate ye Turnpike man. As Master Strange is willing to make ye Turnpike any reasonable satisfaction I desire you would put him in a way to extricate himself out of this Difficulty, wch I shall take as a signall favour.

I accidentally met our High Sherriff[2] at Buckingham who seems desirous to have ye Subscription Book, but I had it not there, but desire you will write a proper receipt & send it to Mr Wallbanks at Buckingham & on ye sherriff's signing it in my presence I am ready to deliver ye Book.

I hope I shall have my Quietus some time in Trinity Terme & shall be very glad to see you here & am

Your very humble serv^t

ffor /

H. P.

Mr Sheppard Attorney at law
  at Lidcott /
    This

1 The "Instruments Executed" book, under 10 Novr. 1749, has this entry: "I executed a Letter of Attorney for Mr Middleton Howard, attorney at law of ffleetstreet, to receive ninety six pounds out of the Exchequer for mee as Sheriff of the County of Bucks". On 2 Aug. 1750 is a similar entry for £28–14–0 "for the surplusage due to mee as late Sheriff of Bucks". In a letter to Mr Moulson of 13 August, not printed, occurs the sentence: "The Plague of my Sherrifalty is almost over tho' I was sorely fatigued last Buckingham Assizes".

2 Henry's successor as Sheriff was Thomas Leigh, of Iver.

CHAPTER XV

NEIGHBOURS AND SOCIAL MATTERS

THE letters collected under this head indicate that social amenities were limited but by no means lacking; the difficulty was in transport, for the bad state of the roads largely restricted visits of pleasure to the summer months.

The Diaries mention several families to whom no letters happen to have been written; thus on 2 June 1726 the Purefoys called on Mr and Mrs Francis Dayrell, of Lillingstone Dayrell; this was the son of Sir Marmaduke Dayrell.[1] In July of the same year they called on Col. Pendlebury of Maids' Moreton; this was presumably the "Col. of the Royal Train of Artillery and Master Gunner of England to the day of his decease, and sub-Governor of the Tower of London during the latter end of Queen Anne's reign" who is commemorated by a monument in Maids' Moreton church; he died in 1731, aged 72. On 21 July 1737 they went to Mr Fermor's at Tusmore, and saw "Mrs Fermor the widow, Mrs Harriott Fermor, Miss Sheldon".

"The widow" was presumably the grandmother of Henry Fermor, as his mother died in 1722. "Mrs Harriott" was possibly Henrietta, an aunt (died 1744); a far more famous aunt, Arabella, was the heroine of no less a poem than "The Rape of the Lock". Henry Fermor married Frances Sheldon in 1736, perhaps "Miss Sheldon" was his sister-in-law. This Henry's son, another Henry, married the daughter of Mr Justice Willes whom we shall meet at Astrop.[2]

These visits were all returned in person; an exceptional entry in the diary under 22 Mar. 1747 runs: "Mr Wentworth's servant man, who came with an How do yee".

Then every summer a series of visits to Astrop Well took place, and a good deal is said about them under Letter No. 576; this was a mere half-day excursion as they generally reached home again in the early afternoon. The other holidays only appear whilst Henry is young and probably before gout troubled him; thus in 1726 on 11 August the Purefoys went to Towcester and dined at "Mr Kingston's White Horse Inn at Tocester", they stayed until 5.30 and then went to "Ld Pomfret's at Easton". This is Nicholas Hawksmoor's magnificent house at Easton Neston,[3] and they apparently went over it, as Henry "conversed with

1 If the pedigree given by Lipscomb (vol. III, p. 33) can be trusted. He is there described as of Castle Camps and Lillingstone Dayrell, but never owned the last-named manor.

2 For particulars of the Fermor family see J. C. Blomfield, *History of Tusmore*, pp. 64–84.

3 Built for Sir William Fermor, who became Lord Lempster (Leominster) in William III's time; his son was made first Earl of Pomfret in 1721.

the house-man & gardiner at Ld Pomfret's"; they returned to Shalstone that night.

On 17 August they went to Oxford, where they spent the night at the King's Arms Inn; the next day they went to Woodstock and to see over Blenheim House.

There were often visits to Stowe, which adjoins the Shalstone estate on the north; during one such visit (on 20 Aug. 1735) is recorded the fact that he spoke to "the Boy that let us in at my Lord's Gardens, Mr Love ye Gardiner, the groom of ye Chambers that showed us my Lord's house, and Mrs Hodgkinson (a fat woman,) 't was her, I think". On 14 Dec. 1750 Henry apparently dined with the (second) Viscount Cobham at Stowe.

There are added several interesting and not unamusing letters to Browne Willis regarding some of Henry's neighbours; the old antiquary did not incorporate much of them in his book, indeed they are nearer to gossip than to historical evidence. He preserved them, however, and two are in the Bodleian Library to-day. (See Plate 25.)

Finally a few letters relating to local incidents have been placed in this chapter for convenience.

No. 554. H. P. *to* JOHN WENTWORTH [CRESSWELL]

Shalstone
29th March 1736

Sir! /

Some time ago you was so kind to proffer mee some carp—if it suits with your conveniency now they will be very acceptable if you send them by ye Bearer—if not appoint a Day & the serv^t shall wait on you again. Wee hope to hear Mrs Wentworth & you enjoy the Blessing of health that wee may have the pleasure of waiting on you here & our best services & respects wait on you Both & I am Sir

Your very humble serv^t
H. P.

ffor John Wentworth Esq at
Lillingston Lovell &c.

The Wentworths had held Lillingstone Lovell since 1546, when Sir Nicholas acquired the estate; the last Wentworth died in 1690 when the property passed to his great-nephew John Cresswell, who assumed the name of Wentworth. The owner of the carp was the second Wentworth-Cresswell; he held the estate from 1697 until 1759. For a full account of this interesting family see *Wentworth of Lillingstone Lovell*, by W. L. Rutton, in *Records of Bucks*, vol. VI, pp. 212–244. There was an old friendship between the Purefoys and the Wentworths, because the will of John Purefoy (1579) was witnessed by his "louinge friende Peter Wentworthe Esquier"—see *Records of Bucks*, vol. XII, p. 124.

No. 555. H. P. *to* THE REV. RICHARD DALBY

Shalstone [&c.]
September the 8th 1736

Sir! /

I am favoured with yours of the 12th August last. I am glad you Ɔcluded your journey safe & that your preferment is like to prove to your mind & hope this will find you perfectly recovered of your fever, but if it should not I am informed there is an excellent medicinall spring at a place called Saint Landulphs in your County of Cornwall, partly of the same nature with Scarborough Spaw waters;[1] probably if you were to drink this Landulph water for a month or so it might restore your Ɔstitution to a due temper & for the future fortifie you against any noxious particles that may arise from the Tin or Copper mines & so mix with the air. As to any Vapours that arise from the sea I don't beleive they will hurt you for I have been at Bristoll where there then was as foggy & thick an air as well could be & it was occasioned by vapours arising from the sea, but I felt no ill effects from it so must attribute your disorders to the efluvia of the mines. Don't be sollicitous about the gelding hee proves extremely well. I have no news to send you but our town of Buckingham is greivously visited with the small pox, the last I heard of it it was in threescore houses, so forasmuch as it is so universall hope it will be soon over. I thank God our Shalstone folks have escaped it hitherto. There never was so great a scarcity of hares as with us at present & but a few Partridge & Pheasants. This last season at Astrop Wells has afforded more Divertion than usuall & there

1 Landulph is in the S.E. of Cornwall on the River Tamar, and N. of Saltash. There is a "Holy Well" ¼ mile W. of the church, the water of which seems to be chalybeate. Some carved stone-work which probably covered the well at one time lies about the church and in the garden of Lower Marsh Farm. The spring-water was formerly used for baptisms. (Information kindly given by the Rev. I. P. Jenkyns, some time rector of Landulph, now of Calstock). It is difficult to know how Henry heard of it, as it is not mentioned in Dr Shaw's book on Scarborough referred to in Letter No. 339, nor in any other book on mineral springs known to the editor.

has been much Dancing & pleasantry there among the young folks. Myself & the rest of your ffreinds here are heartily glad that wee are like as to have you among us next summer & that you are so good as to think of us tho' at so great a Distance & when you come into these parts of the world I assure you no one of your freinds will have more satisfaction in seeing you than, Sir! /

Your affect: ffreind & ĥĩe serv.^t
H. P.

P.S. / My mother joins with mee in our service & respect & shall be glad to hear of your health & successe in your schooll.

ffor /
The Revd Mr Dalby
    at Helston in Cornwall
By way of London /

No. 556. H. P. *to* THE REV. RICHARD DALBY

Shalstone [*&c.*]
Sunday, August 28th 1737

Sir! /

    I was not favoured with yours of the 18th of last July till above a fortnight after the date, so suppose 'twas a mistake at ye Post Office; however I am glad to hear your spavin mare was able to perform her journey to your satisfaction.

    I am sorry to hear the Cornish air agrees no better with you, when you was in your native countrey Oxfordshire I don't remember any complaints from you for want of health; your situation at present seems to mee so difficult that none of your ffreinds can venture to say anything about it, Interest you say inclining you to Cornwall & the prospect of health to Oxfordshire. As to our affairs of husbandry & grazing, wee have fallowed, stirred & laid up most of our fallow Land, & the harvests here are generally gotten in, but those who are so unfortunate to be behind hand will have the worst on't especially for their barley, it being very showery weather. Cows fetch a very poor price here & I suppose dry Cattle are proportionably cheap, it being most folks' opinion Hay will be very dear in these parts this next winter & calves, which wee send to Leighton in Bedfordshire for the better price, fetch almost nothing at all. Wee have had plenty of apricots, peaches

24-2

& plumbs & nectarines, but shall have but very few apples or pears. However I can't advise you about your stay in Cornwall, I heartily wish you better health & all manner of prosperity & with my mother's & my service & respects to you I am

Your very humble serv.^{t}
H. P.

P.S. / I had almost forgot to tell you here is the greatest scarcity of Hares that has been known. Wee have got a new sort of wild Cats, almost the colour of a polecat which haunt all the gentlemen's woods hereabouts, & have destroyed most of the young Leveretts already, I have killed one of them with some difficulty in my Cowpasture; when the Dogs pressed her hard she ran up into a tree, but wee got her down agen & then the dogs demolished her tho' She fought well for her Life & tore the Dogs greivously. Mr Price of Westbury his huntsman has killed about half a dozen of these new sort of cats, but I don't hear any of the other gentlemen have as yet taken it in their heads & go about to suppresse them.

Wee have pretty plenty of Partridge & pheasants.

At your leisure a line or two that you have better health will be a signall favour.

ffor /
The Revd Mr Dalby[1] at
Helston in   Cornwall
By London /

No. 557. H. P. *to* THE REV. WILLIAM PRICE

Shalstone [*&c.*]
July y^e *30*th *1738*

Sir! /

Wee shall draw of[f] our hogshead of red Port some time this week towards ye latter end, if you please to have any send for it before 't is drawn of[f].

1 From an entry in an account-book it seems that Mr Dalby's first name was Richard. One is tempted to identify him with Rd Dalby, B.A. of Brasenose Coll. in 1727–8, who was son of the rector of Upper Heyford, Oxon. J. C. Blomfield, *History of Upper Heyford*, 1892, p. 52, however states that the Rector's son (unnamed) was buried 20 Aug. 1737, and our Letter No. 19 proves that Mr Dalby was alive (even "boisterous") in 1742. In 1752 Henry dined with a Mr Francis Dalby who lived at Croughton, with a wife and three daughters. See Letter No. 579. There was also Mrs Purefoy's god-daughter, Sally Dalby, to whom Letters Nos. 130 and 216 are addressed.

My mother has some white Damask come down[1] for window curtains & there will be more than will be used; if any of your family should want any let them come & see it, my mother esteems it a great pennyworth. Wee both join in service to you all & I am

Your very humble serv.
H. P.

ffor /
  The Revd Mr Price
    at Whitfeild /
       This

No. 558. H. P. to THE REV. WILLIAM PRICE

Shalstone
Wensday Octob.^r the 25th 1738

Sir ! /

Yesterday I fished a pond & I think you mentioned some time ago you had occasion for some store ffish, wch if you have if you would send your servant over too morrow morning with things to carry 'em in, I shall have about 100 Brace of store carp at your service. My mother & self join in our service & respect to yourself & ffamily & I am Sir !

Your very h̶t̶e̶ serv.
H. P.

ffor /
  The Revd Mr Price
    at Whitfeild
       This

In the afternoon of the 26th the Diary duly records the appearance of "Mrs Sukey & Kitty Prices of Whitfeild, & their servant man".

No. 559. E. P. to MRS SUSAN PRICE

Shalstone
Novemb.^r 11th 1738

Dear Sukey /

Wee were coming yesterday to Whitfeild in hopes to wait on M.^r & Mrs Price, but were prevented of the pleasure of seeing you all by reason the Axtree of the Chariott broke in Westbury ffeild[2] so wee were forced to send for the Coach to have us home; wee thank God no other harm happened to us. This accident will hinder our coming to you this moon, so hope wee shall see some of your family here soon. I had the 3 couple of Chickens & have ordered the bearer to pay you 3 shillings, I have ordered the

1 See Letter No. 170 ordering this damask.
2 On 4 Oct. 1749 the coach was overturned near Brackley as the result of the "ax-tree" breaking.

bearer to go to Radson for a Pigg if you think it is not gone. Wee both join in service & respect to M.ʳ Price & all the ffamily & I am

Your affect. Godmother
E. P.

ffor /
   M.ʳˢ Susan Price¹
    at Whitfeild
      This

P.S. My dairy maid is very sickly & goes away, if you hear of ever an one pray let mee know.

Whitfield is 6 miles from Shalstone; the difficulty of travelling in November and the necessity for moonlight is an indication of the state of the roads. The Diary records during the afternoon: "out in the Chariott in Westbury ffeild (where the chariott axle chanced to break)".

No. 560. E. P. *to* MRS SUSAN PRICE

Shalstone
5.ᵗʰ January 1741

Dear Sukey /

I shall be glad of your company & any of your ffamily & M.ʳ ffletcher² to dine with us on Thursday next; now there is a moon I hope to have more of your company. If you can't come on Thursday let mee know by the bearer if you can come on ffriday, if you can't come this week let mee know what day you can come the week after this that comes in, the next week being our washing week. Wee give you all the compliments of the season & I am

Your affect: Godmother
E. P.

ffor /
   M.ʳˢ Susan Price at
     Whitfeild /
       This

No. 561. E. P. *to* THOMAS ROBOTHAM

Shalstone [&c.]
May the 23.ᵗʰ 1742

I beleive M.ʳ Robotham thinks wee are gone to Cheltenham, but wee have been prevented by our Coachman's being ill of a Rheumatism this month; his year was up last Thursday so wee

1 On 31 Aug. 1752 Henry was at Astrop and recorded in the Diary that he saw there "M.ʳˢ Rushworth (late Sukey Price)".
2 See Letter No. 577.

are in hopes hee will be well to go away soon. I have hired my old servant William Baker again, I cannot yet determine the time I shall go my Journey, the small pox is broke out afresh that way and it is terribly at Brackley & Mr Lisle[1] of Imley as well as many others have died of it. It has been particularly fatall to the men over it has to the women.

I rece^d your pickled salmon, the pot of anchovies, & six Sevill oranges wch were all very good & wee return you thanks for them. The salmon was very good but jumbled into peices & the liquor all run out. I suppose you rece^d my order to pay the £7. 15s. 6d. to Mr Moulson. I have sent you with your butter a stone Bottle wch I desire you to get filled with the very best sallet oyll & sent as soon as may be. Wee shall be glad to hear of yours & Mrs Robotham's good healths & with our hearty service & respects to you both

I am

Your humble servant

ffor /   E. P.
   Mr Robotham...
      London

No. 562. E. P. *to* MRS WALLBANK

Shalstone
July the 13th 1743

If it is agreeable to Mrs Wallbank & she is not otherwise engaged I will come & dine with her on Tuesday next, being the Buckingham Assize.

And if it is so I desire you will give mee leave to bring some of my Chickens & Bacon &c., and favour mee with your answer by the Post Boy who brings our news on ffriday next. Our compliments attend Mr Wallbank & yourself & Miss, and I am

Your humble servant

ffor /   E. P.
   Mrs Wallbank at
     Buckingham
      This

1 This was Fermor Lisle, of Evenley (as it is now spelt), whose death, unmarried, in 1742 is recorded in the pedigree printed in Baker, *History of Northamptonshire*, vol. I, p. 612. His mother was a niece of Sir Isaac Newton.

No. 563. H. P. *to* JOHN WENTWORTH [CRESSWELL]

Shalstone
8ᵗʰ Septembʳ 1744

Sir! /

I am informed the Way of the World will be acted this night at Westbury. It is to begin about half hour after 5 a clock. I hope wee shall have the ffavour of your companies to drink a Dish of Tea & then to wait on you thither.

Our Compliments attend you both & I am Sir!

Your very humble servant

H. P.

ffor /
John Wentworth Cresswell
Esq at Lillingston Lovell
This

Perhaps the notice was too short; the Wentworths did not attend, but the rector and his reverend brother went, and there Henry spoke to "the man who held the coach door, Mʳˢ Bowles, wife to Dʳ Bowles of Brackley, Mʳ ffienes Trotman, the stranger gentlewoman who sat by mee in yᵉ Playhouse, & a stranger gentleman I spoke to in yᵉ parlour, Mʳ Richᵈ Greenville", etc. etc.

Congreve's play was first produced in 1700.

The Purefoys went to plays at Westbury on 17 Sept. and 16 Jan. (O.S.) 1735, and on 11 July 1737, but we are not told the names of the plays performed. On 2 Aug. 1745 they also went to see "King Richard the 3ᵈ". Perhaps this play was repeated, because a month later, 5 Sept. 1745, Earl Verney's steward writes to him: "Mʳ Price of Westbury plays Richard the 3ʳᵈ this Night" (*Verney Letters of the Eighteenth Century*, 1930, vol. II, p. 197). See also Letter No. 570.

No. 564. H. P. *to* THE REV. WRIGHT HAWES

Shalstone
December yᵉ 21ˢᵗ 1744

Sir! /

I desire your acceptance of a peice of sturgeon wᶜʰ I have sent by the Clerke's boy, & my mother desires you will let Mʳ Starkey know she will have his neck chine if it is not of an old sow. She would have it weigh about 20 pounds & cut thick & handsome, & she will not exceed three pence a pound, but you may get it cheaper if you can, & she must have it too morrow

night or on Saturday morning betimes, or else not at all. I entreat
your answer by the Lad about the Chine. Wee desire Miss Haws &
yourself & Mr Matthew Haws to accept of the compliments of the
season, & I am, Sir!

Your very humble serv^t

ffor /
H. P.

  the Revd Mr Wright Haws
    at Siresham
          This

Both Mr Robotham and Mr Moulson were sent a chine and a turkey,
but there was a little delay, so perhaps the rector failed to buy at
3*d.* or under.

No. 565. E. P. *to* HARRY WALLBANK

Shalstone
June the 17th 1745

Sir! /

  My son being one of the Commissioners ab^t the Charity at
Gawcot[1] attends at the Crosskeys on Wensday next & if it is
agreeable to you & Miss Bet: I will take a Commons with you
on that day & be with you between one & two a clock. Let mee
know by the bearer if you are not otherwise engaged. Our compliments attend you all & I am

Your humble serv^t

ffor /
E. P.

  Mr Wallbank a Surgeon
    at Buckingham
          This

The following letters, written within a fortnight of each other, form
an interesting pair.

1 It is not clear why Gawcot[t] is mentioned; the Commissioners actually
met at the Town Hall, Buckingham, and dined at the Cross Keys Inn there.
The Charity was that founded by Sir Simon Bennett, of Calverton, in 1631,
and included a sum of about £20 p.a. for the poor of Buckingham; the
income arose from the impropriate tithes of the manor of Bourton, adjoining
Buckingham (*Victoria County Hist.* vol. IV, p. 310). The Commissioners were a
very distinguished body including Sir Charles Tyrell, Mr Lowndes (thrice
knight of the shire), Mr Denton, Mr Risley, Mr Pollard, and the great Browne
Willis. On 9 July Henry paid Mr Risley his "share of the Reckoning when
the Com^{rs} met about the Charity of Sr Simon Bennett"—5*s.*

No. 566. H. P. *to* HARRY WALLBANK

Shalstone
September ye 21th 1745

Sir ! /

Since you are so oblidging to give us an Invitation wee intend to come & take a commons with you toomorrow about one a clock & hope wee shall have your good company. Our compliments attend you all & I am Sir !

Your humble servant
H. P.

ffor /
Mr Wallbank a Surgeon
at Buckingham
This

The Diary shows that they actually went, on Saturday, 21 Sept., "to Mr Wallbank's at Buckingham on visiting"; the date of the letter is presumably a slip, it must have been written on the 20th.

No. 567. E. P. *to* HARRY WALLBANK

Shalstone
October the 5th 1745

I expected Mr Wallbank would have sent mee word by the Postboy when my son should have come to receive ye money of him, which you not having done I desire you will appoint a day that you will pay it, by this day fortnight. Our compliments attend you all & your answer hereto by ye bearer will oblidge

Your hte servant
E. P.

ffor /
Mr Wallbank a Surgeon
at Buckingham
This

Perhaps the money came promptly, for the very next day the son writes in a very different tone.

No. 568. H. P. *to* HARRY WALLBANK

Shalstone
Sunday 6th of Octob^r 1745

Sir ! /

Our maid Betty Evans whose sister lives with Mr Thompson tells us Mr Thompson intends us ye favour to dine with us. I suppose hee will come from Buckingham; wee shall be in hopes of seeing you & Miss Betty & Mr Passelow with him. It would be kind if you would let us know ye day before that wee may be at home. Our compliments attend you all & I am

Your humble servant
H. P.

ffor /
   Mr Wallbank a surgeon
     at Buckingham
         This

No. 569. H. P. *to* RISLEY RISLEY

Shalstone
Sir! /
August the 10th 1746

I am summoned on the Grand Jury, but since that have an unexpected call to Northampton, but shall return home by Thursday night. I must entreat y^e favour of you to make my excuse to the Judge (when I am called over) for my non=attendance, wch will much oblidge

Your most humble servant
H. P.

P.S. Our compliments attend yourself & Mrs Risley & Mrs Hook, & hope for the favour of your company's at Shalstone soon

ffor /
   Risley Risley^1 Esq
   at Chetwood /
         This

As it turned out, the excuse was not very good because, after rising at 4.0 a.m. on 12 August, "wee were in ye Coach setting out for Northampton, but the Revd Mr Haws fell from his horse in Shalstone street by Salmon's house that was pulled down, wch prevented our Journey".

A week later Henry had the chance of explaining matters to Mr Risley because they met at Whaddon Hall, where there was a dinner-party. The Rev. Mr Hawes had recovered from his fall for he was present, and so were Mr Wallbank, the surgeon, Dr Knap, the physician, Mr Prance,^{2} the mayor of Buckingham, and the Rev. Edward Troutbeck, the vicar of Westbury. "Mr Brown Willis & his 3 Daughters, & his 2 men servants & servant maid" received them.

1 The Risleys acquired the manor of Chetwode Priory at the Dissolution, Risley Brewer succeeded his uncle and took the name of Risley in 1739; he was sheriff 1744, and died 1755 (*Victoria County Hist.* vol. IV, p. 166). A slab just in the middle of the chancel in Chetwode Church says: "He was a gentleman of great hospitality".
2 Lipscomb gives the name as Thomas France.

No. 570. H. P. *to* JOHN WENTWORTH [CRESSWELL]

Shalstone
Sunday August 24ᵗʰ 1746

Sir!

They act the Play at Westbury too morrow night to be sure, & they say they also act on Wensday night & ffriday night next. I hope you will favour us with your Company too morrow at Dinner & to take a Bed with us. Your answer by yᵉ bearer will oblidge

Your most humble servant
H. P.

P.S. Our compliments attend yourself & Mʳˢ Wentworth

ffor /
  John Wentworth Cresswell Esq
      at Lillingston Lovell
                    This

The Wentworths did not come; the Purefoys attended Friday's performance (we do not learn the name of the play) "at Mʳ Campbell Price's". For an account of the Price family see Letter No. 583 *ad finem*.

No. 571. H. P. *to* SAMUEL PASHLER [PASSELOW]

Shalstone
Octob: the 4ᵗʰ 1746

Sir! /

I shall let down my fish pond on Tuesday morning next & entreat yᵉ favour of your Company about 10 a clock. Pray don't mention yᵉ fishing to any body. My mother joins with mee in our Compliments to self & Mʳ Wallbank & Miss Barrett & I am Sir!

Your humble servant
H. P.

ffor /
  Mʳ Passelow at Mʳ Wallbanks
    at Buckingham
                 This

On Tuesday, 8 October, Henry was "at the Pond bank on ffishing the upper pond"; the rector attended and various others, including "two little boys who stood by the upper pond", but Mr Passelow was not present. On 29 Sep. 1743 Goodman Archer of Tingewick and another man received 1s. "for fishing the Roundabout Pond".

No. 572. E. P. *to* THE REV. DR DAVID TRIMNELL

Shalstone [*&c.*]
Octob.ʳ the 4.ᵗʰ 1747

Sir! /

I am favoured with yours dated the 19ᵗʰ of last month & am much obliged to you for your kind invitation to Lincoln, but the winter comes on so fast that wee durst not afford ourselves the pleasure of waiting on you there; but if you should come into this Countrey before the Astrop Season wee shall be proud to wait on you & your ffamily at Shalstone. Since I had yᵉ favour of seeing you last my son has had the Jaundice & hee was so bad wᵗʰ it that I was afraid I should have lost him, but I thank God now hee is somewhat recovered. [Wee are obliged to you for your good Intentions but]¹ the Match you propose is no ways agreeable. Pray make our Compliments acceptable to Mʳˢ Trimnell & Miss & accept the same from Sir!

Your very humble servant

ffor /

E. P.

The Revᵈ Dʳ Trimnell
at Lincoln
By way of London

Is it possible to assume from the penultimate sentence that a match between "Miss" and Henry had been suggested? This letter is addressed to David Trimnell, born in 1675 at Abbots Ripton, Hunts, and a member of a family which was well versed in church preferment, one of his brothers becoming Bishop of Norwich and later of Winchester; whilst two more held livings. David matriculated at New College, Oxford, in 1693, was made M.A. in 1701, and D.D. in 1716. In 1708 he was made rector of Stoke Hammond, Bucks, and apparently retained the living until his death in 1756. He was made Archdeacon of Leicester in the Cathedral Church of Lincoln 17 May 1715, and Precentor of the same Cathedral in 1718; in that capacity he took precedence after the Dean, and so lived at Lincoln. He was a constant visitor at Astrop Wells, and Henry Purefoy also met him occasionally at the Assizes at Buckingham. (See Foster, *Alumni*, 1892, vol. IV, p. 1510. The editor is indebted to Canon Foster, F.S.A., for some of the above facts.)

¹ The words in brackets have been interlined in order to tone down the refusal.

No. 573. E. P. *to* CATHERINE WILLIS

Shalstone
May the 28th 1748

This is to acquaint Miss Catherine Willis that I expect to go from Home very suddenly, so can have no thoughts of waiting on you to Lord Cobham's Gardens, and give you this Trouble that you might not be disappointed. My son joins with mee in our Compliments to yourself & all your ffamily & I am

Your humble servant
E. P.

ffor /
    Miss Catherine Willis at Brown
    Willis's Esq. at Whaddon Hall
           This

Possibly this was a polite refusal, as there is no other evidence of a contemplated journey and they did not in fact leave home at all; a week later mother and son invited themselves to dine with the Wallbanks.

There is a famous account of Browne Willis's daughters in a letter by Miss Talbot; she says that there were two "Lambs", "very good and very insipid", and two "Lions" who had "a little spirit of rebellion, that makes them infinitely more agreeable than their sober sisters" (Nichol's *Literary Anecdotes* (1812–1815), vol. VI, p. 204).

There were actually five sisters, and Catherine, to whom this letter is directed, was a twin with Gertrude, according to the pedigree given by Lipscomb (vol. IV, p. 11). We do not know whether they were Lions or Lambs.

On 21 Aug. 1749 the Purefoys dined at Whaddon Hall and "Miss Kitty and Miss Gatty" are mentioned, so is another sister Mary, who was the wife of the Rev. Edward Harvey. "Mr Owen (keeper of the Bodleian)" was also there.

No. 574. H. P. *to* JOHN WENTWORTH [CRESSWELL]

Shalstone
Octob^r the 22th 1748

Sir! /

My mother has a She ass & foall about 2 months old; if you or Mrs Wentworth have a mind to drink the milk my mother will lend it you as long as you have occasion for it, if you please to send a servant over for it. Wee beg leave to desire yourself & M.rs Wentworth to accept of our Compliments & I am Sir!

Your very true servant

ffor /
   John Wentworth Esq.
   at Lillingston Lovell
        This

H. P.

No. 575. H. P. *to* SAMUEL PASHLER

Shalstone
Sunday, August the 27.th 1749

Sir! /

I shall have an haunch of young fat Venison for dinner on Tuesday next & desire the favour of yours or M.r Wallbank's and Miss Barrett's good company to eat some of it. M.r & M.rs Haws will be with us then & dinner will be on y.e Table by 2 o'clock. I hope for your answer by the Bearer that wee shall see you. My mother joins with mee in our compliments & I am in hast, Sir!

Your very true servant

ffor /
   M.r Pashler at
        Buckingham
        This

H. P.

The Diary of 29 August records that "young M.r Pashler of Buckingham, the Rev.d M.r Haws and his wife" profited by the invitation.

No. 576. H. P. *to* THE REV. DR BOWLES

Shalstone
August the 15.th 1750

Sir! /

Wee propose to go to Astrop on ffriday morning next & hope for your good Company's, having two places in the Coach for you. Shall call on you about 8 o'clock & with our Compliments to you all I am in hast, Sir! /

Your very humble serv.t

ffor /
   The Rev.d D.r Bowles
    at Brackley
        This

H. P.

On Friday, 17 August, they went accordingly, taking with them the Rev. Doctor, his wife, son, Miss Lisle Bowles,[1] and one of her sisters. There was quite a crowd there: "Lord Lymington & the honŏble Master Wallops his three brothers, young Master Cartwright of Aynho & his Tutor the Revd Mr Parker,[2] Sr. Henry D'Anvers, the Revd Dr Trimnell, the Revd Dr Grey & his wife, Captn Thicknesse, the woman at the well, Dr Brown Willis, a clergyman whose name I have forgot"— and many others, named and nameless.

Viscount Lymington was so called in 1743 when his father took the title of Earl of Portsmouth; he was born in 1718, married 1740, M.P. 1741–9, and died in 1749. The three brothers with him at Astrop all predeceased him, and his son succeeded to his grandfather's titles in 1762.[3] The Cartwrights had lived at Aynhoe since 1615;[4] the Danvers had been at Culworth since 1439,[5] and continued there until the death of the last baronet in 1775. The Rev. Dr Grey was author of *Memoria Technica* and was rector of Hinton and chaplain to the great Nathaniel Crewe, Dean of Chichester, Bishop of Oxford, Bishop of Durham, and, after his brother's death, Lord Crewe of Steane. He married Joyce, sister of Philip Thicknesse, which probably explains the presence of Capt. Thicknesse at Astrop.[6] More will be said of him presently.

Tradition ascribes the chalybeate blessings of Astrop Well to St Rumbold who was born at Kings Sutton hard by; he is also associated with Buckingham, though he only lived three days, and his name is preserved there in "St Rumbold's Lane".

More historic discovery of the virtues of the waters is ascribed by Anthony à Wood to Dr Richard Lower in 1664; Aubrey gives Dr Thomas Willis, grandfather of Browne Willis, credit for it, and John Morton in 1712 says[7] that the spring "has been of note now above 40 years". This is supported by the account of it given by Celia Fiennes[8] in the time of William III: "Thence I went to Astrop where is a Steelé water much ffrequented by ye Gentry, it has some mixture of Allum so is not so strong as Tunbridge. There is a ffine Gravell Walke that is between 2 high Cutt hedges where is a Roome for the Musick and a Roome for ye Company besides ye Private walks. The well

1 Fermor Lisle (see Letter No. 561) had presented the Rev. Doctor, who had married his sister Elizabeth, to the living of Brackley in 1729 (Baker, *Northants*, vol. I, pp. 576 and 612).
2 A fortnight later the Diary calls the tutor "the irreverend Mr Parker". The young man was Thomas (1736–1772), whose marriage to the daughter of Gen. Desaguliers took many splendid pictures to Aynhoe Hall, where they still remain; the lady's own portrait by Hogarth is also there.
3 G. E. C., *Complete Peerage*, 1895, vol. VI, p. 280.
4 Bridges, *Northants*, vol. I, p. 137; Baker, *Northants*, vol. I, p. 548.
5 Baker, *Northants*, vol. I, p. 605.
6 H. A. Evans, *Highways and Byways in Northants*, 1924, Chapter XVII.
7 *Natural History of Northants*, p. 281.
8 *Through England on a Side Saddle*, 1888, p. 23.

To face p. 388

Plate 24. ASTROP WELL

runnes very quick, they are not curious in keepeing it, neither is there any bason for the spring to run out off, only a dirty well full of Moss's which is all changed yellow by the water. There are Lodgings about for ye Company and a little place called Sutton".

According to Baker,[1] Dr Radcliffe of Oxford patronized it "and in 1749 a new well at Sutton, half a mile from the old Spa, was opened. Astrop was then in the height of its popularity and could boast of its public ball every Monday, and breakfasts, cards, dancing, and ordinaries for ladies and gentlemen every Friday during the season". William Bray says[2] the well is "now out of fashion. The lodging houses are miserable. Dr Short says nature and art have combined to make this a paradise of pleasure,—I doubt it will require a warm imagination to discover in it any resemblance of what we suppose Paradise to be". It is only fair to give Dr Short's account of the Spa in 1740, as it is extremely good and tells us much of interest; the well-water, he tells us,[3] "is the product of Lime Stone, Iron Stone, and sandy Clay, in which may be found calcarious and ferruginous petrefactions, full of shells, and, in the Clay below, the Selenites. The water is a noble, brisk, very spiritous, clear pleasant tasted chalybeate, considerably lighter than common water, it springs up into a close strong Bason full of holes at bottom, and empties itself by a long neat gutter, cut out of Freestone, both which it lines with a ragg'd small furr, of a light pale coloured Ochre, and all along its course leaves a strong variegated scum...the spring discharges between 3 and 400 gallons of Water in an Hour. So very subtle and volatile is its Chalybeate Spirit, any solid ponderous Body laid a few days in the Bason, contracts an indelible black colour; the same Tincture it gives the Fæces of its Drinkers, and sometimes to their mouth and teeth. On the same side of the Brook with the Well is a house with pallisadoes before it, from this the Company go under a Shelter into another very large Sashed, Wainscoted, boarded floor room, where they walk, drink coffee or Tea, and in the afternoon meet, converse, or entertain themselves with some Diversions; out of and behind this is a noble, dry, fine gravel walk 140 yards long, 6 broad, with a charming close set clipp'd hedge 12 foot high, with several neat Benches on each side; at the far end of it is a stately large garden house, where at right angles from this turns off another shaded walk 45 yards long, at the end of which are conveniences for the drinkers to retire when their Waters operate. On the other side of the brook from the Well, is a fine Tea Room, dancing room, and a large Kitchin &c, and near this a convenient shop. In the Town there is a large Ball or Assembly Room. Thus Nature and Art have combined to make it a paradise of pleasure".

1 *History of Northants*, vol. 1, p. 703.
2 *Sketch of a Tour*, etc., 2nd edit. 1783, p. 29.
3 *The Natural Experimental and Medicinal History of Mineral Waters*, vol. II, p. 47, 1740. The same account was abbreviated, and by no means improved, by Dr John Rutty in *A Methodical Synopsis of Mineral Waters*, 1757.

One feels at least that Dr Short speaks from first-hand knowledge; to-day none of these buildings stands, but the "noble gravel walk" is indicated. The doctor then proceeds to describe the therapeutic qualities of the waters, which he declares to be "singularly good in the first, and beginning of the second stage of consumption; seldom fail in the Jandice, or beginning Dropsies, effectually restore a Constitution shattered by hard Drinking, they are sovereign in Rheumatic pains, stone and gravel; and have restored several that have been melancholly or maniac from Hyppo or Hysteric. But such as reap this surprising Benefit from this Water never drink less than from 3 to 5 Quarts in a forenoon, a sure sign that the modish quantity of a pint and a half, or a Quart is wrong, and as seldom answers with such general great Success".

Whilst all the buildings have gone, except a ruined cottage where perhaps the keeper of the well lived, the well itself remains, and Plate 24 makes a detailed description unnecessary; the water issues from a pipe opposite to the structure shown in a paved enclosure, measuring about 3 yards by 2 yards; the stones forming the floor are discoloured and the water has a faint but agreeable taste of chalybeate. The later well[1] in the village is a replica of the old one, and the water there flowed freely during the drought in the autumn of 1929; a year later it flowed strongly from both wells.

The Purefoys always visited the well during August and September; in 1750 they were there fourteen times between 13 Aug. and 2 Oct. In 1751 eight visits were paid between 19 Aug. and 24 Sept., and in 1752 nine visits between 10 Aug. and 2 Oct. In 1751 besides the local families "the Lady Lucy & Lady Susan Sherrards" were visitors; these were the daughters of Philip, second Earl of Harborough (1680–1750); the first-named died in 1781, the second in 1765.[2] "Breakfasts" were given by local people, Lord Chief Justice Willes,[3] the owner of the Park in which the well is, gave the breakfast on 17 Aug. 1752, Lord Cobham and Mr Richard Dayrell were present amongst many others; on another occasion the Earl of Dalkeith was host.[4] On 9 Sept.

1 The new well, as has been said, was opened in 1749, and, says Baker (vol. I, p. 703), "a breakfast given by Anthony Keck esq, of Leicestershire, in gratitude for the benefit he had received". Henry was present at "Mr Keck's breakfast at Astrop Wells" on Friday, 25 Aug. 1749. Anthony Keck was a Serjeant of Lincoln's Inn; he acquired Stoughton and Thurnby, Co. Leicester, by marriage with Anne Busby, and died 1786. (J. Nichols, *History of Leicester*, vol. II, part II, p. 847.)

2 Nichols, *Leicestershire*, vol. II, p. 346; they were presumably sisters of Bennet, third Earl Harborough, who married the sister of the second Earl Verney, (*Verney Letters of the Eighteenth Century*, vol. II, pp. 236 et seq.)

3 Sir John Willes was a native of Warwick, he was made Chief Justice in 1737 and died in 1761 (Baker, *Northants*, vol. I, p. 695). In 1735 he had acquired the manor of Kings Sutton by purchase from George Kenwick (whose family had held it since 1598), and to this estate he added freeholds in Astrop where he built his seat (Oswald Barron, *Northants Families*, 1905, p. 346).

4 This was the son of the second Duke of Buccleugh, he died at Adderbury, Oxon, in 1750; the breakfast was in 1748.

1755 "the two Master Aubreys and the Lady Say & Seal" were there. The Aubreys were probably sons of Sir Thomas Aubrey, the 5th baronet of Boarstall; Christina, Viscountess Say and Sele, was a very famous lady, of uncertain age but nearing 100 when she died in 1789. She was the daughter of Sir T. Tyrrell of Castlethorpe, and married firstly John Knap, secondly John Pigot of Doddershall, and lastly Richard, 6th Viscount Say & Sele; she was both a beauty and a wit, and said that "she had chosen her first husband for love, her second for riches, and her third for honours; and that she now had some thoughts of beginning again in the same order".[1] Another notable and constant visitor, already mentioned, was the Rev. Dr Richard Grey, and his wife, who was Joyce Thicknesse; her brother Philip Thicknesse tells the story of her being wooed and won and says that Mr Grey was with Joyce and her mother in the garden and "after walking round and round her several times and admiring her person, 'Well', said he, 'Miss Joyce, I own you are too good for me; but at the same time I think myself too good for anybody else'".[2]

In the Diaries one catches glimpses of all kinds of people: "Mrs Watson who keeps the gaming room", "Mrs Towzey of the Gaming room", "the fiddler who collected the money", "a stranger gentleman in a gold Buttoned coat", "a young woman who gave mee silver for half a guinea", and people who sold peaches and "catchup". The game which Henry played was Commerce; on one occasion Miss Sally Willes played with him, on another "Mr Wills (son to the Ld. Cheif Justice) played my cards for mee". On 1 Sept. 1748 we have a reference to "a young lady I danced right hand & left with on the walk"; and on 17 Aug. 1741 we hear of "the Parson who brought mee the Walk Book, and the stranger gentleman who askt mee to play at whisk".

Their visits to Astrop provide numerous entries in the Account-books and prove that they were not expensive:

1736 Aug 12.	Paid our John for him & Ned May to drink & for the standing of yᵉ horses at Astrop	00 : 01 : 06	
— Sep 2	Paid Mrs Budd of Astrop for coffee & tea	00 : 02 : 06	
1741 Aug 17	Paid for our breakfast at Mrs Towzey's at Astrop	00 : 02 : 00	

1 This is given by Lipscomb (*History of Bucks*, vol. I, p. 410) "from actual reminiscences". The *Gentleman's Magazine* of 1789 (vol. LIX, pt 2, p. 764) gives a most agreeable picture of her: "The late Viscountess dressed even at the close of her life more like a girl of 18 than a woman of 90. Her favourite colour in ribbons was pink, and even in the present year she wore muslin gowns and gauze trimmed with ribbons of this colour. Her favourite amusement was dancing and she indulged in it almost to the last week of her life. Her ladyship had an excellent heart, and wishing to see every one as cheerful as herself, if the want of money made them sad, her purse was generously at their service".

2 *Memoirs and Anecdotes of Philip Thicknesse*, 1788, p. 12.

1747 Aug 10	Paid to the Walks & Musick at Astrop	00 : 03 : 00
1750 Aug 13	Gave the woman at the well at Astrop	00 : 02 : 00
—	Paid for breakfast at Astrop	00 : 00 : 06
— Sep 17	Paid my mother Purefoy for two expences at Astrop that was my share thereof to ffriday last	00 : 02 : 10

One of the occasional visitors at Astrop was Mrs Wodhull of Thenford; she was probably the second wife of John Wodhull whom we shall meet later,[1] and mother of the famous classical scholar and book-collector Michael Wodhull, who published a volume of (very dull) poems in 1804. One of these is called "The Tears of Astrop"; it has no local colour, it must be admitted, but a few convivial lines[2] may serve to close this note, already too long:

> "Can the blest swains of Astrop pine,
> When, crown'd with Amalthean horn,
> Such savoury cates, such floods of wine,
> Such slaughter'd hecatombs of geese,
> This chosen* festival t'adorn,
> September, bounteous God, presents?"

* Michaelmas-day, annually commemorated at Astrop Wells in Northamptonshire.

No. 577. H. P. *to* THE REV. WILLIAM FLETCHER

Shalstone
Tuesday Septemb^r *the 10*th *1751*

Wee shall be glad to see M^r & M^{rs} ffletcher & Miss Sill to dine with us too morrow on an haunch of Venison & hope you will not faill to favour us with your Company then, your answer ℔ bearer will oblidge

Your humble servant
H. P.

P.S. Wee both join in our Compliments to you all.

ffor /
   The Rev^d M^r W^m ffletcher
  at   Croton
       This

Mr Fletcher was apparently he who was curate to Mr Price at Whitfield (see Letter No. 560); and afterwards to Mr Lloyd, rector of Croughton; Henry attended the christening of his son William on 24 Aug. 1752,

1 See Letter No. 590.
2 Epistle III, Book I, p. 116 of the edition quoted.

and acted as godfather. Canon J. Willis Price, the present rector of
Croughton, is kind enough to furnish extracts from the registers relating
to Mr Fletcher's family (William, for instance, was buried 3 Oct. 1769);
he thinks that Mr Fletcher was curate at Croughton from 1750 to 1769.

No. 578. H. P. *to* SAMUEL PASHLER

Shalstone
October the 21ᵗʰ 1752

Sir! /

I have considered further of the affair you was mentioning to
mee and as I live 3 miles from Buckingham it will be impossible
for mee to act as a Justice[1] for your Corporation on account of
my ill state of Health; so there will be no occasion for mee to
wait on my Lord on Tuesday.

Shall be glad to wait on you & Mr Wallbank & Miss Barrett
here whenever your leisure will permitt & with our compliments
to you all am Sir!

Your very humble servt
H. P.

ffor /
Mr Pashler at
Buckingham
    This

No. 579. E. P. *to* MRS DALBY

Shalstone
September yᵉ 20ᵗʰ 1753

Madam /

I have received my Hatt & handkercheif & find a bill in it of
twelve shillings & ten pence.

I find my son had the good fortune to winn yᵉ pool; my son
was in such an Hurry hee could not ask you what the Pooll

---

1 Henry had been made a J.P. in 1737, but he never mentions acting as a
magistrate; we have a record of the fact in an Account-book for that year:

Apr. 21th Paid the Landlord at the George inne at Ailesbury my reckoning	00 : 04 : 09
Gave the Hostler & maid there 6ᵈ apeice	00 : 01 : 00
24th Paid Mr Scott the Sheriff's officer for bringing me my certificate of my taking yᵉ Oaths &c.	00 : 02 : 06
21th Paid Mr Hayton the Clᵏ of the Peace for my taking the Oaths in Cotᵗ & for my certificate	00 : 04 : 00

amounted to, but if it don't reach the twelve shillings & ten pence I will pay ye Remainder wth Thanks, & hope to meet you at Astrop toomorrow or on Monday & am

Your humble servant
E. P.

ffor /
Mrs Dalby at
Croton /
This

No. 580. E. P. *to* MRS MARY PRICE

Shalstone
March ye 1st 1748

This is to acquaint Mrs Price my son is oblidged to go to Ailesbury Assizes & I should be glad of your Company for about a week during his abscence, if you are not otherwise engaged. If you have not a conveniency of coming I will send ye saddle Horses for you about 11 a clock on Saturday morning next, or on what other hour you shall appoint. Our compliments attend you all & your answer by ye Bearer will oblidge

Your humble servant
E. P.

ffor /
Mrs Mary Price at
Whitfeild
This

No. 581. H. P. *to* BROWNE WILLIS

Shalstone
January 29th 1750

Sir! /

I am favoured with yours of the 25th of this instant & as to Mr Minshull's ffamily, the Q^{rys} you want to be satisfied about I have enquired after & are as follows:—

1st Q^{ry} What time Mr Richd Minshull (the Horse racer) left Boreton?

Ans^r It was about ye year 1711 when I myself saw 8 or 10 of his Racehorses breathed on ye Common or Green by Monk's house on Straw Litter for a mile round, it being a very hard frost & as I suppose to save his Horses' ffeet.

2ᵈ Qʳʸ Who Mʳ Minshull the Horse racer's mother was?

Ansʳ His mother was Daughter to [Francis] ffinch of Worcester-shire Esq, & reputed a very shrewd & notable Lady for management &c.

3ᵈ Qʳʸ Where Mʳ Richard Minshull the horse racer's father Min-shull died?

Ansʳ After hee had resigned Boreton to the Horse racer hee lived & died at Barton juxta Chetwood in Com̃ Bucks & as it is supposed was buried in the Minshull's Vault in Buckingham Church.

4ᵗʰ Qʳʸ Whose Dauʳ Mʳ Richard Minshull (the horse racer's wife) was?

Ansʳ She was Dauʳ to Sʳ Walter Blount who (I think) lived in Staffordshire but Mʳ Wentworth can tell you where Sʳ Walter Blount lived.

5ᵗʰ Qʳʸ Where Mʳ Richard Minshull (the horse racer) was buried and where he dyed?

Ansʳ Hee died in yᵉ Kings bench prison but what year I can't tell, nor where hee was buried.

Francis Poulton (the weak bigotted papist as you call him,) had an Annuity of £60 a year paid him for his Life by that Mʳ Minshull who cheated him out of his Estate, & there is an old Steward of the Minshull's family now (or lately) alive at Bucking-ham who has seen severall of these rectˢ under ffrancis Poulton's hand for this Annuity amongst Minshull's papers.[1]

Mʳ ffrancis Ingoldsby died in the Charterhouse (where hee was a pensioner) but where buried—cannot find out.

I have some articles of my own family to incert in your Book wᶜʰ if you'll do yᵉ favour to call, & you & your folks to do us the favour to take a bed with us, shall impart to you & am with all due esteem Sir! /

Your obligded hie servant
H. P.

P.S. My mother joins with mee in desiring you to accept of the Compliments of the Season.

ffor /
   Brown Willis Esq Dʳ of Laws
      This

---

1 Browne Willis (*History of Buckingham*, p. 31), used the substance of this paragraph and the actual phrase about Francis Poulton.

The connection of the Minshull family with the manor of Bourton, by Buckingham, lasted for about a century from 1634.[1] The Richard Minshull who owned it in 1642 was an ardent Royalist, and when he was away from home on the King's service, his house was raided by Lord Brooke's troops; a long account occurs in *Mercurius Rusticus*, Chapter IV.

The Ingoldsby family owned the manor of Lenborough, on the other side of the Borough of Buckingham, from the end of the fifteenth century until the end of the seventeenth century.[2] They were equally active supporters of the Parliament, and Sir Richard married Elizabeth, daughter of Sir Oliver, and cousin of the Protector. In the eighteenth century this estate was owned by no less a person than Gibbon, the historian, who had some trouble in selling it.[3]

No. 582.   H. P. *to* BROWNE WILLIS

Shalstone
ffebruary 2ᵈ 1750

Sir! /

I am heartily sorry to hear you are indisposed with a cold & wish your speedy recovery, for if it should please God to take you from us the losse of you would be very sensibly felt. I return many thanks for yᵉ sketch of your History of Bucks you sent mee to look over, & as to Mʳ Minshull's affair Mʳ ffrancis Garvan of the inner Temple in the year 1720 told mee that Dick Minshull the Horse racer presently after yᵉ peace of Reswick, sent a set of fine horses down to Dover to be exported to Sᵗ Germains as a present to the late King James yᵉ second, but the then officers of the port of Dover, getting intelligence that Minshull was a Papist, seized these horses for the Government's use, they being above yᵉ vallue of £5. This Disappointmᵗ piqued Minshull so far that hee declared hee would have as fine horses as any man in England for all the Government, & immediately set up=on breeding & running race horses, & this unhappy branch of conduct hee used to lament & acknowledge was the Occasion & Rise of all his future misfortunes; for I never heard hee was Gamester either at Cards or Dice. As to Mʳ Garvan hee was a Catholick Gentleman & I was favoured with his ffreindship & acquaintance. Hee was a very

1 *Victoria County History*, vol. III, p. 482.
2 *Victoria County History*, vol. III, p. 483.
3 Gibbon's *Private Letters*, 1896, vol. I, p. 186, vol. II, p. 83, and *Autobiographies*, p. 290. According to Browne Willis (*op. cit.* p. 36), Gibbon (the historian's father) pulled down some of the "Capital Manor House"; it still remains a good structure.

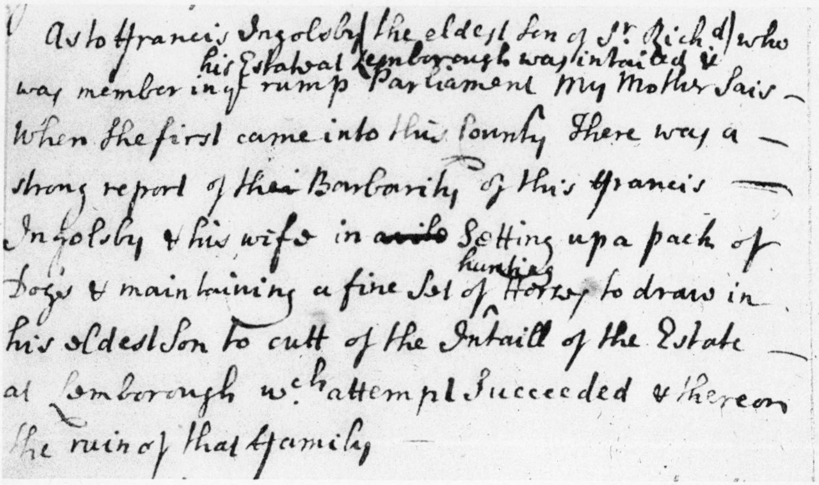

As to Francis Ingolsby (the eldest Son of Sr. Richd.) who
his Estate at Lemborough was intailed &
was member in ye rump Parliament My Mother Sais —
When She first came into this County There was a —
strong report of the Barbarity of this Francis —
Ingolsby & his wife in ~~avile~~ Setting up a pack of
hunting
Dogs & maintaining a fine Set of ^ Horses to draw in
his Oldest Son to cutt of the Intaill of the Estate —
at Lemborough wch attempt Succeeded & thereon
the ruin of that Family —

(*a*)

As to Francis Ingolsby (the oldest Son of Sr. Richard) who was member in the —
Rump Parliament his Estate at Lemborough was entailed & my Mother Sais When
She first came into this County There was a strong Report of the Barbarity of this Francis
Ingolsby & his Wife in setting up a pack of Dogs & maintaining a fine Set of Hunting —

Horses to draw in his Oldest Son to cutt of the Intaill of the Estate at Lemborough
wch attempt succeeded & Thereon the ruin of that Family

(*b*)

H Purefoy

To face p. 396

Plate 25. FACSIMILES OF LETTER NO. 582

(*a*) FROM THE LETTER-BOOK

(*b*) FROM THE LETTER ACTUALLY SENT

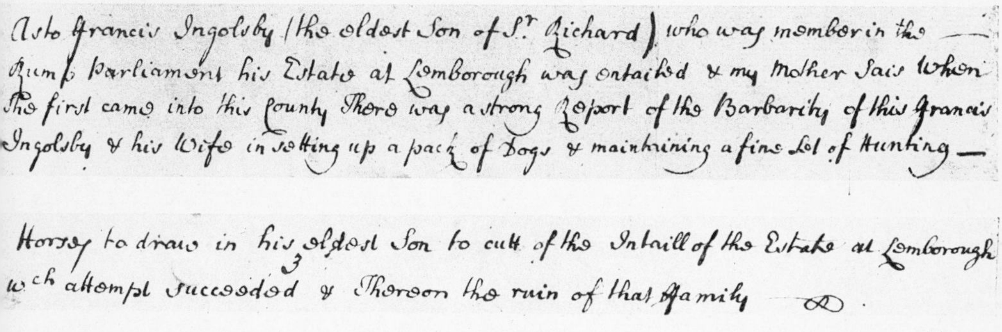

polite gentleman & a man of veracity & much admired & esteemed by late Ld North & Grey & the Visc.^t Mountague of Sussex as well as by everybody else who knew him, & I have been at his Chambers in 1720; they were near the Cloysters in the Inner Temple; his home was in the County of Clare in Ireland & his estate there reckoned about £1.000 a year. This I mention if you should have further curiosity to enquire after Minshull, for Garvan knew as much of him in his Decline of Life as anybody.

As to my own ffamily my great Grandfather George Purefoy kept two coaches & six horses at Wadley in Berks, & fed the neighbouring poor in so plentifull a manner at his Porter's Lodge that at night his servants have brought two basons full of the Twigs of birch brooms to him, every twig denoting a person who rece^d his alms, that hee might know next time what Quantity of Victualls to provide for them; in so grand & hospitable a manner did hee live.

As to ffrancis Ingolsby (the eldest son of Sr. Richard) who was member in ye Rump Parliament, his estate at Lenborough was intailed, & my mother sais when she first came into this county there was a strong report of the Barbarity of this ffrancis Ingolsby & his wife in setting up a pack of Dogs & maintaining a fine set of hunting horses to draw in his eldest son to cutt of[f] the Intaill of the estate at Lemborough, wch attempt succeeded & thereon the ruin of that ffamily.

As to Sr George Moor[1] of Maids Moreton hee was created a Barr.^t 26th July 1665 & as I imagine passed over his estate there to Dr Bate[2] Physician to Oliver Cromwell & King Charles the 2.^d,

[1] He was the son of a cutler, or some say of a grocer, in Fleet Street, and "got" a great estate near Henley. He owned Bobbing Court, Kent, and dying in 1678 was buried at Bobbing (G. E. C., *Complete Baronetage*, 1904, vol. IV, p. 23). If Lipscomb (vol. III, p. 41) is to be trusted, he was "an intimate acquaintance of the noted Titus Oates", which is small commendation for anyone. Lipscomb also says that after selling Maids' Moreton he "retired into Hertfordshire", but one expects that he copied this from Browne Willis (p. 230), who trusted to this letter. If Mrs Purefoy's Sir George had nineteen children he was unlucky to die *s.p.m.*

[2] Dr George Bate was also physician to Charles I when the Court was at Oxford, and was therefore able to enjoy successively the confidence of that unhappy monarch and of his son as well as that of the Protector; but he was a very able man, Fellow of the College of Physicians and of the Royal Society; Pepys thought highly of his *Elenchus Motuum*. He was born in 1608 at Maids' Moreton and died in London in 1669.

whose son[1] Justice Bates enjoyed the same after him, & to whose person and meritt and good Character you cannot be a stranger to. My mother sais when she was a Child & at M.ᵣ ffish her uncle's at Bellbar near Hatfeild in Hertfordshire, there was one S.ᵣ George Moore who hired a seat in a lane by Northall Common & had 19 children followed him & his lady to church there, & she thinks this S.ᵣ George Moor might be the person.

Wee are very much oblidged to you for your kind intentions of giving us your company here & hope the ways will permitt for us to see you here soon, & with our compliments I am Sir! very respectfully

Your most humble servant
H. P.

P.S. S.ᵣ Richard Ingolsby of Wallridge who signed the dead warrant &c. was made a Kn.ᵗ of the Bath at Coronation of King Charles the 2.ᵈ

ffor /
   Brown Willis Esq
   D.ᵣ of Laws at his
   seat at Whaddon
   To be left at the Crosse
   keys inne at Buckingham
       This

No. 583. H. P. to BROWNE WILLIS

Shalstone
ffebruary the 16.ᵗʰ 1750

Sir! /

I am favoured with yours dated the 12.ᵗʰ of this month & would gladly have waited on you at Whaddon hall, but I have received a letter from Town wherein I am informed that about this Time my Lord Duke of Grafton comes down with L.ᵈ Conway to Wakefeild lodge, & that his Grace gives mee leave to wait on him there[2] ab.ᵗ this unhappy affair of killing the Deer. So as soon as I am

---

1 Browne Willis speaks highly (*op. cit.* p. 229) of his son Edward, who was a J.P., not a judge, as one might think from Henry's expression; he calls him "a good Neighbour, and Friend". He died in 1717 and was buried at Maids' Moreton.
2 From the Diary-extract given after Letter No. 607 it will be seen that Lord Conway did accompany the duke.

certain his Grace is come down I intend to wait on him. As to your description of our County Town of Bucks I think it is very full & clear & done with much accuracy & Judgm.ᵗ The present M.ʳ Minshull lives at Ailesbury, is son to the horseracer's younger brother Minshull, & has about £1.000 a year, as young M.ʳ Pashler of Buckingham informs mee & was last year at Buckingham in his chariott & four. As to Stockholt house in Akeley Parish it belongs at present to the Earl of Salisbury¹ & one M.ʳ John Smith rents it of him.

As to old Colonell Wellsbourne Sill of Fulwell I know nothing of his pedigree² but my mother informs mee that his wife was a Shuckborough & a very prudent woman, & having a numerous issue by him left a considerable summe of money in a Topping ffarmers hands at Mixbury, unknown to her husband in order for him to give it her children as they should stand in need of it. But she herself died in Childbed & the ffarmer never gave the money to the children but abused his Trust & kept the money for himself; but according to the superstition of those times this M.ʳˢ Sill was reported to walk & haunt the ffarmer, & her ghost set his cows on fighting so that hee had severall sets of cows gored & killed one another & at last was reduced to poverty. However I find by my writings that in or about the year 1658 this Wellsborne Sill sold one yard land in Westbury Parish to one James Watts a farmer, & the Price's ffamily are reported to have bought the rest of his estate there. This M.ʳ Sill was a sad spendthrift & my mother has heard my father Purefoy say that when M.ʳ Sill came to y.ᵉ estate a Squirrell might passe from ffinmere parke to Mixbury Town thro' the Trees on Mixbury Warren without ever jumping from of[f] ye trees, the trees stood so thick together; but now there is not one tree standing on Mixbury Warren.

1 The Manor of Stockholt, together with manors in Beachampton and Calverton, came into possession of the Earls of Salisbury through the marriage of James Cecil to Frances, a great-niece of Sir Simon Bennet (see *Victoria County History*, vol. IV, pp. 146, 151 and 309, and *Records of Bucks*, vol. V, p. 130). It remained with the Earls of Salisbury until the close of the eighteenth century.

2 Sir John Wellesborne was resident at Fulwell in 1539; he was succeeded by his son John (1562–1611), whose daughter married someone named Sill, and two generations of Wellesborne Sills followed. All the family were "sound Churchmen and staunch Royalists" (J. C. Blomfield, *History of Mixbury*, 1890, p. 15).

This M.ʳ Sill's Chappell at ffulwell house is now Desecrated & turned into a Barn where they thresh Corn. Shuck Sill his son obtained leave of his father Wellsborne Sill to sell the furniture of the Chappell & the wainscot of the house, w.ᶜʰ hee did accordingly to my mother's knowledge.

As to the owners of the Mannor of Westbury by my writings I cannot trace it higher than S.ʳ L'Estrange Mordaunt who was lord thereof in King Charles the 1.ˢᵗ his time, & passed his right therein to one S.ʳ Lawrence Washington,[1] then of the Chancery Office, & S.ʳ Lawrence Washington's executors (being legally empowered) sold the said mannor (w.ᶜʰ had a numerous parcell of ab.ᵗ twenty petty ffreeholders in it,) to S.ʳ ——[2] Littleton of Worcestersh̃, Bar.ⁿᵗ, but it was a wofull purchase to him, for chancing to bring 5 or 6 hundred pounds more than occasion required to the Mannor House at Westbury, where the purchase Deeds were executed, as hee returned to his own home in his Coach & six over Mixbury Warren (then thick with trees & a nest of Robbers,) hee was assaulted there by a noted Rogue who was called Collonell Downs & his Gang, & tho' hee & his servants made a brave resistance they were over powered & S.ʳ —— Littleton was shot in his coach, & they went of[f] with their prize. But his servants raised the Countrey & pursued Downs so closely that hee venturing to leap his horse thro' a live Quick hedge his horse was catched in y.ᵉ hedge & hee taken Prisoner & was conveyed to Oxford Jayll where hee was tryed Ɔdemned & executed & very much by the Interest of my great grandfather George Purefoy who on this occasion stook close to his skirts. This S.ʳ —— Littleton's widow built the present Mannor House at Westbury, but on the losse of her eldest & favourite son grew beside herself, & hating Westbury, thereupon sold the estate to the present Price's ffamily without any consideration for the Timber then growing thereon, so that after the writings were executed her Steward asking her Ladyship

---

1 This is a slip, he was never knighted; the Washingtons sold Sulgrave in 1610, and Lawrence bought Westbury in 1621; Browne Willis says (p. 352) that Lawrence's son sold it in 1639. Lawrence emigrated to America with his brother John and was great-great-uncle of George Washington (Baker, *Northants*, vol. 1, p. 514).

2 Should be Sir Thomas Littleton; his youngest son George married the daughter of the great Sir Thomas Browne.

what Consideration was allowed for the Timber then growing on
the estate, she said "none at all", "Why then, madam," said hee,
"you have fairly given away the estate to the Prices for there is
now growing more Timber on the Estate than the estate is worth".
This account of S.ʳ ——— Littleton's being shot I had from old
W.ᵐ May of Warwick Castle in Bidlesden parish lately deceased
upwards of 80 years of age, & the other of Lady Littleton's selling
the estate to the Prices on these disadvantageous Terms I had
from Mary Hobcraft of Shalstone, who nursed mee when I was
a child & she was dau.ʳ to Chapman, M.ʳ Price's steward.

If I can be of any further service to you in this affair, if you
please to let mee know where you lodge in London you will
allways find mee Sir! with due regard

Your humble serv.ᵗ to command
H. P.

P.S. My mother joins with mee in our service & respects to
yourself & Miss Willis's, wishing you a good Journey.

ffor /
   Brown Willis Esq...
         Whaddon

Roger Price was a London merchant whose son was M.P. for Buckingham in 1702. The father died at Bilbao, Spain, in 1677, but was buried
at Westbury. The son died in 1694, and his son Thomas in 1733, the
estate then passed to Campbell Price (see Letter No. 570, the Rev. R.
Ussher, *History of Westbury*, p. 16, and the *Victoria County History*, vol. IV,
p. 264). He died in 1749 and Henry attended the sale of his furniture
which followed. (See Letter No. 178 n.).

No. 584. H. P. to PETER MOULSON

Shalstone...
ffebruary y.ᵉ 25.ᵗʰ 1740

Sir! /

I send you inclosed my Lottery tickett which I desire you will
sell for mee, for after the 15.ᵗʰ of this next March, as I am informed,
they won't be accepted; be so good to keep the money for it till
further orders. Wee received your kind present of oysters & sturgeon

wch were exceeding good, wee return you our hearty [thanks] for them.

The following Tragedy is true: on Saturday last the Revd Mr Burton[1] of Brackley in Nor͠thtonshire, his servant man being sawcy, hee ordered him to leave his service; instead of that hee went to work in the Barn amongst the rest of ye workmen. Mr Burton coming soon after into the barn hee spoke to him & bad him again go of[f] from his Ground wch the ffellow refusing to do in a sawcy manner Mr Burton stroke him over the back with his cane, on which the ffellow upt with a long fork hee had in his hand & stroke Mr Burton a blow on ye side of his head wch felled him down, & after a groan or two hee instantly dyed. The servants who were by, whilst one held Mr Burton up and the other run for a surgeon, the ffellow who murthered him made his Escape & is not yet taken.

The Clergyman was a man of as good parts & Learning as most in our Countrey & his death is much lamented, Sr Thos Abney the Councill married his sister.

My mother & self join in our Respects & Services to yourself & Miss Moulson & I am with due Esteem, Sir!

Your very h͠te servant
H. P.

ffor /
   Mr Moulson...
      London

P.S. As the Rascall made of[f], hee meeting a servant boy of Mr Burton's, hee told him hee had laid his master in his long sleep & gloryed in the wicked fact.

Pray favour mee with a line or two that the tickett is come safe to you and sold.

There is a brief mention of this incident in the *Northampton Mercury* of 2 March 1740 (O.S.); a fortnight later the same paper advertised a reward of ten guineas to anyone who could "apprehend Henry Kerwood so that he may be brought to Justice". The description of Kerwood follows: "about 5 feet 6 inches high, aged about 18 Years,

1 This was Littleton Burton (born 1676) who held various cures and was Chaplain to the Prince of Wales; he was buried in the College Chapel at Brackley. The full inscription on his grave contains no allusion to his tragic end (Baker, *History of Northants*, vol. i, p. 583). By his will made in 1732 he bequeathed the interest upon £50 to "poor housekeepers" of St Peter's, Brackley.

brown lank Hair, full Eyebrows, grey Eyes, round Shoulders, stoops forward in his walk, fresh Complexion and long Visage, had on when he absconded a light colour'd Coat, Leather breeches, and blue Stockings".

No. 585.   E. P. *to* THOMAS ROBOTHAM

Shalstone [*&c.*]
January y[e] *9*[th] *1745*

I received M[r] Robotham's Łre of 31st of last month together with a codfish, a Barrell of oysters, shrimps & 3 Herrings, for w[ch] wee return you thanks; you mention 6 herrings, I hope nobody took them out of the basket. The ffranks are very agreeable. I hope you rece͞d the hare I sent you last Wensday carriage paid. Hares grow very scarce or else you should have had another. I am sorry to hear there is such a bad Distemper amongst your Cows, I thank God wee have not one cow amiss at Shalstone, nor within twenty miles of us only at Shenley & Newnton Longueville; about 10 miles from hence one M[r] George bought a distempered cow of a London dealer & unfortunately putting her amongst his other Cows hee lost seventeen wc͞h were all hee had. There was the same case at Newnton Longueville, but I don't hear it has spread. Our Butcher, M[r] Ben: King told mee hee had 40 fat cows, the worst of them worth twelve pounds & if y[e] Distemper should fall upon his Cattle it would undo him. Before X[t']mas I had of him a rump & surloin & another Bitt that weighed 6 score pounds, the finest beef I ever eat. Our parishioners have sent a certificate to London that our cattle of all sorts are in good health,[1] so our butter and every thing wee send to Town from hence is highly accepted. My son joins with mee in our services to yourself & Nelly & I am

Your humble servant
E. P.

P.S. I desire in your next to let mee know the name of the fishmonger who sent these oysters & where hee lives, for they were very good, & give him directions to send mee a Barrell of such by M[r] Jones our carrier, who sets out of London at 2 a clock eu̇y Tuesday morning & at 8 a clock a Saturday morning, as

---

1 On 28 Nov. 1745 Henry, his mother, and the Rector set their hands to "a certificate that all our cattle at Shalstone are in good health. NB. This certificate was for young W[m] Strange".

also to send a dozen herrings if they be good & a Łre ℔ post of what they come to & when they come; if they prove well shall use him as our fishmonger.[1]

ffor /
    Mʳ Robotham...
                London.

No. 586. H. P. *to* CHRISTOPHER RIGBY

Shalstone
March yᵉ 6ᵗʰ 1753

Sir! /

My mother's Cookmaid, Sarah Bessant the bearer hereof, was set on by three men who bid her stand & deliver her Money as she came from Banbury ffair. Nicholls, as she sais, held the horse's Bridle whilst Boyle rifled her Pocket for money, but she had none about her so lost nothing. The man who was with her his horse brushed by them & got of[f.] This man & she are served with subpœnas to appear at your assizes as this day, but the man & she are both afraid they will attempt to force them to prosecute these Highwaymen, which will be more expence than she will be able to bear. It will be a great charity in you to put her in a way how to avoid being a Prosecutrix, & if they should choose to make her an evidence only, to instruct her how she may get her charges bore for coming from hence to Northampton, both for losse of Time & as a poor witnesse. This will much oblidge Sir!

Your very humble servant
H. P.

ffor /
    Christopher Rigby[2] Esq
            This

P.S. The man who served the subpœna on Sarah Bessant said his name was John Brown. Hee erased the word Barrett in the writt & instead thereof put Bessant; Qʳⁱᵉ whether this is not fforgery in altering a name in the Body of a Writt after it is delivered out of the office.

1 See Letter No. 96.

2 Christopher Rigby was one of three of the same name who owned Cosgrave, Northants. One of them was High Sheriff of Northants in 1734; the third sold the Cosgrave estate in 1764 (Baker, *History of Northants*, vol. II, pp. 130–131, and from information kindly supplied by the Rev. H. Isham Longden, F.S.A.).
    The Diary for 24 July 1753 mentions "A man who came from Justice Rigby to summon our Sarah Bessant to Oxford Assizes".

To face p. 404

Plate 26. THE SECOND DUKE OF GRAFTON

CHAPTER XVI

PURLIEU HUNTING

THIS was the one supreme incident in Henry's life and we are particularly fortunate in being able to watch it from beginning to end. The trouble arose in this way: part of the Shalstone estate was considered as lying within the purlieus of Whittlebury (or Whittlewood) Forest; this, "according to the perambulation of 27 Edward I, and excluding the Oxford and Bucks perambulations of the following year, comprised 329 square miles, or 20,480 acres. The whole of this circuit has not however continued to the present day forest land, or in possession of the Crown. It comprises numerous and extensive manors and other freehold estates which have been silently exempted from forest jurisdiction; besides many purlieu woods, or encroachments by the Crown on private property, anterior to and restored by the perambulation, which skirt the boundaries, and *in which the proprietor and the forester have each the right of hunting, or chasing back to the forest, the deer which chance to stray into them*".[1]

The words printed in italics form the key to the whole situation; it had evidently been the custom of the Purefoys and their neighbours to chase deer; they might hunt any deer back to the forest from which they had wandered, but might not "forestall" them on the way back, either by lying in wait for them up a tree, or otherwise. Probably they might kill them in fair chase before they reached the boundary proper of the Forest; but the Forest Laws had been decaying since the beginning of the fourteenth century, and the right to kill any deer may have been one of custom rather than of law. It is quite definitely stated by Manwood[2] that a "purlieu man must not hunt in the Purlieu with any other company but his own servants". The case contained in the following letters concerns the prosecution of a man named Collison, a mason of Syresham, who was actually paid a small fee by Henry Purefoy for his attendance at a hunt in the purlieus. We are not told the precise charge against him, but it is easy to suppose that he had no right to pursue the deer as the mere employee of one who might possibly have been allowed to do so himself. According to Manwood, Henry might not engage people to assist him because "the laws of the forest do not allow a multitude of people to assemble themselves together to hunt in the purlieus, because that is *ad terrorem* of the beasts in the forest".

Whatever the precise facts were, Henry, who had just served the

1 Baker, *History of Northants*, 1841, vol. II, p. 77.
2 *Forest Laws*, 4th edit. 1717, p. 297.

distinguished office of High Sheriff, found himself mixed up in a kind of poaching case and his agony of mind can be understood. His efforts to appease the Duke of Grafton, and the way in which the duke toyed with his discomfiture, make most entertaining reading—to us, at least; and the whole business served to stimulate him to unwonted energy, and to make him carry himself with great dignity in "the most troublesome affair I ever mett with".

A few letters dealing with other sporting matters are included in this section; from one we learn that Henry himself did not shoot much, and the Account-books contain many entries like these:

Feb 15, 1734　Gave Mr Townsend of Buckingham (y^e Schoollmaster) for Game he shot for mee $\Big\}$　00 : 01 : 06

Feb 24 —　Gave Billy Townsend then for shooting game $\Big\}$　00 : 01 : 00

Numerous entries relate to the netting of the fish-ponds, but there is nothing to show that a rod and line were ever used.

Henry did not hunt, though this was the period when various packs were being started in his neighbourhood, and Letter No. 341 states that "there are now seven packs of hare hounds kept hereabouts".

Henry's one and only pastime (apart from the Purlieu hunting) was coursing, and the constant purchase of dead horses and cattle[1] show that he must have kept quite a kennel. The Diary for 1741 may be quoted as an illustration of the extent to which he followed this sport:

"On Coursing"

1741 Aug 20　To ffullwell grounds, & Astwick grounds.
　　　　22　— Turweston　　,,　　　　,,　　　　,,
　　　　24　— ffinmere　　,,
　　　　26　— Abbotts ffurze, & Westbury ffeild, & ffinmere Grounds, & Water Stratford Grounds.
　　　　28　— Mixbury Grounds, & Woodhall, & to Astwick Grounds.
　　　　31　— Water Stratford Grounds & Dadford Cowpasture.
　Sept　2　— Whitfeild Cowpasture & Haws Grounds, & Turweston Grounds.
　　　　4　— Mixbury Grounds, & the Common by Woodhall, & Cotsford Castle.
　　　10　— Water Stratford Grounds & Chackmore ffeild.
　　　14　— Chetwood Grounds & ffinmere Grounds.
　　　18　To Stratford hill Ground, & Dadford Grounds, & Luffeild Abbey Ground.
　　　23　— Water Stratford & Dadford Grounds, & Stow Grounds.

1 These were often bought from a man described as a "whitler", the more authentic form according to the *Dialect Dictionary* being "whittawer", and meaning one who works in "white-leather", a collar-maker, a saddler.

Sept 26 — Gawcot Heath & Rowley hill grounds, & the 2
         Grounds by it.

Oct. 1. To Dadford Cowpasture & New Jersey Grounds, &
         Shalstone Cowpasture.

    3 — Turweston Grounds & Westbury ffeild, & Tur-
         weston Wild.

  16 — Dadford Cowpasture & the New Jersey Ground, &
         Shalstone Cowpasture.

  23 — My lower Coppice ground & Dadford Cowpasture.

Seventeen days in about two months argues a considerable keenness in one who did not exert himself unnecessarily. In Letter No. 3 we saw how any disturbance of hares in the breeding season was viewed; indeed the number of hares sent to London as presents, and recorded in the carriers' accounts and letters, was very considerable.

One could compile quite a list of the dogs owned from entries in the Diaries and Account-books:

1744 Dec. 30 This afternoon about 2 a clock died my pretty little
         bitch Chloe.

1750 May 14 Gave our Tho.ˢ Clarke for burieing Killbuck 00 : 00 : 06

1755 Oct 30 To the lane by Rawlins's house (where wee lost Jewell.)

References to racing are few, but on 24 Sept. 1739 Henry attended a Horse Race on a New Course, which was on the Green adjoining Monk's House. The last is still the name of a farm on the Finmere-Brackley road, and preserves the fact that the land once belonged to Biddlesden Abbey.

No. 587. H. P. to MR GARLAND

Shalstone
August the 5ᵗʰ 1748

Mͬ Garland /

I shall go on Purlieu hunting too morrow morning & should be glad to meet you at Siresham Hatch about six a clock in yᵉ morning or sooner. Pray bring no dogs with you but what are fit for yᵉ purpose, & don't mention anything of our going to any-body least it should take Wind & hinder our sport. I am

                   Your humble servᵗ
ffor /
  Mͬ Garland at   H. P.
     Brackley
      This

According to the Diary, Mr Garland attended, with a score of people, amongst whom were the rector, Mr Miller of Wappenham (woodward to Earl Verney), and the nephew of Mr Kendall, the lath-render of Syresham. Henry spoke to a child "who opened the gate for mee at our Town's End by Mr Townsend's house". Mr Townsend's address seems to have been quite appropriate.

The run was short, as they only went to Luffield Abbey grounds; they caught a buck "wch cuts 2 inches thick in fat", and invited the Wallbank family to dinner—Mr Pashler accepted. They also sent venison to Mr Moulson; and later Henry wrote to Mr Moulson that he was "sorry to hear the venison proved naughty, but it was fresh taken & the heat of the weather was the occasion of it".

No. 588.   H. P. to PETER MOULSON

Shalstone [&c.]
July 1st 1749

Sir! /

My mother & self, after desiring your acceptance of our hearty thanks for the kind & generous entertainment wee met with at your house, beg leave to acquaint you without baiting wee got to Mr Blackwell's at Missenden about 6 o'clock, & the next day got safe home. Our Journey was pleasant enough saving that wee had not yours & Mr Vaughan's company. At my coming home ye weather being cooll I went on Purlieu hunting in hopes to get you a Bitt of fat venison wch I had a fair chance for, had not a Rascall discharged his gun at a Deer on the ground & without his getting up in a tree, & shot our old Coachmare in at the Lights & she dropt down dead immediately;[1] and of a bad chance it was a good one, for as our George was on her back when she fell & the Bullet grazed on his leg as it went into her Body. This dismall misfortune so surprized the company that it made them cease pursuing severall fat Bucks & they left of[f] their sport & went home. But they have since taken Heart & are gone again too day, [but] did not get anything. I have sent you by Mr Jones ye carrier in a box my shaving bason & a china Dish wch you was so good as to say you would get your man Aron Moore to mend, who mended yours; it is carriage & porteridge paid. I must desire of you to pay your neighbour Mr Turner the sadler £3. 11s. on my account & take a Receipt in full of him. My mother joins with mee in our good wishes & compliments to yourself & M^r & Mrs Vaughan & George the Second, & to Mrs Williams & I am Sir!

Your oblidged hте serv^t
H. P.

1 The Diary for 16 June 1749 says: "Thence to the Mary Woodside (where the Coachmare was shott)".

P.S. I desire the favour of a line or two soon from you when my mother may tap her white wine, and how long it may be drawn on before 't is bottled of[f]. Hope you & M͏ͬ Vaughan & M͏ͬ Williams will make Shalstone in your way when you come to York races & you shall meet with a very hearty wellcome.

ffor /
  M͏ͬ Moulson...
       London
  Carriage & porteridge paid

No. 589. H. P. *to* THE REV. WILLIAM FLETCHER

Shalstone
Sir! /
Septemb͏ͬ the 12ᵗʰ 1750

I am favoured with yours of the 18ᵗʰ of last month, & the Gentleman for whom I designed my three Hounds is about to remove out of this Countrey & will have no occasion for them, so if you imagine M͏ͬ Rainsford of Brixworth will have occasion for 'em & accept 'em I should be glad to know whether hee would send for 'em from hence, or if I must send 'em to him; & to know how many miles Brixworth is from Shalstone. The hounds are middle sized & thoroughly entred for Hare & Deer. Your answer as soon as may be directed for mee To be left at M͏ͬ Yates sen͏ͬ, the Grocer in Brackley, will much oblidge, Sir! /

Your very ħłe serv͏ͭ
H. P.

P.S. Pray our Compliments to M͏ͬˢ ffletcher

ffor /
  The Rev͏ᵈ M͏ͬ W͏ᵐ
  ffletcher at
      Croton
        This

No. 590. H. P. *to* JOHN WODHULL

Shalstone
Sir! /
Septemb͏ͬ the   1750

The occasion of this trouble from mee is—I was lately discharged from Purlieu Hunting in all the Duke of Bridgwater's Woods by their woodward Garland, an innholder of Brackley, on which thinking myself under an hardship I had a case drawn up by an Attorney to know how far the rights of the owners of the Purlieu woods extended in relation to their mutually hunting in each other's woods,—wch case now lies before Councellor Wills (son to the Ld. Cheif Justice). But hee informs mee that the Generall law is very clear in this point, but before hee can answer my case hee must know the particular Customs of our hunting in each other's purlieu woods. I was yesterday to wait on our good neighbour Mr Wentworth, but hee could not resolve mee sufficiently but recommended mee to you as very knowing & intelligent in this affair. What I would entreat to know of you is whether the constant practice has been for the Purlieu men to hunt & kill Deer & climb up ye trees for that purpose in each others woods as well as their own woods; & if the Deer wee rouze in our own woods should escape into those of our neighbours' woods whether wee can't pursue 'em into our neighbours' woods & justifie getting up in Trees to shoot 'em, & in what case wee may set our Reells, or long strings with feathers to 'em, to awe & keep the deer within the woods & if there have been any p'secutions of the owners of Purlieu woods against any or each other for hunting deer in each others purlieu woods in your Remembrance. If you please to favour mee with an answer hereto by ye bearer & to excuse this freedom it will much oblidge, S^r

Your very humble servant
H. P.

P.S. My mother joins with mee in our compliments to yourself & Mrs Wodull.

To John Wodull[1] Esq
  at Thenford /
   This

1 The addressee was referred to on p. 392, he was apparently the father of Michael Wodhull, translator of Euripides and famous bibliophil; he rebuilt the old family mansion at Thenford c. 1765. John Wodhull died in 1754 (Baker, *Northants*, vol. I, p. 712).

No. 591. H. P. *to* EDWARD WILLES

Shalstone [&c.]
Septemb.ʳ the 25.ᵗʰ 1750

Sir! /

Since I had the pleasure of waiting on you at Astrop I have paid a visit to my good neighbour M.ʳ Wentworth who is 70 & odd years of age[1] & has been a purlieu man these 50 years past, & hee informs mee that hee being no sportsman himself, his servants have all along rouzed & hunted yᵉ Deer in his own woods, & M.ʳ Dayrell's, & M.ʳ Hosier's, & other Gentlemen's woods on that side Whittlebury fforest, & got up the trees & shot deer in these other woods as well as in his own, & that these other gentlemen have took the same Liberty in his woods for that space of Time without any Interruption on either side. But he sais, as there was always a good understanding & good neighbourhood between himself & these gentlemen, this freedom & forbearance on either side may be imputed to these occasions; but that in his opinion they can't strictly speaking rouze deer nor get up in trees in another man's woods, but that they may hunt the deer rouzed in their own woods thro' any other's woods, or shoot 'em there. Besides this I wrote a letter to M.ʳ Wodull of Thenford whose answer to my Queries I send you inclosed. This is all yᵉ Light I can procure you in this affair & I am with all due Respect, Sir! /

Your most humble servant
H. P.

ffor /
  Edward Wills[2] Esquire
  member of Parliament at
  M.ʳ Morgan's Coffeehouse
  in Bath Somersetshire /
  By London /
      ffrank

1 He was 73 at this time, and lived nine years more (*Records of Bucks*, vol. VI, p. 239).

2 This was the son of Chief Justice Willes referred to on p. 390 n. Edward was called to the Bar in 1747, made K.C. in 1756, and Judge of the King's Bench in 1767; he was M.P. for Aylesbury from 1747, and was succeeded in that constituency in 1754 by his brother John. Edward died in 1787, and is buried at Burnham (Oswald Barron, *Northants Families*, 1905, p. 347, and Lipscomb, vol. III, p. 218, for the somewhat fulsome inscription on the elaborate monument to his memory; it curiously omits his Christian name). His great-grandson, the Rev. G. E. Willes, was Vicar of Burnham, and died there in 1901 (W. H. Williams, *Burnham, Bucks*, 1925, p. 38).

No. 592. H. P. *to* MR BUSH

Shalstone
Octob.ʳ the 10ᵗʰ 1750

Sir! /

I understand by a Tennant of mine that Mʳ Warren of Stratton
Ardley wants some hounds; I have two couple of staunch ones
from 17 to 19 inches, none of 'em exceeding 3 years of age.
I design to lay down my hunting or otherwise I should not part
with 'em, they being favourite hounds. They are at Mʳ Warren's
Service on giving my man half a guinea. Pray favour mee with
a line next Wensday directed for mee to be left at Mʳ Yates senior,
a grocer at Brackley, to know if hee accepts them & if hee dos my
servant shall bring 'em over to him. I am Sir!

Your humble servant
H. P.

ffor /
— Bush Esquire
at Stratton Ardley
Carriage paid two pence

No. 593. H. P. *to* PETER MOULSON

Shalstone [&c.]
October the 13ᵗʰ 1750

Sir! /

I am favoured with yours of the 15ᵗʰ of last September & heartily
congratulate yours & Mʳ Vaughan's safe return to Old England.
I desire you will send mee by the next return of Mʳ Jones yᵉ
carrier half an hogshead of your oldest and best white mountain
wine together with a ₤re ℔ post that I may know when to send
for it, as also yᵉ price of it that I may order you payment. Wee
both desire to know how George the Second dos. I am informed
that the Duke of Grafton has either filed an Information or com-
menced an action of Trespasse against mee for killing a Deer in
the Purlieus. As I am not conscious to myself of having offended
any ways against the fforest it is amazing to mee, & if you can
Oveniently enquire out the Truth of it & let mee know thereof
it would be a favour. It must be the Vermin of the fforest who
have falsely accused mee & I hope his Grace will not proceed
against mee without letting mee know wherein hee thinks mee

faulty, or let mee have an opportunity to clear myself. My mother joins with mee in our compliments & I am with due esteem, Sir!

Your very humble servant
H. P.

ffor /
Mᴿ Moulson...
    London
Carriage paid and portridge paid with an half hogshead.

P.S. You need not trouble yourself to go to the Duke of Grafton for since I wrote my letter I find 't is an idle Report only, & the Duke intends no such thing.

No. 594. H. P. *to* PETER MOULSON

Shalstone [&c.]
Octobᴿ the 18ᵗʰ 1750

Sir! /

I am favoured with yours of the 16ᵗʰ of this instant October & have this morning sent for the Mountain wine with orders to put this in the post, for yesterday at Brackley market I heard by a Lawyer that my Lord Duke of Grafton had ordered a case to be laid before the Attorney Generall to question my right of hunting in the Purlieus, &, in case hee did not judge mee to have a right to hunt in the purlieus, to file an Information against mee for killing deer. As my ffather & ancestors have always hunted in yᵉ purlieus without interruption I have done yᵉ same within these four or 5 years, and I am not conscious to myself of having ever tresspassed on the forest in any one shape. If his Grace designs to call my right of hunting in the Purlieus in Question I must beg the favour of him not to file an information against mee immediately, but to give mee leave to lay before him my case wherein shall be contained my right & title to hunt in the purlieus & then to condescend to let mee have his answer whether hee approves of it or no.

If you nor any ffreind of yours can't come to speak with his Grace I have enclosed a letter wᶜʰ I desire you will seall it & let it be conveyed to his hands as soon as possible, for the Terme begins the 23ᵗʰ of this month, but if you think you can secure my interest in the affair without delivering the Letter you may lay it by.

Wee are heartily sorry to hear you are ill & wish your speedy Recovery & hope George the Second will live with his Mama to be a comfort to her & M̠ͬ Vaughan, for I myself could not speak till I was 2 years old. My mother joins with mee in our compliments & desiring you to excuse this trouble am with due esteem Sir!

Your very humble servant
H. P.

P.S. This matter is the more surprizing to mee as I never heard the Duke was displeased [with] mee till lately. Sure I am I would have waited on his Grace about it had I known of it when hee had been in the Countrey.

ffor /
  M̠ͬ Moulson
    in London

No. 595. H. P. to THE DUKE OF GRAFTON

Shalstone [&c.]
Octob̠ͬ the 18ͭʰ 1750

My Lord Duke /
   I am informed that I am so unhappy as to have fallen under your Grace's displeasure on account of having killed a deer on Whittlebury fforest ground which upon Honour I never did, and that you imagine I have no right to hunt in the purlieus. My father & our ancestors before him have always hunted in the purlieus without interruption & for myself I have onely followed there [sic] example for four or five years past; and I entreat the favour you will give mee leave to lay before your Grace my right & title to hunt in the purlieus, for I hear you design to apply to the Attorney Generall to have an information filed against mee on account of this affair, w̠ͨʰ will be very hard on mee if you do so, by reason not any one gentleman in the fforest gave mee the least Intimation that you was offended with mee. If I had heard anything of it I would have waited on your Grace when you was in this Countrey in order to have cleared myself, w̠ͨʰ I hope you will still give mee leave to do & not to proceed against mee till

you have seen my case & have honoured mee with your answer thereto, & that you will be assured that I am with all due esteem

Your Grace's most obedient and most humble servant

To /
   His Grace the Duke
     of Grafton
       Humbly present

H. P.

This letter is addressed to Charles FitzRoy, second Duke of Grafton, born in 1683 and died, owing to a fall from his horse long before, 6 May 1757. He was very fond of hunting and continued to hunt until he was 70. According to Swift's additions to Bishop Burnet, he was "almost a slobberer, without one good quality", but according to Lord Waldegrave, although he "usually turned politics into ridicule and had never applied himself to business, and as to books was totally illiterate, yet from long observation and great natural sagacity he became the ablest courtier of his time, with the most perfect knowledge both of the King and Ministers". Londoners owe to him the making of the New or Marylebone Road, which was violently opposed by the Duke of Bedford.[1]

The admirable book *Chief Justice Coke, his family and descendants*,[2] contains a good deal about this duke who was an intimate friend of the Earl of Leicester of the first creation. The earl called the duke "Baldassar" or the "Gran Corteggiano", and the duke in turn nicknamed the earl "Trot". Both were enthusiastic architects and virtuosi and evidently had much in common; on one occasion the duke wrote to "My Angell Trot", inviting him to Euston to meet the Duke of Cumberland; the letter was merely addressed to "Trott", and, says Mr James, "his Grace of Grafton must surely have been in his cups when he wrote such an address".

No. 596. H. P. *to* BROWNE WILLIS

Shalstone
October the 18ᵗʰ 1750

Sir! /

My Lord Duke of Grafton (as I am informed) has ordered his Lawyer to lay a case before the Attorney Generall in order to have an information filed against mee by him for killing Deer in the purlieus, as not being a lawfull purlieu man. My father &

1 G. E. C., *Complete Peerage*, 1926, vol. VI, p. 45.
2 By Mr C. W. James, 1929; the quotation is from pp. 250 and 256.

ancestors allways hunted in the purlieus & their right was never
called in Queon & as I claim under him & them I look on myself
to be a legall Purlieu man. The old men in this Parish say there
were 250 acres & upwards of my ground that were Disafforested
& name the very place (To witt) Dickens's hedge, where the
Bounds of the forest ended. This should seem to prove that Shalstone is one of the forest Towns, but how to prove it so unlesse
it be by Doomsday Book or some ancient Records I cannot tell,
so entreat ye favour of you to let mee know as soon as may be
what Records & where I must search on this occasion. It would
be exceeding kind of you if you would call & take a commons
with us as you come from Aynhoe, then you might favour mee
with instructions &c, for the Terme begins the 23th of this month
& then they may begin against mee. But if your leisure will not
permitt you to favour mee with your Company I must entreat
ye favour of a line or two to be left for mee at Mr Wallbank's
at Buckingham, & with my mother's compliments am Sir! in hast

Your oblidged hte servant

H. P.

ffor /
　Dr Willis /
　　This

18th Octob^r 1750

Sir! /

Please to see ye inclosed sent to Dr Willis. Have Company so
no more but

Your oblidged hte serv^t

H. P.

ffor /
　Rev^d M^r
　W^m ffletcher

No. 597.　H. P. *to* PETER MOULSON

Shalstone [&c.]
October the 27th 1750

Sir! /

Since I wrote to you last I am informed that his Grace the Duke
of Grafton Insists that there are no persons who have any Right
to hunt in the purlieus saving only such as have a right for their
Cattle to bite on the fforest ground. Now there are the three

To face p. 416

Plate 27.   DUNNEY BAXTER'S QUART POT

parishes of Shalstone, Westbury, & Bidlesdon whose respective owners for the time being have time Immemoriall gone on hunting in the purlieus, and yet have no Bite on ye forest. I have received so many affronts from the inferiour people of Whittlebury forest that before[1] I heard of his Grace's Resentment I had laid aside the thoughts of going on purlieu hunting any more, & have given away my hounds, so that being the case I can't imagine how any storm should be raised against mee on this account. It never was in my thoughts to invade any man's right whatsoever & there is no gain in purlieu hunting, but an expence. I hope you will have the honour soon to wait on his Grace & to acquaint him of these particulars as well as the rest, as far as you think proper. I have had the good fortune to catch two brace of woodcocks yesterday w^ch, together with a Cheese of my mother's making, I desire your acceptance of & with both our compliments to you & thanks for all favours I am with much respect Sir!

Your obliged hle servant
H. P.

ffor /
 Mr Moulson...
   London
 with a Basket. Carriage paid

No. 598. H. P. *to* DUNNEY BAXTER

Shalstone
Novemb^r the 4th 1750

Mr Baxter /

I propose to dine at your house too morrow & desire you will get a couple of ffowlls killed too night & boyled with bacon, & a small shoulder of mutton roasted, to be on ye Table at one o'clock. Pray be at home yourself because of paying you the 10s., & let us have ye Ground room on the left hand as wee come into your house, wch will oblidge

Your freind to serve you
H. P.

ffor /
 Mr Dunney Baxter[2]
   This

---

1 See Letter No. 592.
2 Mr Dunney Baxter kept the "Lord Cobham Arms" Inn at Buckingham; the licence was surrendered in the middle of the nineteenth century and the Buckingham Post Office and Reynolds the grocers occupy the site; the archway

No. 599. H. P. *to* JOHN POLLARD

Shalstone
Novemb[r] the 4th. 1750

Sir! /

Our worthy freind D[r] Brown Willis dos mee the favour to dine with mee at our County town of Bucks too morrow & intends to call on you as hee goes by to look into Manwood's fforest Laws,[1] if you have it by you, in behalf of mee who am threatened by his Grace the Duke of Grafton ab[t] the Purlieu hunting. If it should not suitt with your conveniency to be at home, pray leave this book out, if you have it, for the Doctor to look on, which will much oblidge Sir!

Your very hñe servant
H. P.

P.S. My mother's & my complim[ts] wait on Mrs Pollard & yourself

ffor /
  John Pollard Esqre
  at ffinmere /
        This

No. 600. H. P. *to* PETER MOULSON

Shalstone [&c.]
November the 6th 1750

Sir! /

I am favoured with yours of the 3[d] instant & desire your acceptance of my hearty thanks for your kind endeavours to serve

to the inn-yard, and much of the structure of the inn remains, thus at the end of the yard four-stall stables stand on each side, and were used for the stage-coach horses; the original partitions and recesses by the windows for brush-lockers remain. Beyond the yard is a garden, now about an acre in extent; it contains a very fine garden-house, completely overgrown with vegetation and likely to become ruinous. Near to it are a pair of statues on plinths in Portland stone, representing a shepherd and shepherdess. These are weathered but in a fair state of preservation; possibly they were given by Lord Cobham, who died in 1749 and was succeeded by his sister who was soon afterwards created Countess Temple. She died 6 Oct. 1752 and was succeeded by her son as Earl Temple. On 4 Nov. and ever afterwards the "Lord Cobham's Arms" is called "Earl Temple's Arms" by Henry in the Diaries.

1 There is a copy of the 4th edit. (1717) at Shalstone now, but there is no proof that it was Henry's—or perhaps he bought it after this letter was written.

mee. But whilst my Lord Duke of Grafton has such generous intentions of ordering mee a brace of Bucks, Mr Smith of Shelbrook lodge & the other fforesters are prosecuting mee & my ffreinds here with uncommon ffury, for there is one Mr Joseph Harris, a Bankrupt & a man of a very indifferent character has made information on oath that one Wm Collison, a mason, with 4 other men who were hunting with mee, killed a Deer on, & took it of[f] from the fforest ground on the 15th of August last. As to the Ground it was half a mile from the forest pales, but whether belonging to the forest or no I can't tell. The Deer lay in the Ditch & the head & the legs on the Bank, & the Dogs with the deer, & no soull with them. Then two of the men came & the deer was dead; some say 't is fforest ground & some not, it was a very poor deer, & I would not give half a crown for it. Upon this information Wm Collison was apprehended & had before a Justice & would immediately have been sent to Northton Jayll had not I & some of his ffreinds been bound in a Recognizance of £75 for his appearance at next Northampton Assizes; but the fforesters were against accepting Baill, so I was forced to attend again at the sessions at Thrup, where the Justices accepted the Baill & Collison was set at Liberty. It was a very wett day & I was wett to the skin & at these Sessions I met Mr Smith of Shell-brook, & I asking him how he could use mee so ill by prosecuting in [so] clandestine a manner without giving mee any notice, hee answered that hee had very strict orders from my Lord Duke of Grafton to set this prosecution on foot & to continue it till hee had orders from his Grace to the contrary, & that 't was none of his own Doings; & that his Grace, as soon as hee has paid his Devoirs to the King, will go to Euston Hall & stay there till X^tmas. So I must entreat the favour of you, as soon as you can after you receive this, to wait on his Grace & to entreat of him to give orders to his secretary, Mr Modocks, to favour mee with a line or two that his Grace Osents that this prosecution against this Collison & others may be withdrawn, & that his Grace also Osents that the Recognizance wee have entred into for Collison's appearance may be vacated, & Mr Smith sais if I can show him such a letter hee will put an end to the Prosecution. If his Grace should be gone to Euston, if you can't write to him yourself I

must entreat you to let mee know what you would advise mee
to do, w.ᶜʰ will much oblidge, Sir!

Your most humble servant

H. P.

P.S. My mother joins with mee in our compliments to you.

ffor /
 M.ʳ Moulson in
 London

The Diary tells us all about the visit to "Thrup", that is Thorpe
Mandeville; Henry left home at 9.15 and called at "M.ʳ Woodull's
at Thenford, thence to the 3 Rabbitts inne at Thrup". Mr Wodhull
we have already met (Letter No. 590). The "3 Rabbitts" still stands
under the name of "The Three Conies", with a sign depicting them
on each side. It is a three-storeyed stone building, with a sundial
fastened to the front and bearing the date 1622. The house may not
be so old as that, but it is a large structure, where one might not be
able to dine as Henry did, but where most superlative ale, brewed at
Hook Norton, Oxon, is to be procured. The only names in the Diary
which look like those of magistrates are the names of "M.ʳ Woodull
and S.ʳ John Dryden", who presumably formed the "Session".

No. 601. H. P. *to* PETER MOULSON

Shalstone [*&c.*]
November the 18.ᵗʰ 1750

Sir! /

I am favoured with yours of the 10.ᵗʰ of this instant and M.ʳ Ranby
mistakes my case, for I am not guilty of anything myself in relation
to this deer, for I gave the people expresse orders to give it the
fforesters if it was killed on forest ground (as I always did before
that,) for I was not present at all at the place where the deer was
killed, nor in sight of it; but the people then told mee it was killed
far enough from the forest ground & then I rode away with a
gentleman who was with mee & saw no more of them. I am
informed if it is forest ground it is not within the forest, and the
3.ᵈ & 4.ᵗʰ of William & Mary expressly sais the Deer must be
killed within y.ᵉ forest or else 't is not criminall. The reason I &
my freinds gave such large Baill for W.ᵐ Collison was the fforesters

would have dragged him to Jayll on Joseph Harris's oath that hee killed ye deer, wch oath so soon as Joseph Harris had made, two women of credit, who chanced to stand by the deer when it was killed, appeared & made oath that Wm Collison was not at all on the forest ground nor in assisting the killing the deer, nor dragging it from the forest ground, as they call it. So the Justices of Peace, being shocked at this contrary evidence, accepted our baill. Collison is a Tiler by trade & if hee had gone to Jayll hee would have been ruined. I gave him sixpence to sewell[1] for mee & hee was only a spectator & had no share in the sport. As to Joseph Harris's character it is well known within ten miles round this place. I hope for the future my Lord Duke will treat mee as a gentleman for at present I think I am treated as a deer stealer; I really myself nor any body here can conjecture what Mr Ranby means by a ffine, for I myself am no criminall neither will I give any security not to offend. I am informed Mr Peter Dayrell killed deer on this very spot of ground & offered to try it at Law with the foresters, but they never tryed it. I have lately seen a gentleman who will soon wait on the Duke at Euston hall, who will lay ye whole case before his Grace, & when I have his answer I will acquaint you thereof, in the mean time desire you'll enquire of some of his Grace's family in a private manner whether hee is gone to Euston hall, or, if hee is not, when hee goes down there, wch pray acquaint mee of as soon as you can & then you shall have my answer. On going to the Justices twice in extreme bad weather I was in such pain & in such hurry & confusion that I forgot to thank you for your kind present of herrings, wch I lived on for two days, & since that wee have received your kind present of oysters, for both wch wee return thanks, & on Wensday last I sent you by Jones (carriage paid) an hare, pheasant, & a brace of woodcocks, wch I desire your acceptance of. Pray take care you don't mention anything of this to Mr Ranby for hee is a freind to Joseph Harris, & has set the Duke against mee as I am told; I wish I had an opportunity of once speaking to his Grace. My

---

1 Wright (*Dialect Dictionary*) gives it only as a substantive: "A line of feathers fastened on twine and placed a foot or two from the ground in the open parts of a forest, to keep the deer within bounds". He quotes Turberville, *Book of Hunting* (edit. 1575), p. 98: "Anything that is hung up is called a sewel". The word, and thing, are still known to pheasant-shooters.

mother joins with mee in our compliments & thanks to you for your care & attention on this affair & I am with all due esteem, Sir!

Your oblidged ħte serv.ᵗ
H. P.

P.S. Since I wrote this I receȡ yours of the 15ᵗʰ instant & will be sure to observe your directions & return you abundance of thanks.

ffor /
  Mᵣ Moulson
    in London

No. 602. H. P. *to* PETER MOULSON

Shalstone [&c.]
Decemb.ᵣ the 23ᵗʰ 1750

Sir! /

I am favoured with yours dated 15ᵗʰ of last month & am much oblidged to you for your kind endeavours to serve mee in this affair. I am afraid wee have not succeeded with the Duke because I have not heard from you; I have often sent to Shelbrook lodge to Mᵣ Smith but hee is never at home, but I hope to meet with him there too day, & wish it were made an end on, for here is a sad clamour in yᵉ Countrey about it. I should be glad to know who are my adversaries, sure I am I have never gave anybody occasion to be so in any respect, & when this Deer was killed I was half a mile of[f] from it. Wee beg your acceptance of a neck Chine & a Turkey cock (carriage paid) together with the Compliments of the Season. Wee have stopped sixpence with the Carrier for yᵉ oysters, & they are but 6 pence a Barrell coming down, & please place yᵉ 6ᵈ to my account. The Postman has also deducted mee 3ᵈ for overcharging the letter, so I continued to pay yᵉ postage & am wᵗʰ much respect, Sir!

Your oblidged ħte serv.ᵗ
H. P.

P.S. I hope you had the small present of an Hare, Pheasant, & brace of woodcocks.

ffor /
  Mᵣ Moulson...
    London
  With a basket, carriage paid

No. 603. H. P. *to* LORD COBHAM

Shalstone [&c.]
January the 3ᵈ 1750

My Lord /

I have receᵈ the honour of your letter dated 25ᵗʰ of last month wᶜʰ I should have answered sooner, but company came in upon mee & prevented mee. I return you abundance of thanks for your kind Interposition in my behalf & beg the continuance thereof, for I am informed my Lord Duke is not yet thoroughly appeased. My mother joins with mee in our desire that yourself & Lady Cobham will accept of our humble respect & the Compliments of the season, & I beg you'll be assured that I am with all due esteem, my Lord

Your Lᵈᵖᵖˢ most obedient &
oblidged hie servant
H. P.

ffor /
The right honoᵇˡe the Lᵈ Cobham¹
in Pallmall /
London
Frank

No. 604. H. P. *to* PETER MOULSON

Shalstone [&c.]
January the 20ᵗʰ 1750

Sir! /

I am favoured with yours dated 22ᵈ December last & as I hinted in my last to you that I was going to Mʳ Smith & found him at home & hee told mee that hee could not draw a promise from the Duke not to prosecute, but that his Grace was in so good a Disposition towards mee that I had no reason to fear anything of that sort. I should be glad to be satisfied there was a finall end of this affair & am extremely obligged to you for your good offices on this occasion, as likewise for your kind present of Raisins & Almonds & a Barrell of Oysters, & hope you received our small

---

1 This was presumably Richard Grenville Temple, who became Earl Temple when his mother died in 1752; the viscounty of Cobham had been bestowed on his uncle (Sir Richard Temple, the 4th Bart.) who died in 1749; in October of that year Richard Grenville Temple's mother was made Countess Temple. Cobham was therefore a mere courtesy title in 1750–1.

present of a Chine & Turkey, & my mother & self wish you an happy new year & many of them & I am with all due respect Sir!

Your very humble serv.ᵗ
H. P.

ffor /
    Mʳ Moulson in
      London

No. 605. H. P. *to* PETER MOULSON

Shalstone [&c.]
January yᵉ 30ᵗʰ 1750

Sir!

I am favoured with yours dated 24ᵗʰ of this month and Mʳ Smith has neither called on mee himself, as hee said hee would, nor sent mee any word about my affair. I am afraid hee is not my reall ffreind. I shall acknowledge it as a great favour if you will give mee your Company here to go with mee to the Duke when hee comes down; for if Mʳ Smith should faill mee it will be absolutely necessary, for I am afraid I shall have no information when the Duke comes unlesse from you. My mother joins with mee in our compliments to you & I am with all due esteem Sir!

Your oblidged hte servant
H. P.

P.S. Desire your acceptance of an hare fresh catched.

ffor /
    Mʳ Moulson . . .
      London

No. 606. H. P. *to* JOHN LAND

Shalstone
Sunday March 3ᵈ 1750

Sir! /

When I waited on the Duke of Grafton last Wensday his Grace said I must wait on Mʳ Smith to know the decision of this affair about the deer, & his Grace was to go to Town as yesterday. I am under a great difficulty as to the Recognizance of £75 wᶜʰ myself & others have entred into for Will. Collison to appear at next Northampton Assizes, to abide such Judgmᵗ as the Coᵗ shall award &c. as to the affair of the Deer. The Justices have acted wrong for this affair is not bailable & the man ought either to have been

committed or else set at Liberty. I desire your opinion whether
the Recognizance cannot be cancelled in private or whether it
must be carried to the Assize for that purpose, or whether the case
being not bailable if the recognizance signifies anything, & whether
Collison, & the rest of us who are jointly bound therein, must go
to the Assize or no. Pray let mee know what day the Assizes at
Northampton are, for as soon as I have your answer, wch I entreat
by ye bearer, I will write to Mr Smith & am Sir!

Your very humble serv^t
H. P.

P.S. Be so good as to take a dinner wth us the day you come this
week to talk over the affair of my Co^t & then wee can have more
time & let mee know ye day ⅌ bearer.

ffor /
Mr Land   Attorney at
Law at   Buckingham
                This

One of the Account-books has the following entries:
1750

Aug 30	Paid Mr Land (attorney at law) for drawing up the case about the Purlieu hunting & in full	00 : 05 : 00
Sep. 11	Gave Councellor Wills with the case on the purlieu hunting	01 : 01 : 00

No. 607. H. P. *to* JOHN WODHULL

Shalstone
March the 27th 1751

Sir!

I have been to wait on the Duke of Grafton ab^t this troublesome
affair. Hee drank my health at dinner but when I came to desire
him to withdraw his prosecution hee referred mee to Mr Smith
of Shellbrook lodge, who went with mee to my horse & told mee
hee should never have done anything in the affair unlesse I had
waited on the Duke, & when I told him I would waite on him
at Shellbrook about it hee told mee hee would call on mee at
Shalstone very soon, but hee not coming I went on Monday last
to Shellbrook, but Mr Smith was gone from home & Mrs Smith

told mee hee would not be at home under 4 or 5 days; so must desire you would acquaint mee by ye bearer whether anybody from ye Duke of Grafton has been with you to withdraw the prosecution; if they have not, the recognizance wee have entred into must be drawn & sent over on Saturday next to Northampton by your clerke or some safe hand (that being the first day of the Assizes there), & it must be delivered to the Clerke of the Assize on that day, & Mr Collison must appear then, as I am informed, & if no prosecution hee will be discharged the last day of the Assizes. I beleive it will be necessary for Mr Collison to know where your clerke or person you send the recognizance by inns at Northampton, that hee may attend him into Co^t with it, so entreat you will let mee know thereof by ye bearer. This has been the most troublesome affair I ever mett with. My mother joins with mee in our compliments to yourself & Mrs Woodhull & thanks for all favours, wishing you both the blessing of health, & I am with all due esteem Sir!

Your oblidged humble servant

H. P.

ffor /
  John Wodhull Esq
    at Thenford /
          This

The Diary records this great occasion in the following way:

> 1750. 27 Feb. 11.20. To my Lord Duke of Grafton's at Wakefield Lodge to dinner, thence to Shalstone at own house at half hour after 9 c. at night.

He "conversed with"

> The Duke of Grafton, the Lord Delawar, the Lord Conway, the Lady Harcourt, Mr Kitt Rigby, & some gentlemen there whose names I know not.

Lord Delawar was John, seventh baron and first Earl De La Warr, born 1693, died 1766; held various Household appointments (G. E. C., *Complete Peerage*, vol. IV, p. 162).

Lord Conway was the second baron, born 1718, succeeded 1732, created Earl of Hertford 1750 and Marquess of Hertford 1793 (*op. cit.* vol. III, p. 403).

Lady Harcourt was presumably Rebecca, who married the second Viscount and first Earl Harcourt; he was drowned in rescuing a dog which had fallen into a well at Nuneham in 1777. She died in 1765 (*op. cit.* vol. VI, p. 300).

Mr Kitt Rigby was no doubt the addressee of Letter No. 586.

No. 608. H. P. *to* JOSEPH SMITH

Shalstone
March the 29ᵗʰ 1751

Sir! /

I was to wait on you on Monday last but you was from Home. I have got a great cold & pain in my Bones in being out in so dismall a Day or otherwise would have waited on you again. My present request is that you will satisfie Wᵐ Collison you will not prosecute him at yᵉ Assize at Northampton when hee goes to appear to have his Bail discharged. Hee promises to be very good & to be ready to serve you on all occasions, so hope you will not prosecute him at all wᶜʰ will oblidge

Your very humble servant
H. P.

P.S. You said I should have yᵉ favour of seeing you at Shalstone or otherwise I would have waited on you before. My mother & I desire our Compliments may be acceptable.

ffor /
Joseph Smith Esq. at Shellbrook
Lodge /
    This

No. 609. H. P. *to* PETER MOULSON

Shalstone [&c.]
March the 30ᵗʰ 1751

Sir! /

I have receᵈ the favour of your łre dated 5ᵗʰ of ffebʳʸ last wherein you told mee you would let mee know when the Duke came down to Wakefeild, as likewise that every thing would be complyed with that I desired & that I should meet with no further Difficulty. I had no account from you when the Duke came down, but had a card from Mʳ Smith of Shellbrook that the Duke was come down, & I waited on him, but did not speak to Mʳ Williams about yᵉ affair neither did hee say anything to mee about it. When I had dined the Duke drank my health & gave mee his Blessing, but when I requested him to withdraw the Prosecution he said I must wait on Mʳ Smith about it. Mʳ Smith went with mee to take horse & told mee I need not come to him but that hee would

wait on mee at Shalstone. Hee never came to mee, so I called
on him on Monday last wch was a dismall wet day & I have had
a pain in my Bones ever since. Hee was not at home so Collison,
as I hope, will appear at the Assize at North'ton to have his
Recognizance Discharged or take his Triall. 't would be a favour
if you'll let mee know when will be ye best time to buy Tickets
in this Lottery. Wee desire you to accept of our Easter hare (carriage paid) & that our Compliments may be acceptable & I am
Sir! with much Esteem

Your very humble servant

ffor /
 Mr Moulson...
H. P.

London
With an hare—carriage paid

Pray in your next let us know how George the second does.

No. 610. H. P. *to* PETER MOULSON

Shalstone [*&c.*]
Aprill the 9th 1751

Sir! /

I am favoured with yours & yesterday I received the favour of
a Łre from Mr Smith of Shellbrook lodge intimating that his Grace
condescended to make all matters easy, & I thank you & M^r
Williams for your good offices in this difficult affair, wch I am
heartily glad wee are rid of. I must entreat of you to get my
mother's gold repeating watch & my gold watch rectified; my
mother's watch has never went since the watchmaker had it in
hand when wee were in London, & mine has been cleaned by
a countrey ffellow & has not gone since; I send them both to
you by Mr Jones ye Buckingham carrier (carriage paid) who comes
into Town on ffriday morning early. My mother sais George the
second, when hee has done breeding his Teeth, will not be so
crosse, but quite another child, & wee hope when hee is able to
run about wee shall have his company here. If Mr Vaughan
should go to Ireland this year pray let us know, for hee may do
our Parish singular service if hee dos.[1]

1 See Letters Nos. 15 to 17 for an explanation of this.

Wee both join in our compliments to you, & I am wth much esteem Sir!

Your obldged humble serv^{t}

ffor /
   Mr Moulson in
      London
   post paid 3^{d}

H. P.

After this it seemed safer to buy venison than to hunt for it.

No. 611. H. P. *to* JOHN HURST

Shalstone [*&c.*]
June ye 29th 1751

Sir! /

When I had the pleasure of waiting on you at Mr Wallbank's you was so good as to offer to direct mee where I might have a fat Buck in Yardley Chase at £3. 5s.; if you would favour mee with a line or two per post of what Keeper I might have this Deer & where to direct to him, or if you would give orders yourself to have a fat Buck sent over here from Yardley Chase any Wensday or Saturday morning at y^{t} price to be here by 10 o'clock in the morning, I would give him 5s. for bringing it over. It must be killed either on ffriday or Tuesday because part of it is to go to London by the Buckingham carrier who sets out on Wensday & Saturday mornings. This will much oblidge Sir!

Your humble servant

ffor /
   Mr Hurst Attorney[1]
   at Law at Newport Pagnell
          This
   Carriage paid twopence

H. P.

P.S. Wee must have it by the 25th of July or not at all.

It arrived and a haunch was sent to Mr Moulson on 14 August; early in September Mr Hurst again secured a fat buck, of which the shoulders and sides were sent to the faithful Moulson.

1 Mr Fred Bull, F.S.A., kindly says that John Hurst was at Newport Pagnell in 1728, his will was made in 1766. His son, Geo. Pitt Hurst, continued his practice, and died, "an eminent solicitor", in 1817.

As final proof that all was forgiven and forgotten by the duke we have this letter:

No. 612. H. P. *to* PETER MOULSON

Shalstone [&c.]
July ye 4th 1753

Sir /

This morning my Lord Duke of Grafton sent mee half a Buck wch was killed yesterday. I desire you to accept of an Haunch of it sent carriage paid by Mr Jones our carrier who comes into Town on ffridays. My mother desires to join with mee in our Compliments to you & I am with due Esteem Sir! /

Your very humble servant
H. P.

ffor /
   Mr Moulson
     in
    London

No. 613. H. P. *to* EDWARD TROTMAN

Shalstone
Thursday 11th January 1738

Sir! /

Our little black bitch Chloe goes to heat & you was so kind to promise mee your least Dog hound to ward[1] her, so I have sent the servant for him. Hee shall be taken the utmost care of and returned to you again safe in 2 or 3 days. Wee were in hopes of waiting on you & Mrs Trotman at Shalstone before now, & with our Compliments for the season I am, Sir!

Your very humble serv^t
H. P.

ffor /
   Edward Trotman Esq at
    Shellswell /
       This

Edward Trotman, to whom this letter is addressed, obtained Shelswell by marrying Mary Fulmer, the niece of the fifth Viscount Saye and Sele, who had purchased it about 1720. Edward Trotman lived at

---

1 This is the third verbal meaning in Wright's *Dialect Dictionary*; he quotes its use in Nottinghamshire, and says that it is used also in East Anglia.

To face p. 430

Plate 28. FIENNES TROTMAN

Shelswell until his death in 1743, and is buried at Newton Purcell. His son, Fiennes Trotman, succeeded to the estate and enlarged the house, which remained an imposing mansion until it was pulled down in 1875. An interesting sketch of the old house is included in the Rev. J. C. Blomfield's *History of Shelswell*, 1890, p. 12, this note is taken from that valuable work, to which the reader is referred for a most interesting account of the destruction of Shelswell Church early in the seventeenth century; the lay owner not only carried out this wanton act of sacrilege but inclosed and appropriated the churchyard and rectorial glebe.

The Trotmans purchased Bucknell, Oxon, from the Eweres "for a very small pecuniary consideration", and in 1775 Fiennes Trotman also inherited Siston Court, Co. Gloucester, from his cousin Samuel. He died in 1782, aged 59, and is buried in Newton Purcell Church. His daughter married P. T. Wykeham, of Tythrop House, near Thame (Rev. J. C. Blomfield, *loc. cit.*, and Dr F. G. Lee, *History of Thame*, 1883, col. 440).

Plate 28 shows Fiennes Trotman with his hand resting on the medal and diploma awarded to him by the Royal Agricultural Society in 1768 "for planting Scotch firs". His name occurs frequently in the Purefoy Diaries.

No. 614. H. P. *to* THE REV. THOMAS PRICE

Septr the 29th 1739

Sir! /

My man Thomas Chandler acquaints mee that you took an Hare out of the mouth of my Greyhounds in Shalstone Cowpasture on Thursday last in the afternoon, and would not deliver it to him tho' he askt you for it. As the hare was caught by my own Greyhounds & on my own Ground I look upon it to be my property. It disappointed mee from sending it to London as too Day so I desire you will deliver it to the bearer. I am

Your humble serv^t

H. P.

ffor /
The Revd Mr Thos Price[1]
at Buckingham /
This

[1] He seems to have been the son of the Rev. William Price and brother to the Miss Prices of Whitfield, whom we have met so often in the Letters; he was instituted to the vicarage of Buckingham in 1725 and was not succeeded by another vicar until 1772, according to Lipscomb, vol. II, p. 574.

The next letter should have been written by Henry, but, as has been said, Mrs Purefoy generally wrote to Mr Robotham. Plate 13 shows a fowling-piece at the top, but it does not bear Mr Pickfat's name.

No. 615. E. P. *to* THOMAS ROBOTHAM

Shalstone [*&c.*]
September y 28*th* 1745*

I desire Mr Robotham's acceptance of an hare sent this day with your Butter & the Gunn, & the rec.^t for the gun inclosed herein, wch let Mr Pickfat see, hee lives in Holborn by Beaufort Buildings Corner. As to the flaw in the stock it was there when I had it, and the gun has not Mr Pickfat's but another name on ye Lock, wch makes mee think it was a second hand gunn. However hee warranted it mee as a good one in ye presence of my mother, & I never tried it but lately nor has it been let of[f] but 4 times & that within this fortnight. Mr Haws & our William let it of[f] twice each, & it recoiled so upon them that they durst not venture to let it of[f] any more. Let Mr Pickfat know this & let him change it for a gun that will shoot flying; & pray my service to him & desire him to let it be a good usefull gun, tho' I am not a marksman myself my freinds may use them. I desire you will send a pound of good mustard seed, the last was so wee could not use it. With our respects & service to yourself & Mrs Robotham, I am

Your humble servant
E. P.

P.S. Pray when you have showed the receipt to Mr Pickfat send it again to mee. If it is troublesome to you to have ye Butter & fetch it so far as Warwick lane, let mee know & I will send you no more. Since I wrote this I received your letter & heartily wish to hear better news, & am glad you got safe to Town.

ffor /
    Mr Robotham...
            London
    Carriage paid
    With a gun & hare.

No. 616. H. P. *to* JOHN WENTWORTH [CRESSWELL]

Shalstone
Saturday ffeb^ry 8th 1745

Sir!

I have lately had a present made mee of a large Greyhound Dog which is an exceeding good one for a Deer; if you have occasion for one of that kind if you send your servant over any time next week for him, hee is at your service. Wee desire you & Mrs Wentworth to accept of ye Compliments of ye Season & I am Sir!

Your very humble servant
H. P.

ffor /
John Wentworth Cresswell Esq
  at Lillingston Lovell
   This

No. 617. H. P. *to* MR PARKER

Shalstone
Sunday 26th June 1748

Mr Parker /

I am informed by your father that you have two young Buck hounds, a Dog & a Bitch, about a year & quarter old each. I desire a line or two ℔ bearer if they be entred & fit for present use, & what you vallue them at. If they be fit for my Turn I may be your Chap for them & am

Your freind to serve you
H. P.

ffor /
Mr Parker the Keeper at
  Hillersden
   This

APPENDIX A

RULES FOR MANAGEMENT OF OPEN FIELDS

Manor of Shalstone⎱ *to wit a Court Baron of* Henry Purefoy Esqre
in C.º Bucks   ⎰   *there held the* 12th *March* 1750

𝕽𝖚𝖑𝖊𝖘 & 𝕺𝖗𝖉𝖊𝖗𝖘 at this Court made and agreed
by the Homage for the better Regulation and Good
Government of the Fields within the said Manor.

First It is ordered That no Person shall keep or depasture more than
two Cows or horned Beasts, or two Horses or Mares for or in
respect of one yard land, on pain to Forfeit for every Offence 3^s 4^d

Also it is order'd That no Person shall keep more than three Ewes and
Lambs or five dry Sheep for or in respect of one yard land in
Summer and eight Sheep for or in respect thereof in Winter, when
the least or Middle field lyes fallow, and only four Couples or
six dry sheep in Summer & Eight sheep in Winter for or in respect
of one yard land when the biggest or East and West fields lye
fallow, And that the Stint thereof be made on or before the Five
and Twentieth day of March in every year. On pain for each
offence   3^s 4^d

Also that the Lott ground in the Common fields shall be lotted yearly on
or before the twentieth day of May and that the same shall not be
Mowed (except only between Allhallowtide and Candlemas[1]) but
Flit[2] with Horses, upon pain for every offence   3^s 4^d

Also That the Cow pasture shall be Hained[3] yearly at Candlemas and
remain Hained till the First day of June following in which time
no Beasts shall be suffered to go or depasture there (except only
the Haywards Cow till the fifteenth day of April and not longer)
upon pain for every offence   3^s 4^d

Also That the Wheat Field shall be hained yearly at the Feast of All
Saints upon Pain for every Offence   3^s 4^d

1 Allhallowtide is 1 November, and Candlemas is 2 February.

2 To "flit" is to move a tethered animal.

3 Meaning: "cattle shall be excluded in order that grass may grow".
The keep upon some "winter hained" pasture was advertised for sale in
Bucks newspapers in 1930. The "Stint" mentioned above is the limitation of
animals to the area available for grazing.

Also   That a good & sufficient Bull shall be found & provided yearly untill the next Court is held for the service of the Comͦon herd by the occupiers of Four of the Farms of the open ffield Land, to wit John Franklin, Aron Gibbs, Will. Scott, & John Boorten [3 words illegible] (such Bull to be Common) and the sᵈ Aron Gibbs to find such Bull for this next year, then the sᵈ John ffranklin, Wᵐ Scot, & Jno. Boorton & Aaron Gibbs severally & alternately to find the same yearly afterwards till the next Court is held; and in case of death of any of the sᵈ occupiers or other discontinuance of their occupacion of the sᵈ field Land Then the succeeding occupier or occupiers thereof to find the sᵈ Bull as afrsd upon pain that every person making default herein [illegible] shall forfeit for every default the sum of 20ˢ and that if any dispute shall at any time happen to arise touching the finding such Bull the same shall be decided (?) by the Lord of this Manor.

Also that every cow put or turned into the Comͦon or Cowpasture shall be Tipped or Nubbed¹ on both Horns at or before the age of 2 years & if any Tipp or Nubb come off to be putt on again within 3 days upon pain for every offence   4ᵈ

Also that the Herd's plott & the Church mead shall not be flitt with any Horses mares or colts. Upon pain for every offence   3ˢ 4ᵈ

Also that for every Cow put or turned into the Common or Cowpasture shall be paid yearly to the Fieldsmen on or before the 29ᵗʰ day of September in each year 6ᵈ, and that the Fieldsmen shall collect the same of the respective Commoners and forthwith pay the same to the Owner of the Bull for the time being. On pain each Commoner for every default   3ˢ 4ᵈ

Also that no Person shall Fork² or Tye any Cow before the Common Herd in the open field or Cow pasture. Upon pain to forfeit for every offence   3ˢ 4ᵈ

Also   That no Person shall suffer any Colt of a month old or upwards to go lo[o]se in the Comͦon Fields till after the same fields are ridd of Corn and Grain. Upon Pain for every offence   3ˢ 4ᵈ

Also   That no person shall Bait or Tye any Cattle upon his own ground or elsewhere so as to Prejudice or Trespass on his Neighbour till the Harvest is inned. Upon pain for every offence   3ˢ 4ᵈ

Also   That no person shall suffer his Swine Hogg or Pigg to go or be turned into the Common fields till Harvest is ended, or at anytime to go unringed there. Upon pain for every offence   3ˢ 4ᵈ

1 This is the same word as "knobbed".
2 Not given by Wright with this meaning.

Also   That no person shall mow his ground in the Open Field above or more than Once in any one year. On pain for every offence 3^s 4^d

Also   That no Horse Common shall be Let or Set to any Foreigner or persons not Inhabitant of Shalstone. On pain for every offence
10^s

Also   That the Fieldsmen shall find a Mole catcher[1] yearly to be employed in the Open fields and Cow pasture, and that his Wages shall be paid by the Commoners proportionably on Easter Tuesday in every year, On pain Each Fieldsman or Commoner making default herein   3^s 4^d.

Also   That the Fieldsmen do and shall yearly when and so soon as Corn or Grain in the open fields of Shalstone is ripe hire a Crow Keeper to Shoot and keep the Crows and other vermin from destroying the same. On pain in default of   3^s 4^d

Also   That each persons Leys and Greensward ground and such ground which hath been lately ploughed further than usual in the Open fields and Cow pasture shall be marked and meted out from the other by the Jury or Homage, or the major part of them, on or before the 1st day of May next. On pain each Juryman making default the sum of 20^s

Also   That all the Jury or Homage residing in Shalstone (except only such as shall be excused by the Foreman for some reasonable cause) shall yearly in Easter week or the next week after go round the open fields and Cowpasture and see that all the Stakes, Meteholes[2] & Meerstones[2] be in good Repair and in their right places, and fill up any vacant places where necessary, And in case a cart shall be wanted for carriage of Stakes or Meerstones for doing thereof the said Jury shall hire such Cart and the occupiers of the Open field shall pay for the Charge of the same in Proportion to their land therein. On pain to the Defaulter for each Default   3^s 4^d

Also   That the hayward or Cowkeeper for the time being do keep the Cowpasture Gate next the Wood Green and that next Westbury Lane and the gate next the Woodway in good & sufficient Repair and shall be paid the charges thereof by the occupiers of the open field in proportion to their land therein. On pain to the Defaulter for each default   3^s 4^d

1 The Account-book, under 31 Mar. 1741, shows a payment of 6s. 6d. to Goodman Rd. Evans for mole-catching "in the open ffeild and in the Lower Bushy Close to this last Lady day".

2 We have here two pure O.E. words: *Metan*, to measure, and *gemære*, a boundary. For the last word see the *Dialect Dictionary* under "mear"; the word still lingers in Bucks as "Maraway", the name of a road in Weston Turville parish: it used to occur still nearer Shalstone in Hillesden parish.

Also That every Hayward or Cowkeeper shall repair as often as necessary and keep in good repair the Evershaw Lane Gate next Shalstone Cowpasture at his own proper Charges, And that the occupiers of the said Open field land in proportion shall find Timber for it. On pain for each Defaulter to pay 3ˢ 4ᵈ

Also That the Fieldsmen shall cause the Cowpasture Hedge to be well repaired before every Five & Twentieth day of March in each year and so shall keep the same in repair untill Harvest be inned. On pain for each default   10ˢ

Also That the Hayward shall be paid twopence for every Horse, Cow, Bull, Sheep, Swine, or other beast he finds or catches Trespassing in any of the said fields of Shalstone, And in default of Payment thereof such Hayward is hereby Impowered to Impound the same and give notice and detain the same in the pound 'till the person injured be satisfied his Damage for the Trespass and also the Hayward the said 2ᵈ ℔ head.

Also That such person or persons who shall Mow or Trespass on another's Grass or remove Stakes or Meer Stones or stop up the Meteholes shall forfeit & pay for each offence   3ˢ 4ᵈ

Also That when and as often as the lord of this Mannor shall cause any of the Shalstone Moors or other places in the open fields of Shalstone to be dugg or trenched, then and so often the occupiers of the said Slades,[1] Moors, or places so trenched shall within 3 weeks after trenching thereof remove the Dirt or soil dugg or thrown thereout & lay the same on heaps one pole distance from the trench and carry away the same & lay it upon their respective plowed lands before the first day of March next after the said trenching, And where the Trenches shall lye between two owners or occupiers then each of them shall carry a like part to his land. On pain of each default to pay 20ˢ

Also That when and as often as the Lot Moors or fenny Ground, by Estimačon 10 Acres in the East field of Shalstone, shall be trenched the Occupiers of the Open field land for the time being shall in proportion of 3 Poles to each yardland take away the Soil to be dugg and lay the same on an Heap one pole distance from the Trench within 3 weeks' time after the same shall be trenched as aforesaid and carry away the same before the first day of August then next ensuing yearly to their respective ploughed lands as shall be directed by the lord of the Manor. On penalty of each Defaulter   20ˢ

1 This is another O.E. word, *Slæd*, a valley. It is exceedingly common in field-names and can be used of a strip of greensward between two woods, or of a strip of swampy ground.

Also   That the said occupiers of the said Open field for the time being untill the next Court is held shall in like proportion yearly & every year between the second day of November & second day of ffebruary in each year Throw out the Dirt and soil from the trenches in the said Moors or fenny Ground and carry away the same before the second day of ffebruary yearly and lay it on their respective ploughed lands. On penalty of each default   20^s

Also   That the said Occupiers of the said open field for the time being shall yearly and in every year between the second day of November and second day of ffebruary throw out all the Dirt and cleanse and preserve in like Wideness and Depth all the Trenches on their respective lands and Ground, as well those already made as those which hereafter shall be made thereon and where the said Trenches lye between two or more each of them shall do a proportionable part, on pain of each default   20^s

Also   That every occupier shall Plough his ground in the Open field not further than where it hath constantly or antiently been ploughed or should of right be ploughed, and shall on or before the Twentieth day of May next lay down for Greensward what ground thereof hath been ploughed otherwise with Grass seed as the Jury shall mete out. On pain for each default   20^s

Also   That the ffieldsmen shall yearly make a Rate or Levy equal in proportion to and upon each yard land in the Open field to reimburse the Charges of repairs of the Cowpasture Hedges and their other charges & expenses in their said office and the respective owners or occupiers of these Lands shall pay the same. On pain in default of   20^s

Also   That every Fieldsman and Hayward do take due care that the Orders aforesaid be duly observed and kept, And in case of their Refusal or Neglect therein shall forfeit and pay for each offence
3^s 4^d

Also   That the Lord of this Manor his heirs and Assigns with the Consent and Approbation of the Majority of the said Jury or Homage then living in Shalstone shall and may before another Court create and make a new hayward and ffieldsmen or Jurymen or any of them in case of Death or removal of the present Hayward or ffieldsmen or turn them out for Neglect.

Also   That the Fieldsmen or in their default the Lord of this Manor or his Bailiff or other person he shall appoint shall and may have power till the next Court to distrain the goods and Chattels of every Defaulter of keeping the said Orders and to sell the said Goods in like manner as goods distrained for rent to satisfy and pay the penalties, And that the ffieldsmen shall after notice thereof within ffourteen days collect or distrain for the Penalties of each default of the due Observance of these Orders. Under pain for each offence 3ˢ 4ᵈ

Also That no Ridgill¹ sheep or lamb shall lye in the open ffield after Holyrood Day² till Sᵗ Andrew's Day.² Under pain for each offence 3ˢ 4ᵈ

Also That all the Penalties of the Breach of the aforesaid Orders shall be equally divided between the lord of the said Manor and the ffieldsmen, vizᵗ One moiety thereof to the Lord and the other to the ffieldsmen.

Fieldsmen chosen { *John Franklin* & *Aron Gibbs* }

Hayward chosen *William Harburd*
Mole catcher *John Mumford*

In witness whereof we the Jury have herewith sett our hands:

John Franklin	*Aaron Gibbes*	The mark of
The mark of	*Wᵐ Sinnell* (?)	**X**
X	*John Boorton*	*William Scott*
William May		*Richard Boorton*

APPENDIX B

SUGGESTED SALE OF THE ESTATE

The following letter was written long before our books begin, it actually went through the post and was somehow returned to Shalstone. It bears date "Tuefday July the 9ᵗʰ 1720", and is written throughout with long f's. Henry was only 23 at the time and may have been more impulsive than he afterwards became; he was certainly sanguine if he expected to sell an estate for 60 years' purchase. The letter is addressed "for Charles Creagh Esqʳᵉ at Mr Cofby's at the red perriwigg in Thirl-Street near Lincoln's Inne, London;" it is defective but the part relating to his estate is clear.

1 A name applied to an animal when its testicles have not descended into the scrotum, such an animal would not be impotent. The word "ridgy" is still used in this sense in Bucks. Given by Wright under "ridgel".

2 That is from 14th September until 11th December.

28-2

Dear Charles /

I send you inclofed a particular of my eftate which I think, since money is so plentifull, I can't do better than difpofe of it for threefcore years purchafe wch is here given for Mr Minfhull's eftate & others which are not nearly so improveable as mine. My Mother tells me you are not of opinion for me to sell, but I hope I don't proceed amifs, for at 60 years purchafe it fetches me 23.320£ befides the surplus of the eftate, & I am sure 't is a much more pleasant, creditable & Improveable eftate than any that has been sold hereabouts. At this Price my Mother's eftate comes to 3.000£, Her jointure 3.000£, Her debt 2.000£, In all 8.000£, which if you take out of the 23.320£ there remains to me 15.320£, befides the Surplus of the eftate. I think this may make my fortune. All the wife people think Land will fall agen in some few years. I find there is good Interest to be made of money at prefent wth care takeing upon good Securities. This will...my Income upon a moderate Intereft to as high as I shall defire, wch I shall take rather then run any rifque.

I leave it to you whether the advowson shall be sold or not, I think it will be Policy to keep it, for it may be if the eftate is ever sold agen I, having the Parfonage, may come in for it.......

> I am
>
> Your honour's
>
> sincere freind
>
> H. PUREFOY.

If you Advertize it let it be in the Evening Poft. I set out for Briftol in a day or two. If you don't write to me there I shall think you are unkind. You may have directions where I lodge there from my Mother.

The "Particulars" are as follows:

To be sold

The Mannor of Shalftone in the County of Bucks scituate within 3 miles[1] of Buckingham and 3 miles of Brackley wth the Mannor houfe, Gardens, Orchard, Barns, Stables, Dovehouse, & other convenient Outhoufes, & ffishponds, together wth the ⅌'petuall advowfon of the parrifh Church of Shalftone, the parfonage worth 90£ ⅌ ann.

Being a ffreehold eftate confisting of Two hundred eighty four acres of Inclofed Ground and Twenty three yard Lands of Arrable & Meadow ground in ye open feild of Shalftone capable of great Improvement by Inclofing.

The Cowpafture adjoining to the s^d Open feild for 72 beasts to go on confisting of 143 acres wth the herbage & Timber thereon. The Open Coppice 34 acres wth the herbage & timber thereon. A right of Commoning for Cattle on 1500 acres of ground, being common for horfes & cows.

A Mill wth the Meadows & arrable Land adjoining thereto let at 14£ ⅌ ann. together with a ffishery a confiderable way down the River Ouze.

N.B. The Eftate lies w^thin a Mile of Brackley Green, in a very wholfome and pure air and let at 382£ ⅌ ann. old rents.

1 This should be "4 miles" in each case.

APPENDIX C

LIST OF SUBSCRIBERS TO SHERIFF'S FUND
TAKEN 27 JULY 1749

To the bare list of names which follows the present editor has added the name of each parish of residence, where the identity of the person was fairly certain, and the year in which he served the office of sheriff.

	Name	Remarks	Date of shrievalty
1	Sʳ Wᵐ Bowyer	Denham	
2	George Denton	Hillesden	
3	Sʳ Wᵐ Stanhope	Eythrope	
4	Thomas Kensey	Chilton	1746
5	John Wilks[1]	Aylesbury	1754
6	Richard Lowndes	Winslow	1737
7	William Drake	Amersham	
8	Thomas Hill	(?) Little Kimble	
9	John Adams	(?) Swanbourne	
10	William Hayton	Ivinghoe	
11	Sʳ Charles Tyrrell[2]	Thornton	
12	Thomas Willis	Bletchley (son of Browne Willis)	
13	Philip Herbert	Kingsey	
14	Thomas James Selby n.p.[3]	Wavendon	1739
15	Ralph Holt	Loughton	
16	Charles Wodnoth	Maids Moreton	1753
17	Matthias Rogers	(?) Castle Ho, Buckingham	
18	William Basil	(?) Beaconsfield	
19	Thomas Eyre	East Burnham	
20	John Pollard n.p.	Leckhampstead	1735
21	Sʳ ffrancis Dashwood	West Wycombe	
22	Sʳ Thomas Snell	Brill	
23	Sʳ Thomas Lee	Hartwell	
24	John Vanhattem	Dinton (see No. 60)	1761
25	Richard Warr	(?) Hughenden	
26	Alexʳ Townshend	Thornborough	1750
27	John Wells	Wavendon	
28	John Knap[4]	Little Linford	
29	George Wright n.p.	Gayhurst	

1 Wilkes married Miss Mead 1748, and was living at the Prebendal, Aylesbury, in 1749.

2 As a matter of fact Sir Chas. Tyrell died January 1748 O.S., evidently his name had not been removed from the list. See p. 367.

3 Can "n.p.", which occurs a dozen times, stand for "not paid"? Mr Selby made the Lowndes family his heirs in a will productive of much litigation; for an entertaining account of him see *Cole's Paris Journal*, 1931, p. 397 *et seq.*

4 Actually died 14 Jan. 1747.

	Name	Remarks	Date of shrievalty
30	Tyringham Backwell[1]	Tyringham	
31	Henry Uthwatt n.p.	Great Linford	1755
32	Henry ffynes n.p.	Wing	
33	S[r] Philip Touchet Chetwood	Chetwode	
34	Thomas Edwards[2]	Terrick, Ellesborough	
35	John Theed	(?) Edlesborough	
36	Humphry Paine		
37	Lester Selman	Chalfont S[t] Peter	
38	John Robinson	(?) Broughton, or North Crawley	
39	Hugh Barker	Mursley	
40	William Guy n.p.	Marsh Gibbon	
41	Henry Purefoy	Shalstone	1748
42	Anthony Turney	(?) Cublington	
43	Tho[s] Sheppard	Lidcote (the Under-Sheriff)	
44	John Bristow	Ellesborough	1752
45	Lancelot Charles Lake[3]	Aston Clinton	
46	Henry Lovebond	Oving	1751
47	John Ansell	Great Missenden	1758
48	Henry Geary		
49	Valentine Knightley	Haversham	
50	John Revett	Chequers, Ellesborough	
51	Richard Smith	Padbury	1724
52	John Warren	(?) Little Marlow	
53	Henry Cooley n.p.	Cheddington	
54	S[r] Charles Palmer	Dorney	
55	S[r] Charles Jones Wake	Hanslope	
56	S[r] Charles Bagot Chester n.p.	Chicheley	
57	David James n.p.	Woughton	
58	S[r] Richard Atkins n.p.	Newport Pagnell	
59	Crail Crail	Britwell Place, Burnham	
60	John Vanhattem n.p.	Dinton (see No. 24)	1761
61	Barn. Backwell	Tyringham	
62	Rich[d] Greenville	Stowe	
63	George Tash n.p.	Iver	
64	Christopher Towers n.p.	Iver	
65	Rich[d] Dayrell n.p.	Lillingstone Dayrell	

1 This is the grandson of Alderman Edward Backwell, the London banker and goldsmith, so often mentioned by Pepys. His mother was daughter of Sir Wm Tyringham who sold Tyringham to the Alderman in 1675. (*Vict. County Hist.* vol. IV, p. 483). Barnaby Backwell (No. 61 in our list), was son of Tyringham Backwell and died a few months after his father in 1754.

2 Author of *The Canons of Criticism*. Born 1699; died 1757.

3 Father of Lord Lake.

Additions, Regulations, New Orders & Alterations made to and in the Articles annexed—

At a meeting of the Subscribers the 14ᵗʰ Day of January 1747.

It is Resolved that [here follow 51 names out of the 65 quoted] be appointed a Committee and that any five of the said Committee are hereby impowered to make any additions, new orders or Regulations touching the matters contained in the said articles as they shall from Time to Time find necessary.

Resolved that the eleventh clause in the Articles annexed be repealed and instead thereof that any person after the 12ᵗʰ day of ffebruary next and before the first day of November 1748 may become a subscriber to the said articles on payment of five Guineas into the hands of the Treasurer for the time being, to be added to the stock, and that any person whatsoever qualified to serve the office of Sherriff of the county of Bucks and omitting to become a subscriber before the 1ˢᵗ day of November 1748 shall and may at any time afterwards betwixt the 12ᵗʰ day of ffebruary and the last day of October in any year (except when the office of Sherriff is vacant by Death) be admitted as a Subscriber to the said articles on payment of ten guineas into the hands of the Treasurer for the time being to be added to the Publick Stock, anything in the said articles contained to the contrary notwithstanding.

Resolved that Thomas Hill a subscriber to the annexed articles be appointed Steward for the purposes in the said Articles mentioned.

Resolved that Thomas Sheppard a subscriber be appointed Treasurer and receiver of the subscriptions and is hereby impowered to pay and disburse thereout what shall be necessary for the purposes in the said articles mentioned.

Resolved that the Son of a subscriber to the said Articles shall be admitted to the benefitt of the Subscription on his paying five guineas into the Hands of the Treasurer on or before the first day of November next after his ffather's Decease.

26ᵗʰ *July* 1749.

Present Sʳ Wᵐ Bowyer, Barronᵗ, George Denton, Richard Lowndes, Thomas Hill, Wᵐ Hayton Esquires, & divers other subscribers to the sᵈ articles. It being represented by George Tash Esq that Hee & Seüall other Gentlemen of the County of Bucks had not due notice of the sᵈ articles so as to become subscribers thereto within the Time thereby limited for five Guineas It is therefore Resolved for encouraging the said subscription that any Person for the future shall and may become a subscriber to the said Articles on payment of five Guineas into the hands of the Treasurer for the Time being at any time betwixt the twelfth day of ffebruary and the last day of October in any year (except when yᵉ office of Sherriff is vacant by Death) anything in the said Articles or Additions contained to the contrary in any wise notwithstanding.

APPENDIX D

UNDERTAKING BY SERVANT WHO CONTRACTS SMALL-POX

An incomplete "paper" of the kind referred to in Letter No. 235 seems worth preserving, it is in Henry's best hand-writing:

Be it Remembred this...day of October in the year of our Lord God one thousand seven hundred and fifty four That Elizabeth Purefoy of Shalstone in the County of Bucks widow hath hired Priscilla Matthews of...in the county of...to be her meniall servant for the space of a year from the date hereof for the wages of four pounds lawfull money to be paid at the end of the said year's service Provided nevertheless that if she the said...shall at any time of her said service be visited with the Distemper of the Small Pox and the said Elizabeth Purefoy shall pay or Tender or cause to be paid or tendred to the said Priscilla Matthews so much money in Proportion to the said wages for such Time as the said Priscilla Matthews shall have then continued in the said service That Then and at all times from and after the said Payment or Tender the aforesaid Hire to be void. In Witnesse whereof the parties abovenamed have hereto set their Hands, the date above written—

Witnesse hereto.

APPENDIX E

LOTTERIES

In June 1737 (Letter No. 377) enquiries are made about the Bridge Lottery; this evidently refers to the second Act, which became law 21 June 1737. By this £700,000 was to be raised by issuing 70,000 tickets of £10 each; a tenth of these were entitled to prizes and the blanks were valued in the Act at £7. 10s. 0d. each. Both blanks and prize tickets were subject to a deduction of 14 per cent., thus furnishing £98,000 for the building of Westminster Bridge. Subscribers of fifty tickets and upwards were to have 3 per cent. "praemium". The Act also gave authority to levy tolls on the bridge at specified rates, and fixed the remuneration of the Bank of England for receiving and paying the money at £3000. The 3 per cent. discount, the £3000 for the Bank of England, and £10,000 for estimated expenses were to come out of the 14 per cent., making, said its opponents,[1] "a most exorbitant praemium for the loan of about £60,000 neat money".

The use of the word "praemium" where we should say "discount", and of the word "neat" where we should say "net" may be noticed; it is also of interest to see that 200 members of the Lords and Commons, who formed the Commissioners, decided upon the lotteries in the Jerusalem Chamber, Westminster Abbey.

As regards the State Lotteries, the usual plan was to pay in stocks, at 3 or 4 per cent., or in Exchequer Bills; the terms varied from year to year, but we may illustrate the principle by referring to the Lotteries in which the Purefoys appear to have been interested. Letters 330 and 331 were written in the beginning of 1747 N.S., and may have referred to the lotteries of 1746; the terms for these were as follows:

1745. £500,000 raised by 50,000 tickets of £10 each; prizes from £10,000 to £20, blanks £6, about 6 blanks to a prize. Payment in 3 per cent. stock.

1746. For the same amount and on the same terms as in 1745, except that the rebellion of Prince Charles Edward had the effect of making the stock carry 4 per cent., and every purchaser of ten tickets received £9 p.a. for his own or any other life.

Letter No. 335 was really written at the end of 1747, when the conditions were much the same, without the annuity; the sum to be raised was one million pounds.

Letter No. 336 expressly names the "Lottery for the year 1748"; this sought to raise £630,000, on similar terms to those given above.[2]

Letter No. 540 relates to a lottery to raise £600,000, not quoted in the list referred to above, but it is mentioned in the *Gentleman's Magazine*; it was drawn at the Guildhall, and did not finish until 28 December.

The Purefoys, it will be noticed, had fairly good luck in the way of prizes; they seem to have sold their tickets rather than accept stock.

1 Taken from *A Short Narrative of the proceedings of the Gentlemen concerned in obtaining the Act for Building a Bridge at Westminster* &c. printed for T. Cooper, 1738, 70 pp. Charles Labelye, the Swiss engineer who built the bridge, published in 1751 *A Description of Westminster Bridge*, which confirms that there were two Acts, the first, for £625,000, does not seem to have gone very well.

2 These particulars are taken from "A List of State Lotteries" given in *The Lottery Display'd; or The Adventurer's Guide*, 1771. For extracting these particulars regarding lotteries the editor is indebted to Mr C. White.

INDEX

VOLUME II begins at p. 213. Where the text is supplemented by the addition of biographical notes on a person the entry is given first, preceded by (*biog.*). An obsolete or local word, or one with unusual connotation, has double quotation marks.

Abington, Northants, referred to, 190
account books described, xxiv
— — ordered from stationer, 285
accountant, Mr Yates a bad one, 66, 84
— Mr Wilson a worse one, 67
advertisement of theft in *Evening Post*, 131
— — insertion refused, 132
— of Mr Porter's case, 257
Aëte family and Shalstone, xv
de Aëte (or Ayete), Lawrence, 270
aethiops, a form of iron oxide, 329
"aha", a sunk fence, xix n.
"aild", ailment, 173
Akeley, Stockholt Manor in, 399
"alamode" hood, 296
alapeen, a mixed fabric, 198
alarum clock, common one wanted, 132
— — will not go, 114
— — with pendulum, 118–9
— — — — knocks hard, 120
anchovies, pot of, 379
Annesley v. Earl of Anglesey, 277
annuities, 4% bank (1746), 205
apparitor, a greedy one, 26
apple trees, named varieties, 93, 97
— — scions of summer jenneting, 369
ash-poles for sale, 37
— trees for sawing, 38
asparagus beds, 94
— three rows are best, 95
ass, how to treat one in milk, 229, 230
ass's milk for the Wentworths, 386
asses forbidden on the common, 3
assizes at Aylesbury (1748 O.S.), 367, 369, 394
— — Buckingham (1743), 379
Astrop Well, full description of, 388–92
— —, the Spa, 374
— the water mentioned, 306
Aubrey family of Boarstall, 391
axle-tree of chariot breaks, 377
Aydon, Dr John, quoted, 326
Aylesbury, "George" inn, Henry dines at, 359, 393 n.
— — — — stays at, 369
— Quarter Session records for Easter, 1738, quoted, 11
— stage coach from London, 244

Aynhoe, Browne Willis at, 270, 369, 416
— mentioned, 388

Backwell, Tyringham, (*biog.*) 442
Baker, William of Culworth, letter to, 41
— — the coachman, wants a place, 317
"bale", the handle of a bucket, 331
Banbury Fair, horse-dealing at, in 1739, 169–71
— — adventure following, in 1753, 404
— Market, cattle buying at, 163
"banging" hare, 225
bank annuities in 1746, 205, 206
barber, agreement with one, 293 n.
"bargain", a small farm, 30, 73
barley for malting, 75
barn preferred to stable by tenant, 51
Barns, an ironmonger of Buckingham, letter to, 85
barometers, price list of, 112, 113
Barrett, Miss, of Buckingham, letters to, 149, 323
basilicon, 326
Batchelor, Richard, of Buckingham, makes Mrs Purefoy's monument, xv
Bate, Dr George, (*biog.*) 397
Bath, visit to, 352–6
— Mr Peirce, surgeon of, 336
baulk of land measured, 42, 43
Baxter, Anthony T., of London, letters to, 99, 100, 101, 104–6, 303, 304, 309, 320, 322
— Mrs Anne, letter to, 324
— Dunney, innkeeper of Buckingham, letter to, (*biog.*) 417
— Shem (father of Dunney), 284
— — Henry's friends to put up at his house during assizes, 367
Baylis, Edward, of Helmdon, letter to, 25, 55
— — proves "very rough", 27
Baynham, Rev. J. H., quoted, 24
beans, kidney, 93
— Windsor, 91, 95
"bed of beef", 144
bedstead, a low one, 99–101
beer, stale, stolen, 128, 131
— strong, ingredients of, 130 n.
— — stolen, 131, 132

Belchier, cabinet-maker of London, letters to, 98, 107, 111, 177
Bell, of Aylesbury, letter to, 26
Bellingham, Catharine, Lady, marries George Purefoy III, 269
Beloe, T., his *Sexagenarian* quoted, 276
"bengall", a fabric, xxvi
Bennell, tanner of King's Sutton, letters to, 38, 109
Bennett's, Sir Simon, Charity, 381
— — — mentioned, 399
Bernard, Thomas, attorney of London, (*biog.*) 190
— letters to, 193, 200
— takes Mrs Purefoy for a fool, 193
— is disillusioned, 193
— is taught his business, 201
— mandate to pay rent, 222
— Mrs, letters to, 187, 188
Berry, C. W., quoted, 75
Bessant, Sarah, and the highwaymen, 404
"betties", flasks so called, 71, 78
bible, Church-, a second-hand one, 23
Bicester, character of natives, 135
— Statute for hiring servants, 152
Biddlesden Abbey, desecration of, 2
— parish and Lord Grey of Wilton, 4, 6
Birmingham coach, 64, 361
bitters disagree with Henry's stomach, 339
blacking ball for shoes, 103, 203
Blake, J., of Bicester, letter to, 40
— Mrs, of Bicester, letter to, 95, 139, 150–2
blankets from Witney, 82
Blencowe, Judge, of Marston St Lawrence, 278
Blenheim House visited by Henry, 313, 373
Bloxham, a Buckingham brazier, letter to, 112
blue, for washing, 84
blunderbuss, not to recoil, 118
— wanted complete, 255, 258
bohea tea, 65, 67–9
— — 14*s.* a lb., 356
— — "almost all green tea", 68
— — "so ordinary I could not drink it", 69
Bolton, Major, of Cheap St., Bath, 353–4
book-binding, 274–5, 277, 281, 286
book-buying by Henry, 273–4

bookseller, the great Tom Payne, (*biog.*) 275
boots, Russia leather tops for, 299
— half jack, 299
— — — too tight, 311
bottling of port, advice needed, 290
Bourton, (Buckingham,) and Minshull, family, 396
Bowles, Rev. Dr, letter to, (*biog.*) 387–8
Bowyer, Sir William, serves on Grand Jury, (*biog.*) 370
Boyce, John, mercer of London, letters to, 295–6, 298
Brackley, remains of Hospital of St John and St James, 29
— Castle, site of Mr Leapor's garden, 92
— "Crown" inn at, mentioned, 254
— market-day, xxiii
— murder of clergyman at, 402
— stone pits, 51
brandy, French, wanted, 236, 256
— how to distinguish French from "the other", 75
breeches, instructions for making, 297, 301, 303
— should have buckle behind, 316, 321
— too shallow in the seat, 323
— uncomfortable to wear, 302
brewing pipe needs cleaning, 87
Brickhill, T., of Farthinghoe, letter to, 157
bricks and tiles, contract for, 57
Bridgewater, Duke of, forbids purlieu-hunting, 409
Briscoe, S., London goldsmith, letter to, 122
Bristol, air at, thick and foggy, 374
"broad-board", 46
broad-cloth, blue, 258
Brodrick, Mrs A., letter to, 135
— Dr Lawrence, of Mixbury, (*biog.*) 135
brown paper, 131
brushes not to be charged when paint bought, 50
— rubbing, 82
— shoe, 203
— tooth- (1751), 348
"buck", washing, 145, 149 n.
buck, fat, from Yardley Chase, 429
buckhounds wanted, 433
— to be given away, 412, 433

Buckingham afflicted with small-pox (1737), 61
— Fair, horses wanted at, 169
— marble, 47
— wants a J.P., 393
— vicar of, seizes a hare, 431
— "Lord Cobham Arms" inn at, 284, 417 n.
— "Crosskeys" inn at, 381
Buckingham, History of, by Browne Willis, its compilation, 266–7, 271–2
Buckingham, J., his character, 134
buckles and button, 116
— behind breeches, 316, 321
— harness-, break like glass, 181
Budd, Richard, stationer of London, letter to, 286
"budget", a leather container, 175
bureau, boxes for pigeon-holes in, 287
Burton, Rev. L., of Brackley, murdered, (biog.) 402
Bush, Mr, of Stratton Audley, letter to, 412
Butler, Susannah, letters to, 127
butter supplied to Mr Robotham, 232
— marked with a heart, 161
— price of, 158–60, 190
— not paid for, 158
— carriage of, 190 n.
— strong in June, 313
— bitter when leaves fall, 161
buttons, brass, 307, 314
— crystal, set in gold, 235
— gold, for livery hats, 316
— hole at fob for watch-chain, 303
— silver breast, 195
— — for breeches, 306
— — twist, 311
— silvered with cat-gut stalks, 313
— shirt, 116

Ɔ, con-, xxi
cabbage seed, 96
Caenby, Lincs, Manor of, 241
"calamanco", a fabric, xxvi
calendar, reformed, 24
calico, sprigged, 105–6
cambric, 104–5
— price of, 303
canary on the fret, 73, 76
candles made to order, 82
candlestick, well-constructed, 177
Cant, Mr, lawyer of Grantham, 248–9
"capuchin", a genteel one, 319, 320

carcavalla, 79
Caroline, consort of George II, death of, 216
carp wanted, 373
— offered, 377
carriage, see "chariot" and "coach"
— duty on, 179
carrier, Buckingham and London, Eagles, 76, 115
— charges, 90
— Eagles, Mrs, 308
— Jones, 23, 200, 206, 341, 403
— Meads, 79
— Webster, 50, 100
— Brackley and London, Old Eagles the father, 88
— fails in business, 290
— Oxford to Northampton, 8
— — — calls at Brackley, 9, 89
— — — for bringing oysters, 422
— time on the road, xxvii
— acts as paying agent, 87, 89
carrier's man a great rascal, 88
— woman, crossness of, 90
Cartwright family of Aynhoe, (biog.) 388
cash, payment of by carrier, 87
— method of remitting to Bath, 352, 357
castors for bedstead, 100
— for easy chair, 306
catalogue of Henry's library, 273
cats, wild, a new sort, 376
cattle to be bought at Banbury, 163
— sold under distraint, 33
— in common fields, rules for, 435
— see also under "distemper" and "heifer"
Caversfield and the Vaux family, 102 n.
Cecill, James, London lawyer, letter to, 292
Chabbert, J., London goldsmith, letter to, 116
chairs of walnut, 102
"chairwoman", charwoman, 138
Chalfont St Giles, coach stops at, 360
chalybeate water of Astrop, 389
— — of Landulph, 374
Chamberlayne, G., see "Denton, G"
chambermaid, duties of, 149
"chance", luck, 123
change, wrong, 66
"chap", customer, 187, 198, 199, 223
chaplain to peer allowed two livings, 227

character, form of written, xxix
chariot axle breaks, 377
— window breaks, 175
Chebsey, G., Buckingham brush-maker, letter to, 82
cheese, strong, for servants, 70
Cheltenham, letter to postmaster of, 331
— waters bottled, 333–4
cherry trees, named varieties, 93
— — need pruning, 94
chest, iron fireproof one, 74, 103, 130
Chetwodes of Chetwode, xxxii n.
Chetwode, Risley family of, (*biog.*) 383
children, the suckling of, 291
chimney-sweeping, 83
china plate broken, 86
chine, cut thick and handsome, 380
chintz, 101, 104, 105–6
Chitty, H., quoted, 18
chocolate, too high dried, 72
— very good, 182
Christmas present acknowledged before received, 79
church, Shalstone, notes upon, 1
— — repairs needed, 21
— — timber for repairs, 22
churn, made by Richard Newsham, 251
— old one makes butter taste, 251
cider makes Henry sick, 72
— price of, 73
Clanfield, tilemaker of Eydon, letter to, 57
Clark, Sir Ernest, quoted, 180
Clarke, Mrs S., of Scarborough, letters to, 260–1
Clarke-Jervoise connections, 264–5
"clatting", xxvi
cleaning and dipping cloth, 195
clock, the great one, strikes twenty-one, 119
— — — repairs to, 121
— — — striking part will not go, 123
— — — gains, 125
— our little one won't go, 115
— little one on the great stairs, 123–4
— table, month hand amiss, 121
Clopton, Sir Hugh, referred to, (*biog.*) 262, 353
cloth, blue, must be "all of one peice", 300
clothes, directions for making suit, 301
— too tight when Henry grows fat, 315
cloves, 68
coach, a light one wanted, 178, 358

coach, Aylesbury Stage-, 244
— Birmingham, at Buckingham, 361
— — at London, 64
— London and Bath, 356
coachman wanted, 134, 136, 317
— example of moderate intelligence in, 166
— in trouble, 156, 361
coachmare to be sold at Northampton, 164
— to be bought, 169
— cannot swallow hay, 171, 175
— shot when purlieu hunting, 408
— with a sprain, 173
— wanted for Sheriff's coach, 367
coat, directions for making, 301
Cobham, Lord, has good mantelpieces, 58
— — death of, xxxii n.
— 2nd Lord, Henry dines with, 373
— — — letter to, (*biog.*) 368, 423
Cochrane, A. W. S., quoted, 269
cocoa, 68
codling very good, 62
— far from good, 203
coffee berries, 65, 67–9
— — new roasted, 218
Coke, Mrs, of Hillesden, (*biog.*) 154–5
Coleman, of Launton, letter to, 137
— Deborah, in trouble, 138
colic, rum a cure for, 78
Collison, William and the Purlieu case, 419–21
— his recognizance, 425
— his bail at Assizes, 427–8
colt, sale for cash, 157
commerce, played at Astrop Well, 391
— disposing of the pool, 393
"commons", a dinner, 31, 270, 382
common fields, rules governing, 434–439
condolence upon Mrs Robotham's death, 228
— — Mr J. Fish's death, 195
— — Mr Robotham's death, 231
— — Mrs Porter's death, 260
Conway, 2nd Lord, at Wakefield Lodge, (*biog.*) 426
— — — mentioned, 398
cook, duties defined, 153
— sober one wanted, 139
— "tite lass" wanted, 152
— stammering one will do, 140
— prefers marriage to service, 146

cook in trouble, 133, 139
Cooper, schoolmaster of Brackley, letters to, 274, 275, 277, 285, 288
Coppin, of Market Street, letter to, 327
"corinths", fresh currants, xxvi
corn for horses should be demanded, 219
Corner, E. M., quoted, 343
Cornwall, effect of mines on the air of, 374
Coryndon, William, London dentist, letters to, 345–7
Cosgrave, home of the Rigby family, 404
Cossins, London grocer, letter to, 65
— succeeded by Wilson and Thornhill, 67
cotton for morning gown, 322, 324
coursing from Aug. to Oct. 1741, 406–7
Court Baron, Mr Welchman to keep it (1739), 28
— — in 1750, 29
cow commons at Biddlesden, 4, 6
cowl for a chimney, 161, 229
cows, distemper amongst, 403
— price of, in 1739, 33
Cox family of Souldern Manor House, 253 n.
Coxed, Dr John, of Winchester Coll., letter to, (biog.) 18, 17
Crabb, Henry, of East India House, mentioned, 354, 356
crab-tree stocks for grafting, 92
Creach, boot-maker of Great Turnstile, 311–12
Creagh, Chas, letter to, 439
Cresswell family, see Wentworth-Cresswell
crier, town, to announce timber sale, 40
— — — theft, 112
Croke, Alexander, of Marsh Gibbon, letters to, (biog.) 7, 12, 44
Cropredy, mentioned, 72 n.
Crouch, Col. Guy, quoted, 10
Croughton, rector and curate of, in 1750, 393
Crutchfield, keeper of colour-shop, letters to, 50, 55
— — — mentioned, 221
Crystal buttons to be matched, 235
Culworth, Rye family of, 41 n.
Cumberland, Duke of, where he was 6 Dec. 1745, 202
cummin seed for quit-rent, 36

Cunnington, Mrs Jane, of Lincoln, (biog.) 241, letter to, 246
currants, 66
Cursitor's Alley house, 118, 182–196, 199–202
— — — repairs to, 199
curtains, chintz, 104
— Indian damask, 105
Curtis, London fishmonger, letter to, 63
"cutlets", oatmeal, xxvi

Daffy's Elixir, 312 n.
"daggled", muddy, 280
dairymaid, duties of one, 133, 139, 144, 147
Dalby, Rev. Richard, letters to, (biog.) 376, 16, 164–5, 332, 374–6
— Sarah, letters to, 82, 133, 393
— Mrs Sarah (? mother of above), 393
Dalkeith, Earl of, (biog.) 390
damask, white Indian, 105
— for window curtains, 377
damson trees, 97
Dancer, George, of Buckingham, letter to, (biog.) 289
Danvers family of Culworth, 388
dates, Old Style, xx
Davis, Edward, of Cottesbrooke, letters to, 8–10
— Mary, character wanted, 183
— — proves dishonest, 131
Daws Close, 32, 34
— Corner, a disputed baulk of land, 41–2
Dayrell, Francis, (biog.) 372
— Richard, 390
Deacles, an attorney of Buckingham, letter to, 159
death from cold in 1739, xxix
deer, practice of killing in the Purlieus, 410
De La Warr, Earl of, at Wakefield Lodge, (biog.) 426
dentistry by post, 345–7
Denton, George, of Hillesden, letter to, (biog.) 12
Denton, Mr Justice, of Hillesden, (biog.) 12, 155
desk, table-, 111 (Plate 11)
dial of great clock, 122
diamond ring, "spark" wanted, 116, 118, 130, 216
diaries described, xxii et seq.
— ordered from stationer, 286–7

dimity and vermilion, 101, 106, 309
dinner, self invitation to, 379
"dish-kettle", 280
distemper amongst cows in 1746 N.S., 229, 403
distraint for rent, 32–5
—— —— accounts of one, 33
—— —— after sunset, 34
Dobson and Cockle, lottery agents, 361
doctor will not send in his bill, 328
dogs owned by Henry, 407
domestic animals, Henry's regard for, 352
domestic troubles at Shalstone, 156, 361
Dorney Court, 370
Draper, Serjeant, of Carey Street, 103
drinking, hard, effects of, cured by Astrop waters, 390
drowning accident, 126
dyeing a gown, 317

Eagles, William, Buckingham carrier, letters to, 89, 117
earthquake (1750), 237
Easton Neston visited by Henry (1726), 372
Edmunds, Rev. F., of Tingewick, (biog.) 17
Edwards, J., London fishmonger, letter to, 65
— Thomas, of Ellesborough, (biog.) 442
Elms, J., of Charlton, letters to, 41, 42
Errington, F. H. L., quoted, 227
escrow, 200
estate of Shalstone, computation of its value, xxxi
Evershaw Lane gate, whose responsibility? 1, 437
ewes, rotten ones, 157
— which may stray, 43
excise duty on carriages, 179
Eyre, Richard, of Cottisford, (biog.) 285

fan and ball, ? vane, 60
"fancy", design (both subst. and verb), 106, 107
farm to let, 25, 30, 31, 73
Farmer, Christopher, of Southwark, letter to, 240
farriery, mysteries of, 166–70
fashions, enquiries about, 295, 296, 300, 308, 311, 313, 317, 319

Fatal Effects of Present Rebellion, a pamphlet, 273
Fell, Edward, tailor of Chipping Norton, letters to, 302, 310, 315, 318, 319, 320
—— addressed to him in London, 321
— Francis, of Chipping Norton, 323
felony, compounding one, 130
fencing defective, 43
fender, brass one wanted, 223
Fenimore, of Brackley, letter to, 81
— Mrs, of Brackley, letter to, 147
Fermanagh, Lord, acquires Biddlesden, 2
—— letter to his father quoted, 203
Fermor family of Tusmore, (biog.) 372, 315
Fiennes, Celia, quoted (on Astrop), 388–9
Finmere House described, 364 (illustrated in Plate 22)
fir-pole wanted for ladder, 91, 229
fish, weekly supply wanted, 61
— stinking, 62
— does not keep for a week, 203
— conveyance by carrier, xxvii
Fish family of Herts, to which Mrs Purefoy belonged, xvi n.
Fish, Harry, letters to, 195–6, 256, 319, 320
Fisher, J., London fishmonger, letters to, 61, 62
fishing the pond, 384
flax, no better than 8d. hemp, 83
Fletcher, Rev. William, of Croughton, (biog.) 392, 409
"flit", tether, 434
Florence wine, 71, 78
footboy, pretty strong one wanted, 150
footman-gardener-carter wanted, 136
forest laws, their late application, 405
"fork", 435
Fortescue, Hon. Sir John, quoted, 15
Foster, Canon, F.S.A., quoted, 385
fountain pens in 1750, xxvi
Fowler, Dr G. Herbert, quoted, 36
"fret", to ferment, 73
Frewen, Miss, of Brackley, letters to, 145, 146
Friday, Joseph, who deserted his family, letter to, 13
frocks, servants', 302, 308, 310
— linen, for men servants, 318, 321
fruit trees, grafting, 92, 96

fruit trees named varieties, 93
—— need pruning, 92, 96
—— planting of, 97
Fulwell House, 399–400
"funnel", a cowl for a chimney, 161

galoshes ineffectual, 295
game, shot vicariously, 406
gamekeeper, official appointment of, xxix
Game laws, association to prosecute offenders against, 291, 292
game season (1736), 374
gardener wanted, 149, 150, 156
Garland, of Brackley, letter to, 407
—— referred to (?), 410
Garrett, Buckingham wig-maker, letter to, 293
Garvan, W., a very polite Irish gentleman, 396–7
Gee, Mary, of Farthinghoe, letter to, 151
gelding too airy for Henry, 172
Gentleman's Magazine, 274, 275
"gentlemen of figure", 370
"George" inn, Aylesbury, Henry visits, 359, 369, 393 n.
"gets", gains time, 242, 252
Gibbs, grazier of Farthinghoe, letter to, 172
— James, of Souldern, letters to, 31, 162, 173, 174, 254, 367
———— swindled by R. Porter, 253
gilding, 60
ginger, 68
"ginn", a kind of crane, xxvi
glass for window of chariot, 176, 177
— crown, panes wanted, 349
glasses, seeing-, 130, 348–51
Glover, Lady, and family, (*biog.*) 269, 268
gloves, white thread, 305
god-daughter valued at £500, 292
Good, Mrs, of Carey St., letter to, 360
Gostelowe, Kirton, a footman, of an ancient family, (*biog.*) 140, 141
Gough family of Souldern, (*biog.*) 82
gout, Henry suffers from, 226, 265, 299
— cure for, 236
— and boots, 299
gowns, cotton materials for, 324
grafting fruit trees, 92, 96
Grafton, 2nd Duke of, letter to, (*biog.*) 414 (and Plate 26)

Grafton, 2nd Duke of, Henry dines with, 425–6
——— sends Henry half a buck, 430
——— begins purlieu hunting action, 412
Grand Jury, Henry unable to attend, 383
grate in parlour, setting delayed, 52
—, stove, 106
Greaves, John, of Broughton, letter to, (*biog.*) 24
— James, a tenant, his character, 30
— Richard, London chairmaker, letter to, 108
Greenough, ?druggist of Snow-hill, 348
Greenwich visited by Henry, 359
Grenville, Richard, M.P. (afterwards Earl Temple), letter to, (*biog.*) 368, 423
Grey, Rev. Dr, of Hinton-in-the-Hedges, (*biog.*) 388, 391
Grey de Wilton, Lord Arthur, at Biddlesden, 2, 4, 6
grogram, 220
grounds to powder periwigs, 216, 221, 240
Grub Lane (? at Bell Bar), house in, 195, 198
Guesse, gardener of Preston Bisset, letters to, 94, 95
guinea, 2-guinea piece mistaken, 226
guinea-hen, 117
Gulick holland, 320
guns become rusty, 124
— charge for cleaning, 124
— which recoil badly, 432
Gunn, William, Buckingham mason, letters to, 47
—— requires to be "jogged", 48

Hains, Buckingham carver, letter to, 122
Halford, Rev. C., of Radclive, (*biog.*) 285
handkerchief, cambric, 303
— for neck, 324
Harcourt, Countess, (*biog.*) 426
hare, a "banging" one, 225
— disturbed by hounds in breeding season, 4
— leverets destroyed by snow, 231
— scarce in 1737, 376
hare, seized by Vicar of Buckingham, 431

hare scut as penwiper, 370
— difficult to obtain for different reasons, 223, 224
— not delivered with butter, 90
— identified by cutting claw, 222
— — by sealing with arms, 70, 91, 224, 226
— hounds near Shalstone, 216
harness, buckles for, 181
— neatsfoot oil wanted for, 181
— request to borrow, 180
Harris, Joseph, of Buckingham, letter to, 352
— — his low credit, 354
— — serves Henry a scurvy trick, 355
— — (? same as above) "a bankrupt & a man of a very indifferent character", 419, 421
— Timothy, of Brackley, letters to, 128–9
— of Bicester, letter to, 14
— Mrs, of Bicester, letters to, 16, 156
"harslet", xxvi
hartshorn shavings, 70, 341
Harvest weather (1737), 375
hat, beaver, 131, 307, 317, 322
— "Caroline", for servants, 309
— French, gold & silver ones, 306
— with wide brim, 300
Hawes, Rev. Wright, of Shalstone, (biog.) 19
— letters to, 18–21, 380
— falls from his horse, 383
— would like a suit of clothes, 315
— Mary, her christening, 239
hay, solicitude for its housing, 352
"hayne", to shut up a field for hay, 4, 434
headstall and reins of black leather, 237
Heal, Ambrose, quoted, 67, 123, 177, 305, 311, 348, 351
heifer, adventures of a, 161
heifers at straw, 163
Helston, Cornwall, Mr Dalby at, 374–6
hemp, 83
Herriard, Hants, seat of the Jervoise family, 261–2
herrings support Henry for two days, 421
— three missing, 403
— wanted with roes in them, 64
— — — soft roes, 65
Heyford, Upper, 376 n.

hiera picra for gout, 236
Higgins, Mrs P., letter to, 153
highwaymen, maid's adventure with, 404
Hillesden and the Cokes, 155
— and the Dentons, 12
— letter to gamekeeper at, 433
Hind, Bicester chimney-sweep, letter to, 83
Hobcraft, Nurse, Henry her trustee, 141
— — her funeral, 28
— — was a Miss Chapman, 401
— William of Finmere, letter to, 43
hog puddings, a present of, 348
hogs, fat, the price of, 160
hogshead, an unsound one, 76, 81
hog's sty not pitched, 52
holland, Gulick, 320
— Irish and Dutch, 304
— price of, 303, 322
Holloway, William, of Great Boreton, letters to, 72–3, 132, 134, 136, 170
Holt, Wilts, mineral spring at, 264 n.
— Mr and Mrs, letters to, 159
— Mrs, will say wrong things, 159
Holton, of Buckingham, letters to, 293, 350
homestall, 30
hood, Alamode, 296
— short flourished black one, 313
hoop, a fashionable one needed, 218
Hooton, Buckingham painter, letter to, 60
horse, blind one with lame foot, 165
— chestnut, "heaves at ye flanks", 168
— little one "very little behind", 164
— with hoof trouble, 166–7
— see also under "coachmare", "mare", and "gelding"
horse-hire for prospective servants, 143
horse-meat to be asked for by guests, 219
horse-race near Shalstone in 1739, 407
horse-racer, Richard Minshull one, 396
hospitality on a grand scale, 397
hounds, Buckingham, in 1753, 4
— Henry wishes to breed from, 430
— — — to buy, 433
— — — to give his away, 409, 412, 433
house-boy's conditions of service, 310
Howard, Middleton, attorney of Fleet Street, mentioned, 371
"how do yee", 372

Hows, Betty, of Towcester, letter to, 153
Hughes, William, London attorney, letters to, 4, 6
Hunney Holmes, mentioned, 46
Hunt, old Goodman, a tenant and his rates, 12
— the baker, distraint upon, 32–5
— — his debts, 167
Hunt's Mill, ford at, 127
— — lease of, 36 n.
— — mud from dam, 45
— — mentioned, xviii, 46
Hurst, John, of Newport Pagnell, letter to, (biog.) 429
Hurt, Joseph, of Ludgate Street, letter to, 350
"hurters", xxvi
husbandry and grazing in 1737, 375
Hyson tea, 70, 131, 218

ignorance, advantage of in errand boys, 66
inclosure of Shalstone parish, 25
"indicted", addicted, 152
infants, how to rear when teething, 237
Ingoldsby family of Lenborough, (biog.) 396, 397–8
ingratitude, example of, in a parson, 17
inkstand, silver, enquiries for one, 122
"inn", used as a verb, xxiii
inquest upon a drowned footman, 126
"instruments executed", a book with this title described, xxviii
insurance policy on London house, 192
— — — Shalstone house, 196 n.
insurances a bad investment, 212
investment, difficulty of, in 1745, 205
Ireland, letter to a soldier in, 15
"issue paper", tissue paper, 286

jack, bad effect of eating one, 338
Jaycocks, a case of parochial domicile, 8, 11
Jenkyns, Rev. I. P., quoted, 374
Jervoise, Richard, letters to, 264–5
— Thomas, (biog.) 261
— — mentioned, 239
— — letters to, 262–3, 353
— — death of, 263
— Rev. G. H. J. P., mentioned, 239

Johnson, a Tingewick tailor, letters to, 160, 305, 314
Jolly, a Brackley cooper, letter to, 37
Jones, Conquest, of London, letters to, 34–5, 106–7
— — letter regarding a mare, 167
— Goodman John, of Wappenham, letter to, 1
— John, Buckingham carpenter, letters to, 48–9
— William, Buckingham carrier, letters to, 90, 181
— a Brackley tailor, letter to, 301
— and Horsley, lottery-office keepers, 211
Jordan, Zachary, of Helmdon, letters to, 38, 45
journey-time to London, 359
journey to Aylesbury takes seven hours, 369
Jury, Grand, summoning of, 370
Justice of the Peace wanted for Buckingham, 393

Keck, Anthony, patron of Astrop, (biog.) 390
"keep" of sheep and cows, price of, in 1739, 33
Kerwood, Henry, wanted for murdering his master with a pitchfork, 402
key for sash-door needs mending, 85
Kimberley, Dr Charles, letters to, (biog.) 325–6
"kinchen", 133
kindness to animals, Henry and his dogs and horses, 352
— — — Mrs Purefoy and a turkey, 223
King, a Bicester chair-frame maker, letters to, 102
"King's Head", Islington, 213, 232
"kiver", xxvi
Knibb, J., of Westbury, letters to, 109–10
Knight, J., a London fishmonger, letter to, 64
Knightley of Fawsley family, 268

lace, 323
— at 2d. the yard, 215
— for mob and handerkerchief, 355
— gold, for servants' hats, 131, 309, 316
— silver, 116, 311

lace, silver, for red waistcoat, 305
— — showy ounce, 195
laced clothes, paper to wrap them in, 316
Lake, Henry, a London coachmaker, letters to, 175, 178, 181
lamb (or lamp) black, 50, 56
"lampreys", lampers, a disease in horses, 174
Land, John, Buckingham attorney, letters to, 19, 20, 196, 354, 424
land, purchase value of, 198, 440
Landulph, Cornwall, mineral spring at, 374 n.
Langham, Sir John, of Cottesbrooke, mentioned, 9
lawyer once ill-used Henry, 360
"lay", "ley", pasture, 41–2
Lea, Col. E. T., quoted, 213
lead paint, light blue, 55
— — white, 50
Leapor, P., the Brackley gardener, (biog.) 92, 278
— letters to, 92–4, 96–7, 115, 149
— Molly, poet and daughter of above, (biog.) 278–80
Leghorn hat, 221
Leicester, Earl of, friend of 2nd Duke of Grafton, 415
Leigh, Thomas, of Iver, succeeds Henry as Sheriff, 371 n.
Leighton Buzzard, a good market for calves, 375
leisure, a maid's, employed in spinning, 147
Lenborough, manor of, 396
letter-books, particulars of the, xix et seq.
letters, difficulty of delivering, 16
— of attorney, 205, 208, 236
Lewes, Francis, of Stanford, Notts, letter to, (biog.) 140
"lift" of beef, xxvi
Lillingstone Lovell and the Wentworth family, 373
Lindsay, Mrs, quoted, 345
Linnee, Hannah, steals beer, 128–9
Linseed oil, cure for a cold, 333
Lisle, Fermor, of Imley, death of, 379
Littlecote, hamlet of Stewkley, 366
liveries, servant's, 85, 308, 321
liveries, see also under "frocks"
living of Shalstone, presentation to, 18

Lloyd, Henry, a London mercer, letter to, 308
lobsters boiled when dead, 215
lodgings in London required, 358, 360
London, visit to in contemplation, 357
— — in 1749 for six weeks (various tradesmen named), 358–9
London Evening Post, advertisements in, 257
— — — distribution of, 284–5
Long, Lady, of London, letter to, (biog.) 134
Longden, Rev. H. Isham, quoted, 404
Longley, of Carey Street, Henry lodges with in 1743, 122, 360
Long's Warehouse, Covent Garden, hoop from, 218
— — — — (in address), 308
looking-glass, 98
"Lord Cobham Arms" inn, Buckingham, 417 n.
lotteries, 81, 204, 207–8, 210, 212, 245, 252, 340, 361
— finance of, 444–5
lottery-tickets, registration of, 210–11, 361
Loveday, Mrs, of Brackley, letter to, 180
Lovell, a painter of Bodicote, letter to, 56
Low, John, of Studham, letter to, 137
Lower, Dr Richard, his tincture, 312
— — and Astrop Well, 388
Lucas, John, of Westbury, letters to, 45, 163
— — mentioned, 3
lucerne seed wanted, 236
Luke, Sir Samuel, and the Knightley family, (biog.) 268

mace, 69
mackerel, orders for, 61, 64
maid servant, the duties of one, 145
Malaga (wine), price of in 1748, 80
malting barley, 75
manteel hood, 296
mantelpieces of marble, ill-set, 55
— — polishing, 57
— — — defects, 53–4, 58–60
Manton, J. O., quoted, 227
Manwood's Forest Laws, copy needed, 418

Manwood's *Forest Laws*, quoted, xxix, 405
marble, black, red, and white, 53
— Buckingham, 47
— counterfeit suggested, 58
— polishing, 57
— Turkey, 55
mare, bay, throws Henry, 174
— strong black one wanted, 171
— with sprain in shackle joint, 173
mares "resty and gamesome", 174
marriage, books for and against, 283
Marsh Gibbon and the Croke family, 7
mason, a neglectful one, 51
— orders to a, 51-2, 55
Mason, Mr, of Islington, letter to, 235
May day, xxv
May, Edward, a coachman, his character, 135
— — — deserves sympathy, 155
— William, distraint upon his cattle, 34
"mazzardly", knotty, 39
Meads, Z., a carrier, letter to, 160
Meredith, Charles, a London hatter, letters to, 305, 307, 309, 317, 322
— Hugh, London attorney, letters to, (*biog.*) 183-5
— — first mentioned, 71
— — churlish, 189
"meteholes" and "merestones" in common fields, 436
"mete stakes", xxvi
milk, ass's, how to manage the ass, 229-30
mineral springs, at Astrop, Northants, 388-91
— — — Holt, Wilts, 264 n.
— — — Landulph, Cornwall, 374 n.
Minshull family of Bourton, (*biog.*) 394-6, 399
mirror ordered, 98
— received, 242 (and Plate 10)
Missenden, Great, Henry stays at the "White Hart", 359, 408
mole-catcher in the common fields, 436
money, difficulty of remitting to Bath, 352, 354, 355
Monger, Lt.-Col., death of, 245
— — mentioned, 88
moonlight needed for visiting, 329, 377-8
Moor, Sir George, of Maids Moreton, (*biog.*) 397

Morgan, of Lee, letter to, 39
morris dancers, xxv
Morshead, J. F., quoted, 202
Moulson, Peter, London wine-merchant and general agent to the Purefoys, letters to, (*biog.*) 213, 23, 70-4, 76, 79, 80, 111, 182, 184, 188, 199, 201, 204-12, 213, 219, 221-2, 224, 227, 235-7, 290-2, 340, 347, 356-8, 360-1, 401, 408, 412-13, 416, 418, 420, 422-4, 427-8, 430
Moulson, Mrs, wife of above, letter to, 226
"mounds", fences, 196
mountain wine, white, 71, 76
— — oldest and best, 412
— — strong, not sweet, 72
— — too new and sweet, 80
mourning, order for, 310
— limited, 216, 245
— second, 217, 323
mud from mill-dam, who owns? 45
muffetees, French silk ones, 341
Mulford, London clockmaker, letters to, 118-20
Murcott, of Buckingham, order to pay money, 210
Murray's regiment at Dublin, 15
mushrooms, pickled, 86
mustard, 23

nails must not be mixed, 85
neatsfoot oil, 181
nectarines, named varieties, 93
Newbottle, sale at, 109
Newsham, Richard, engineer, (*biog.*)251
newspapers, how distributed, 284
New Style, reformed calendar introduced, 24
Newton Longville, cows at, distempered, 403
night caps, material for, 309
Northampton and the rising of 1745, 202
"nubbed", knobbed, 435
nutmeg, 66, 69

oak, cut by mistake, 39
— crying the sale of, 40
— hard-wood and lop for sale, 38
— the buyer to pay for felling, 40
— trees for Shalstone Church, 22
— — — Rectory, 21

oatmeal, xxvi, 66
"occamy", xxvi
Onion, Matthew, associate of R. Porter, 255
Oriel College, Henry at, xvi
— — Henry's rooms panelled, 186
oven, arbitration about the cost of, 49
"over", more than, 379
Owen, Mr, Keeper of the Bodleian, dines at Whaddon Hall, 386
oysters, 63–5, 161, 403
— price of, 229–30
— "as good as ever I eat", 198
— at the end of March, 284
— at the end of April, 226
— "too small & watry", 231
— "black as ink", 62

Paddon, Mrs Alice (daughter of Henry's nurse), letter to, 28
— Thomas (her husband), letter to, 141
paduasoy, a fabric, 302, 307, 310
paint, 50, 55
painter, orders to a, 56
painting a London house, when needed, 184
— — — cost of, 189, 191
— parlours at Shalstone, 56
Palmer, Northampton carrier, 9
— — — letter to, 89
Palmer, Sir Charles, of Dorney, on Grand Jury, 370
— London stone cutter, letters to, 53–4, 58–60
pan, brass, stolen—and recovered, 112
paper, brown, 131
— various kinds of, 286–7
parcel rates, agreement for, 90 n.
Parker, Charles, a mason, letters to, 46, 51
— — a very unworthy man, 52
— a keeper at Hillesden, letter to, 433
Parkins and Sitwell, of London (sell castors for chairs), 306
Passelow (or Pashler), Saml, of Buckingham, (biog.) 278
— letters to, 342, 384, 387, 393
Patey, W. J., quoted, 338
Payne, Ollive, a Brackley baker, letter to, 49
— James, his son, letters to, 154, 276–7, 280–2
— brothers, booksellers, (biog.) 275–6

peach trees, 93, 97
pear trees, named varieties, 93
peas, early, 95
— Hotspur, 91, 95
— Rouncival, 236
peeling, a fabric, 296–7
Peirce, Jeremiah, Bath surgeon, letters to, (biog.) 337, 336, 338
— — his goodness and humanity, 338
Peirson, A., saddler, letter to, 175
pencil, a silver one, $4\frac{7}{8}$ ins. long, 131
Pendlebury, Col., Master Gunner of England, 372
Pennell, widow, a painstaking person, 26
pens, Dutch, 286
pen-wiper made of hare's scut, 370
pepper, black, 68
— Guinea, 66
Pepys, S., quoted, 213
periwig, dark brown preferred to grizzle, 293
— unruly one, 293
Perkins, James, of Tingewick, letters to, 21–2, 43, 46
Perne, Miss, plays a prank, (biog.) 136
petticoat, quilted calico one wanted, 303
— — unsatisfactory, 304
— under, 309
— whalebone hoop, 308
pewter dishes bruised, 123
— — how to scour, 280
Pickfat, London gunmaker, referred, to, 432
Pidenton, of Brackley, letter to, 302
pigeons devoured by cat, 250
Pilsworth, Charles, of Oving, (biog.) 7
— — — mentioned, 8, 11
"pitching", paving, xviii n., 52, 193
Pitts, Dr Humphrey, of Oxford, letter to, (biog.) 340
plaster for Mrs Purefoy's leg, 326, 329, 332, 336–8
plate, broken, must be replaced, 86
Plautus, Echard's translation of, 281
plays performed at Westbury, 149, 380, 384
ploughing in common fields, 438
ploughs, wooden, 45
plums, named varieties, 93
pluralities, authority to hold, 227
— distance apart of livings, 19

poaching in 1732, xxiv
pocket-book from Samuel Saunders, 252
pocket sheriff, what he is, 365 n.
poems by Molly Leapor, 278–80
pole of deal to make ladder with, 91, 229
Pollard, J., of Finmere, (biog.) 364
— — — letters to, 363, 365, 418
pond fished, 384
port, best old red, 70
— daily ration of, 61
— injured by bad corks, 290
— sent in a rotten hogshead, 76, 81
Porter, Leonard, death of, 217
— Ralph, letters to, 242–4
— — references to, 234, 260
— — marries an heiress, 240–2
— — little indiscretions of, 246
— — extravagance of, 246–7
— — villainy of, 249–61
— — reported (wrongly) as hanged, 259
— Mrs, mother of above, letter to, 246
— — — — death of, 260
Portuguese coins as English currency, 227
postal difficulties, 16
— service, xx
postmaster of Cheltenham, letter to, 331
— of Greenwich writes to P. M. of Brackley, 257
Post Office and newspaper distribution, 284
Potford, mentioned, 43
— subject to spates, 267
Potts, Samuel, of G. P. O., London, letters to, (biog.) 284, 285
Poulton, Francis, "a weak, bigoted Papist", 395
— Catherine, in trouble, 137
Pratt, J., Helmdon clockmaker, letters to, 85, 119, 121, 123–5
— — — farrier, letters to, 166–7, 169
Pretty, Rev. William, rector of Herriard, letter to, 263
Price family of Westbury, (biog.) 401
— Campbell, of Westbury (sale, 1749), 109
Price family, plays acted at their house, 380, 384
— Rev. William, of Whitfield, letters to, (biog.) 3, 77, 376–7
— Mrs, of Whitfield, letter to, 77

Price, Mrs M., of Whitfield, letter to, 394
— Susan, of Whitfield, letter to, 140, 377–8
— her eligibility in marriage market, 292
— Rev. T., of Buckingham, letter to, 431
— Canon J. Willis, quoted, 393
Profily, Dr, his Treatise, 282
promissory notes, some sporting ones, xxviii
public affairs, small mention of, xxi
public house disqualifies for domestic service, 144, 153
Purcell, Buckingham Shoemaker, letters to, 295, 299
Purefoy family, Browne Willis's letter about, 266
— — arms of, x (and Plate 8)
— — Henry's letter about, 267–70
— George, Henry's great grandfather, 268–9
— — — — anecdote of, 397
— Knightley, Henry's grandfather, 270
— Sir Henry, Bart., forgets his family in his will, 270
— Mrs E., (biog.) and character, xvi
— — — her fondness for truth, 152
— — — her interest in an old servant, 155
— — — will not be put upon, 185
— — — rebukes Mr Bernard, 201
— — — chides Mr Robotham, 225
— — — instructs Mrs Cunnington, 247
— — — hopes to retain her integrity while, 226
— — — not at home in washing week, 378
— — — has a bad leg, 243, 246, 323, 326, 329, 332, 336–8
— — — has a fever on her spirits, 72
— — — falls down stairs backwards, 204, 221, 330
— — — has epidemic cold for twenty weeks, 237
— — — very ill in her stomach, 341
— — — size of her waist, 218, 308
— — — her letters of condolence, 195, 228, 231, 260
— — — her monument, xv
— — — letter to from Henry, 369

Purefoy, Henry, (*biog.*) and character, xvi
— — champions the poor, 5
— — kind to animals, 352
— — visits Bath (1742), 262, 352–6
— — — London (1749), 358–60
— — his interest in celibacy, 283
— — solicitude for his clothes, 297–8
— — — for his periwig, 293
— — struggles with half jack-boots, 311
— — as High Sheriff, 366–70
— — as a J.P., 393
— — as commissioner for a charity, 381
— — ill-used by a lawyer, 360
— — his library catalogue, 273
— — not a great smoker, xxvii
— — does not claim to be a marks-man, 432
— — as a sportsman, 405–7
— — at Astrop Wells, 388, 391
— — thinks of selling Shalstone (1720), 440
— — makes a will (1742), 288
— — has always been loyal, 368
— — is not a criminal, 421
— — accused by vermin of the forest, 412
— — hurts his wrist, 335
— — thrown by bay mare (1749), 174
— — — by Jenny mare (1756), 330
— — suffers from jaundice (1747), 385
— — — — gout (1743), 265
— — — — colic (1742), 257
— — contracts a pain in his bones (1751), 428
— — much fatter in 1745, 315
— — feels ill after eating jack, 339
— Mrs R., quoted, 309, 311
Purlieu hunting, 405 *et seq.*

Quarter Sessions at Aylesbury, 1738, extract from the records, 11
— — 1748, mentioned, 44
quilting, 99, 100
Quincy's *English Dispensatory*, 281
quit-rent payable in cummin seed, 36

raisins in the sun, 66
— the large sort of, 68
— bad ones, 69
"rand", 64
ratteen, blue, 258

Rayner, Dr Alexander, letter to, (*biog.*) 332
— — — death of, 336
razors, 293
— to grind, 89
"rearing", 203
rectory of Shalstone repaired (1744), 20
"reels" in hunting deer, 410
Reeves, London stationer, letter to, 287
repairs to house in London, 184, 188–192, 199
rice, 68–9
Richard the Third acted at Westbury, 380
"ridgill", 439
Rigby, Christopher, of Cosgrave letter to, 404
— — at Wakefield Lodge, 426
Rinehill, a field-name, 43
ring, diamond wanted for a, 116, 130, 216
Risley, Risley, of Chetwode, letter to, (*biog.*) 383
rivers, season for cleaning, 22, 46
roads, petitions for their construction, xxx
— state of (1744), 314
— — of, in autumn, 353
Roberts, Francis, of Willesden, 269
Robins, Bucknell farrier, letters to, 165, 168, 171
Robotham, Thomas, of Islington, inn-keeper and London agent to the Purefoys, letters to, (*biog.*) 213, 36, 62, 78, 88, 90–1, 103, 115, 117, 130, 132, 161, 186, 189, 192, 194, 197–8, 203, 213, 214–20, 223–6, 228–231, 240, 242, 244–5, 248–59, 283, 298, 300, 306, 311–13, 317, 348–9, 354, 356, 378, 403, 432
— — attempt to break into his house, 214
— — in sad disgrace, 225
— — stays at Shalstone, 313
— — death of, 231
— Mrs, a former servant, 240
— — death of, 228
Rose, Benjamin, of Deddington, letter to, 86
rosemary, a cure for a sore breast, 335
rouncival peas, 236
Rous, Anthony, and the Glover family, (*biog.*) 269
rubies, real and imitation, 118
ruffles for cambric shirt, 304

rum good for colic, 78
Rumbold, St, 388
Russ, Miss, quoted, 337
Russell, Mrs (niece of Mrs Robotham),
letters to, 231–4
Rye family of Culworth, 41

sack whey, 74
— shared with friends, 77
St James's Evening Post, advertisement
for, 131–2
salad-oil, 217, 379
sale at Biddlesden (1742), 110
— — Maids' Moreton (1737), 110
— — Newbottle (1747), 109
— — Westbury (1749), 109
Salisbury, Earls of, and Sir Simon
Bennett's estate, 399 n.
salmon, pickled, "jumbled into
peices", 379
salmon, "tale" of, 225
Salmon's *Modern History*, 273, 275–7
salt, 84
sand (for writing), 286
Sandford, Mary, Henry's grandmother, 271
sashes for gentlemen's nightgowns, 115
satin, 8s. a yard, 217
— beautiful green, wanted, 317
Saunders, Samuel of St Paul's Church-
yard, 252
savoy biscuits, 341
Say & Sele, Christina, Viscountess,
anecdotes of, (*biog.*) 391
Sayer, Henry, of Biddlesden, (*biog.*) 2
— — and some cottage tenants, 5
— — letter to requesting a warrant,
128
— a Buckingham chandler, letter to,
82
scarlet fever very rife in 1742, 353
"scuttle bone" (bone of cuttle-fish), 288
seal affixed to hare sent by carrier, 91
sealing wax, 286
"sear cloth", cerecloth, 330
Seawell, H., of Syresham, letter to, 157
sedan-chair wanted, 108, 215
seeds, vegetable, various, 95–6
Seeley, B., Buckingham bookseller, 274
"sego", sago, 68
Selby, T. J., (*biog.*) 441
servants make mistakes, 222
"serve", to feed an animal, 145, 156
"sewelling", 421

"sewelling", *see also under* "reels"
sewers "choaked up", 199
shagreen silk, 296–7, 306
shalloon, a fabric, 259, 314, 318
Shalstone Church, repairs to, 21–3
— Manor, valuation in 1720, 440
— — and village described, xviii
(see Plates 6 and 7)
— Rectory, repairs to, 20
Sharp, R. F., quoted, 283
"sharps", shafts, xxvi
shaving, annual contract for, 293
Shaw, Dr P., on *Scarborough Spaw
Waters*, 215
sheep, horned Western, 162
— piebald, now at Shalstone, 163
— *see also under* "ewes"
Shelswell and the Trotman family, 431
Sheppard, Goodman, his financial
position, 163
— Joseph, his engagement, 310
— — the state of his wardrobe, 143
— Mrs M., of Cornwell, letters to,
142–4
— Thomas, under-sheriff, letters to,
(*biog.*) 366, 365, 366, 370–1
sheriff, Henry's appointment as, 366
— subscription-list, 363, 365, 368,
371, 441–4
Sherrard, Ladies Lucy and Susan,
(*biog.*) 390
"shewers", sewers, 194
Shillingford, Richard, Buckingham
joiner, (mentioned) xii
— — — — letters to, 39, 40, 56
Short, Dr, his description of Astrop in
1740, 389
"shoull", shovel, xxvi
Showler, Thornborough stone-mason,
letter to, 57
shrimps not good, 203
Shuckburgh, Dr, (Sir Charles), (*biog.*)
156
— Mrs, of Warwick, letter to, 155
shutters recommended to keep out
rogues, 214
Sill family of Fulwell, 399 n.
"slade", 437
sleeve burnt in a sorrowful manner, 314
"slob" (slab) of marble worries
Henry, 58–9
small-pox (1736 and 1737), 36, 61,
243–4, 299, 374
— (1742), 331–2, 379

small-pox (1746), 317, 320
— (1747), 336
— (1749), 358
— fear of infection through clothes, 288
— indemnity from servants, 145, 310
— — actual form of, 444
— reference to inoculation against in 1726, xxii
smith, orders to a, 52
Smith, Joseph, of Shelbrook, letter to, 427
— — is never at home, 422, 425
— — is not a "reall ffreind", 424
"sned", a scythe-handle, xxvi
snow destroys leverets, 231
"snuff", an adjective, meaning "vexed", 221
snuffers, steel ones wanted, 124
soap, best white, 84
Souldern, Gough family of, 82
— R. Porter pretends to buy, 253
South, of Astrop, letter to, 30
Southall, Henry dines at the "Red Lion" inn, 359
sparadrap, a kind of plaster, 338 n.
spectacles and frames, 349–51
— see also under "glasses, seeing"
spelling in the letters, xx–xxi
"spend", to eat, consume, 162
spinach, 96
spirits of wine, 216
spirits, violent, misplaced in a chamber-maid, 148
splatter (or spatter) dashes, 150
spurs and spur-leathers, 299
Stanbridge, of Bicester, letter to, 138
— Martha, litters her clothes about, 138
Stanhope, Sir William, M.P., (biog.) 370
starch, 70
stationers, orders to, 286–7
Steegman, John, quoted, xii
Sterrop, George, London optician, letters to, 112–13
— Ralph, alluded to, 348, 351
Stiles, Brackley ropemaker, letter to, 83
"stint", 434
stirrups of white thread, 115
Stockholt Manor, Akeley, 399
stockings of white thread, 305
stone wanted from Brackley pits, 51
Stonehouse, Sir John, of Amberden, Essex, mentioned, 265 n.

Stowe, reference to the Gardens, 373, 386
Strange, J., a Tingewick smith, letter to, 52
— William, of Shalstone, letters to, 352, 355
— — guilty of indiscretion, 371
Stranks, of Brackley, letters to, 78, 300
street numbering in London in 1738, 187
sturgeon, a welcome gift, 214
— very good, 182, 193
sugar, 65–9
suit of clothes, materials and instructions for making, 301
— — price of, 298
"surprize", meaning alarm, 214
surtout coat for a servant, materials for, 314
suspensory bandage, details of, 342–4
swan shot for a blunderbuss, 255, 258
Syresham, Rev. W. Hawes at, 19–21
— Hatch, a rendezvous for hunting, 407

table, writing, 111
— mahogany, 108
tailor reproved for delay, 317–8
— — for bad fit and material, 298
"tale of a tub", used proverbially, 249
"tale" of salmon, 225
"tap" used of barrel of sturgeon (? caviare), 214
"tap-wort", xxvi
Taylor, a freeholder in Shalstone parish, 17
tea, 65, 67–70
— see also under bohea and Hyson
teeth, artificial, ordered through the post, 345–7
teething of infants, 237, 428
Temple, Earl (Richard Grenville), 368
tenant, character of a prospective one, 29, 30
tenant's covenants in lease of house, 197
tenants, some bad payers, xxx
Thanet, 7th Earl of, and Newbottle, (biog.) 109 n.
Thicknesse, Joyce, anecdote of, 391
Thorpe Mandeville, "Three Rabbits" inn at, 420
— — owners of manor, 141
"Three Tuns" inn at Banbury, 170

tiles, 306
— contract for making, 57
— "figured", 106
— pattern at supplier's discretion, 107
— with a ship on them, 195
— in the parlour fallen down, 47
timber carriage, pins missing, 41
— to be paid for before removal, 37
tincture for preserving teeth, 348
Tingewick and Rev. F Edmunds, 17
tippet of ermine, 319, 320
Titchburn, of London, letters to, 342–3
tithe, trouble with rector about, 17
tobacco, Henry's small indulgence in, xxvii
toll on corn through a turnpike, 371
tooth-brushes in 1751, 348 n.
tortoise-shell rim to glasses (1737), 349
Tower of London visited by Henry, 359
town crier for sale of oak timber, 40
Townsend, Rev. Richard, and tithes, 17
— — — death of, 224
treacle, 84
trees, fruit, need grafting, 92, 96
— — — pruning, 92, 96
— — named varieties, 93
— marked for sale, 37
trenching in the common fields, 437
Trimnell, Archdeacon, letter to, (biog.) 385
— — gossips, 247
Trotman, Edward, of Shelswell, letter to, (biog.) 430, 85
— — has his house well painted, 56
— Fiennes, his son, (biog.) 431 (Plate 28)
Troutbeck, Rev. Edward of Westbury, letter to, 335
"truss", 342–4
truth, need of in Mrs Purefoy's household, 152
"tunnel", for funnel, the cowl of a chimney, 359
turkey, old cock given to Mr Robotham, 224
— tenderness towards one, 223
— at 4d. a lb., 81
Turland, a bone-setting family, letters to, (biog.) 330, 335
turnpike, tolls on corn, 371
Tusmore House, mentioned, 315
Tyrell, Sir Charles, death of, 367, 441

"ꭒ", ver-, xxi
"umbles", 198
"umbrello", xxvi
"unked", akin to "uncouth", 119, 369
Unton, Sir Edward and the Knightley family, 268

"vaillings", valence, 104
valentines, xxv
vane (?) gilding one, 60
Vaughan, G., laceman of London, letters to, 238, 311, 316
— marries Miss Moulson, 227, 357
— has a son, 205, 213
— called upon to answer Mr Moulson's servant's delinquencies, 238
Vaux, William, of Caversfield, (biog.) 102 n.
veal ordered from a shoemaker, 144
venison, shoulders and umbles, 198
— — sent to Mr Robotham, 186, 197, 229
— for dinner, 387, 392
— proves "naughty", 408
vermilion, a fabric, 101–2, 309
Verney, 2nd Earl, and Biddlesden, 2
Verney Letters of the Eighteenth Century quoted, 2, 203, 253, 328, 330, 380
Verney Memoirs quoted, 348
Verney, John, a footman, drowned, 126
vinegar, 84
vines, named varieties, 93
"voider", xxvi

wages of servants, 127 et seq.
waist, size of Mrs Purefoy's, 218, 308
waistcoat, a gaping one, 297
waistcoats, Henry well supplied with, 321
— instructions for making, 297–8
Wallbank, H., the Buckingham surgeon, letters to, (biog.) 328, 75, 148, 179–80, 328–30, 333, 338–9, 341, 369, 381, 382
— Mrs, letter to, 379
"ward", to copulate with, 430
Ward, Mrs, London china-dealer, letter to, 86
Waring, William, farrier of Shipston-on-Stour, letter to, 171
Warr, Mrs A., letter to, 158
warrant needed for timber-thieves, 44
— — for beer-stealing, 128–9
Washington family and Westbury, 400

watch, new-fashioned and a good goer, 115
— repeating, goes true, 214
— — misbehaves, 242, 252
— badly cleaned and repaired, 193
— will not go since cleaning, 428
Waterman, of Whittlebury, letter to, 37
Watts, Brackley plumber, letter to, 87
— Whitfield tailor, letter to, 154
Way of the World acted at Westbury, 380
Webster, the carrier, letters to, 87–8
Weedon family of Souldern, Oxon, 253
Welchman, J., Brackley attorney, letters to, (*biog.*) 29, 27–9, 32, 34–5, 75, 129, 163, 288
Wellesbourne family of Fulwell, (*biog.*) 399 n.
Wentworth-Cresswell, J., of Lillingstone Lovell, letters to, (*biog.*) 373, 29, 30, 282, 333, 335, 373, 380, 384, 386, 433
— — — on purlieu hunting, 410
— — Mrs, letter to, 334
— — — recommended to Mr Baxter as a customer, 309
— — Mr & Mrs in London (1749), 359
Westbury, sale at, 109–10
— plays performed at, 380, 384
— estate, owners of, 400–1
Westminster Bridge Lottery, 245, 444–5
— — seen by Henry in 1749, 359
"wetshod", 268
Whaddon Hall, dinner parties at, 383, 386
White, Mrs, a London milliner, letter to, 296
— C., quoted, 269, 445
Whitfield to be visited by moonlight, 377
"whitler", a worker in white-leather, 406 n.
Whitmore, J., shoemaker of Brackley, letters to, 143–4, 150
Whitsun-ale, xxv
Whittlebury (or Whittlewood) Forest, bounds of, 405, 416
— — — mentioned, 411, 417
Whitton, of Westbury, letter to, 168
wigs, taste in, 293
Wilkes, John, M.P., 441 n.
will, orders for drafting (1742), 288

Willes, Sir John, Chief Justice, (*biog.*) 390 n.
— Edward, his son, letter to, (*biog.*) 411
— — — — consulted, 410
— — — — his fee, 425
Willett, Thomas, of Shoe Lane, letters to, 344–5
Williams, Rev. —, of Buckingham, letter to, 3
Willis, Browne, the famous antiquary, letter from, 266
— — letters to, 267–72, 394–401, 415
— — his *History of Buckingham*, 266–267, 271–2
— — — "trade", 267
— — Henry dines with, 383, 386
— Miss C., letter to, (*biog.*) 386
— Dr Thomas, and Astrop, 388
— Rev. William, of Little Billing, covets Shalstone Rectory, (*biog.*) 225
Wilson, London grocer, letters to, 67–9, mentioned, 131, 220
Winchester, Dr Coxed, Warden of, 18 n.
window catches, 85
— of chariot breaks, 176–7
wines, various, 70–80
— an order for, 341
— white mountain, a long while coming, 238
Withers, of Westbury, mentioned, 36 n., 155
Wodhull family of Thenford, 392, 410
— John, of Thenford, letters to, (*biog.*) 409, 425
"woman" preceded by "an", xxiii
wood, thefts of, 44
Woodcock, Benjamin, deserts his family, 12
— — letter to, regarding his wife, 15
— — allusion to his case, 347
— Nan, has a bad breast, 341
wood-drink, when to be taken, 328–9
Woodfield, a Bicester mercer, letters to, 306–8
"wortwale", xxvi
wrappers, cotton, for Mrs Purefoy, 303

"yard" used verbally, xxiii
yardland, what was it in Bucks? 25
Yardley Chase, buck wanted from, 429
Yates, a Brackley shopkeeper, letters to, 66, 70, 84, 149, 313

CAMBRIDGE: PRINTED BY W. LEWIS, M.A., AT THE UNIVERSITY PRESS